WHEELING GLASS
1829 - 1939

Collection of the Oglebay Institute Glass Museum

See Figures 298-299

Gary E. Baker
Holly Hoover McCluskey
Jane Shadel Spillman
G. Eason Eige
James S. Measell
Kenneth M. Wilson

Edited by Gerald I. Reilly

Table of Contents

Funding for this catalogue was provided by an Institute of Museum Services General Operating Support Grant.

Introduction
A Short History of Wheeling and its Glass Industry

Wheeling's contributions to the history of the American glass industry are often overlooked today but in the 19th century the Upper Ohio River Valley Region was the main pressed glass production center of the United States. Pittsburgh was the largest manufacturer of pressed glass while Wheeling, Virginia (later West Virginia) was the other major hub. Although Wheeling's importance as a glass producing center lessened in the 20th century, glassware was made in the city until 1939 when the Central Glass Works closed its doors.

Print, Wheeling in Virginia, *c. 1855.*

Wheeling began as an early Ohio River crossing before the Revolutionary War but the city became a major industrial and transportation hub by the 1850's. A main factor contributing to the city's growth during this period was its location on the Ohio River. Steamboats cruised the great waterway as early as 1811 and by the 1850's hundreds of steamboats docked each year at Wheeling's wharf.

Wheeling's role in land transportation solidified when it was selected as the terminus of the National Road. Initiated in 1810, the macadam road was nearly seventy feet wide and it became a major route for settlers heading for the Old Northwest Territory. A large variety of goods, including glass, was transported on this great east-west highway.

Travelers on the National Road crossed the Ohio River by ferry until the one thousand and ten foot long Wheeling Suspension Bridge, then the longest in the world, was completed in 1849. Still in use, it is arguably the nation's most significant extant antebellum engineering structure. The construction of the bridge was also a political triumph for Wheeling. Pennsylvania had lobbied hard against the bridge, fearing it would inhibit Pittsburgh's growth and river traffic. The rivalry with Pittsburgh for dominance of the upper Ohio Valley continued into the 1850's over railroad construction. In 1852 the Baltimore and Ohio Railroad was completed to Wheeling. Although the Pennsylvania Railroad had reached the Ohio River at Pittsburgh, the Baltimore and Ohio was the nation's first main line railway and first continuous railroad between the Atlantic Ocean and the Ohio River. By bypassing Pittsburgh, goods could be transported to the River from Baltimore in much less time.

Wheeling became a major supply and urban center as thousands of people passed through the city heading south or west. Commerce, industry and population grew to meet the demands of travelers, making Wheeling a thriving center of trade and industry.In 1831, Wheeling was designated a Port of Entry and in 1859 a U.S. Custom House was built in the city.

The Custom House, now designated a National Historic Landmark and known as West Virginia Independence Hall, acquired added significance for its major role in the statehood movement and in the Civil War. It was the site of a pro-Union convention in 1861, the capitol of Union Virginia from 1861 to 1863, and the site of the constitutional conventions for West Virginia in 1861 to 1862. These statehood efforts by Unionist leaders of western Virginia allowed U.S. military commanders to justify an invasion of the area in the spring of 1861. That invasion enabled Union forces to secure the vital transportation routes of the upper Ohio River and the Baltimore and Ohio Railroad. The routes were indispensable in transporting troops and supplies between the east and west and in maintaining economic ties throughout the Union.

After the Civil War, economic and political factors eroded Wheeling's position as one of the nation's key transportation centers. Traffic on the upper Ohio River and the National Road declined as railroad transport increased. New industrial cities, such as Cleveland, Detroit and Chicago appeared on the shores of the Great Lakes. Pittsburgh was in possession of the major rail line to the West, making her the victor in the old rivalry with Wheeling. Also, by 1869, the capital of West Virginia moved from Wheeling to Charleston.

Wheeling nevertheless remained a major industrial center in the state. The city's glass production peaked in the second half of the 19th century as did its fabrication of cut nails. In fact, Wheeling was known as the "Nail Capital of the World." Other major businesses during this period included steel, pottery, coal mining, tobacco processing and breweries.

The active industrial life of the city attracted large numbers of European immigrants, particularly Germans, to the area. Also, workers in most of the local industries formed or joined trade unions and Wheeling consistently led the state in union membership.

All this economic activity made Wheeling, in proportion to her population, the largest manufacturing center in the country during the late nineteenth and early twentieth centuries. The wealth and diversity of the local population was reflected in the large numbers of substantial and fashionable homes built during this period.

The growth of Wheeling's glass industry parallels the city's general industrial development. Besides the geographical and transportation advantages mentioned earlier, Wheeling had abundant timber and coal supplies for fuel. Sand, the major ingredient of glass, was available by pulverizing sandstone quarried in the region. Also, the steady stream of immigrants to the city provided the labor and expertise needed to manufacture glass.

Isaac Duval and Company, founded in 1813, was the first glass house in the Wheeling area. The firm was located in Wellsburg, Virginia, (now West Virginia) a town just north of Wheeling. This company produced high quality cut lead crystal as well as green hollow ware. The first glass concern in Wheeling itself was opened in 1820 by George Carruthers who manufactured hollow ware and window glass.

Although there were numerous glass houses in the Wheeling area, most of the pieces in the Oglebay Institute Glass Museum were manufactured by five major companies, all of which operated within the city limits. Some of these firm's names changed several times during their periods of operation but they are commonly known today as Ritchie (1829-1837); Sweeney (1835-1868); Hobbs, Brockunier (1845-1893); Central (1863-1939) and Northwood (1902-1925).

The Ritchies operated the first flint glass house in Wheeling and they manufactured high quality cut and pressed pieces. George Wilson became a partner of the firm in 1834 and by 1836 the *Western Address Directory* stated that Ritchie and Wilson employed 40 hands and consumed 67,000 bushels of coal. The product they produced was worth $87,000. The Ritchie firm closed in 1837 owing to financial difficulties.

The Sweeney brothers founded their flint glass factory in 1835 and their company became one of the most famous and prosperous glass houses in Wheeling before the Civil War. The award winning glass produced by the Sweeneys was shipped all over the country and the firm had warehouses in Pittsburgh and St. Louis. Sweeney glass was cut in the latest English and American styles of the period. Thomas Sweeney and his son, Andrew J. Sweeney, quit the glass business in 1863. A new partnership, which included Michael Sweeney, operated the North Wheeling Glass Works until 1868 when the firm concentrated their production at a new plant in Martins Ferry, Ohio. This last Sweeney-related glass business failed during the financial panic of 1873.

Hobbs, Brockunier and Company was established in 1845 and grew to become one of the largest and most innovative glass firms in America. This very large production company made fine cut lead crystal, Victorian art glass, fancy pattern glass, lamps and even glass chandeliers. William Leighton, Sr. perfected a soda lime glass formula, which was ideal for use in a mechanical press, while he was a partner of the firm. Hobbs, Brockunier was taken over by the United States Glass Company in 1891 and the factory was closed by the conglomerate in 1893.

During the Civil War a group of glass workers gathered their resources and, with $5,000 in capital, formed a flint glass works called Oesterling, Henderson and Company. In 1865 the business was re-chartered as the Central Glass Company. John Oesterling, the firm's first president, was the company's driving force. Under his leadership Central produced full lines of clear, pressed tableware in well over a hundred patterns. Oil lamps and bar glasses were also made by the company in large numbers.

The volume of Central's production was enormous. Its glass was sold throughout the United States as well as Cuba, South America, Europe and Australia. Despite its success, Central Glass finally succumbed to foreign competition in 1939.

Harry Northwood founded his Wheeling glass firm at the site of the old Hobbs, Brockunier factory in 1902. His father, John Northwood, was a noted glassmaker in England and Harry came to America to seek his fortune in the same business at the age of 21. He worked at both the Hobbs, Brockunier and the LaBelle Glass factories before he opened his own company in Martins Ferry, Ohio in 1888. His company moved to Ellwood City, PA in 1892 and in 1896 the factory moved again to Indiana, PA.

Harry Northwood Company of Wheeling produced colorful pressed glass which appealed to middle class American families. The company is most noted today for its so-called "carnival glass", which had an iridescent, rainbow-like finish. Northwood was the only firm in Wheeling to mark its glass. The capital N underlined and surrounded by a circle can be found on pieces produced between 1906 and 1915.

Harry Northwood passed away in 1919 and the company closed in 1925 owing to financial and legal difficulties.

All of Wheeling's glass houses are gone now but one business related to the glass industry still survives in the city: Island Mould and Machine Co. This company was founded in 1939 by Joseph Dewey Weishar. He and his father had worked as mould makers at the Central factory which had closed the same year. The family owned concern thrived under the leadership of J. D.'s son, Joseph James, who passed away in 1989.

This company, now operated by J. D.'s grandsons, Thomas and John Weishar, has made moulds for numerous glass firms such as Imperial, Fostoria, Fenton, Dalzell-Viking, Degenhart and Steuben. Island Mould also made the mould for Oglebay Institute's miniature Sweeney Punch Bowl.

Although Wheeling is no longer a glass production center, the factories which operated in the city for almost one hundred and twenty years have left a spectacular heritage of glass. The pieces on display in the Oglebay Institute Glass Museum are a tribute to the skill, labor and entrepreneurship of the thousands of people who helped make Wheeling a national glass center.

Portions of the text reprinted from the *Wheeling Heritage Project, Draft Concept Plan*. Prepared by the U.S. Department of the Interior National Park Service - Mid-Atlantic Regional Office Division of Park and Resource Planning. November 1990.

HISTORY AND ACKNOWLEDGEMENTS

In 1991, the National Early American Glass Club held its annual meeting at Oglebay Park in Wheeling. Jane Shadel Spillman, Curator of American Glass at the Corning Museum of Glass, asked the Mansion Museum staff when we were going to publish a catalogue on the Wheeling Glass Collection.

Through her continued encouragement, this project has now been completed. The Mansion Museum applied for, and received, a 1992 General Operating Support Grant from the Institute of Museum Services. These IMS funds were used to help publish the catalogue. Jane Shadel Spillman suggested bringing together a group of glass scholars and historians to write a description of each of the major Wheeling glass companies. Without the combined help and cooperation of Gary Baker, Eason Eige, Beverly Fluty, Jim Measell, Holly McCluskey, Gerry Reilly, Jane Shadel Spillman and Ken Wilson, this catalogue would not have been possible.We also wish to thank Dave Richardson, President of Antique Publications, for his generous support and guidance on this project.

When the Museum Association was formed in 1930 under Oglebay Institute, a cultural non-profit organization, its focus was art and local history. Since the exhibits were held within the Mansion Museum, an historic house, a decorative arts collection of furnishings and accessories also evolved. At this time the Museum Committee did not actively collect glass. In 1937 Mrs. Robert Benton Ewing, Thomas Sweeney's granddaughter, donated several pieces of glass made by the Sweeneys to the Museum. A separate area was established to display this glass which became the nucleus of the Museum's glass collection.

Twelve years later, in 1949, the Museum Committee, under the leadership of Charles J. Milton, Museum Director, established the Wheeling Glass Collection and supported the concept of acquiring items made by the glass companies that had operated in Wheeling.

Two years earlier, Josephine Jefferson had published her book, "Wheeling Glass." She joined a special glass committee made up of several Museum committee members including Mrs. Joseph Bruning who was chairman.

Mr. Carl Gustkey, president of Imperial Glass Company of Bellaire, Ohio and an avid supporter of Oglebay Park and Institute, offered his assistance to the glass committee. He established a fund known as the J. Ralph Boyd Memorial Glass Fund to underwrite research and purchase glass. Mr. Boyd was a glass maker and past-president of Imperial Glass.

With Mr. Gustkey's support, the Museum Committee embarked on a series of fund raising campaigns and established the annual Oglebay Institute Antiques Show and Sale in 1954. A solicitation of all area glass companies to provide funds for the Boyd Memorial Fund proved successful. Contributors included Fostoria Glass, Fenton Glass, Blenko Glass, Viking Glass, Cambridge Glass and Seneca Glass Companies.

The Committee established a number of glass seminars in the 1950's. George and Helen McKearin were among the noted speakers. Through lectures and seminars as well as personal contacts, the Museum brought attention to Wheeling glass. Of the contributors during this time, Mr. and Mrs. Arthur Stifel stand out as the major donors. Through both gifts and purchases, the collection grew by 1959 to over 550 pieces, including the Sweeney Punch Bowl.

In 1962 Mr. Robert DiBartolomeo became director of the Museum and I was named curator. Bob's research increased the appreciation of the importance of Wheeling's glass industry. From 1962 until Bob's untimely death in 1974, the glass collection grew tremendously. Major contributors during this period included the Gustkey family, Karl and Ann Koepke, Mr. and Mrs. Everett Greer, as well as Joseph Weishar. 1,296 pieces were acquired.

From 1976 through 1980, Gary Baker was Museum curator. Through his extensive research of court records, Gary greatly increased the knowledge of the history of Wheeling's glass industry.

Holly McCluskey assumed the position of Curator of Education in 1984. She expanded the educational program of the Museum, especially in relation to the glass collection. Miss Betty Robb, granddaughter of Harry Northwood, became interested in the collection and contributed toward its growth. Beginning in 1990 she and noted Northwood scholar, Dr. James Measell, have worked together to expand the Museum's collection of Northwood Glass. Through their combined efforts, over three hundred pieces of Northwood have been added to this collection.

Since Jane Shadel Spillman first suggested this catalogue, the collection of Wheeling Glass has moved from a gallery within the Museum's historic house to the new Carriage House Glass Center at Oglebay. This collection is displayed and interpreted with state of the art technology.

Oglebay Institute's glass collection is unique because it is devoted to the interpretation and preservation of the glass made in Wheeling.

We thank and acknowledge the 323 individual families and organizations which donated glass for this collection. We dedicate this catalogue to all of them.

John A. Artzberger, Director

Oglebay Park
Wheeling, WV 26003

ISBN# 1-57080-002-2

Chapter One

Bottles and Flasks

See Figure 14

Kenneth M. Wilson

The black and white photographs in this chapter are by Gary Zearott, Zee Photo.

OGLEBAY MANSION MUSEUM: BOTTLES and FLASKS

By Kenneth M. Wilson

As this new nation embarked upon its course, following the successful conclusion of the Revolutionary war, bottles and window glass were in great demand. As the population grew from 3.9 million in 1790 to 12.9 million in 1830, and gradually improving transportation fostered commerce, the demand for all sorts of bottles grew steadily. This demand -or lack of supply- was noted in a number of contemporary accounts. On April 7, 1789, a Baltimore newspaper stated:

> No factory is more wanted, says a correspondent, than a capital glass manufactory for bottles similar to those of Bristol, in Great Britain. Considerable orders for Philadelphia beer and porter are now in the city, some of which cannot be executed for want of proper bottles. While France is discouraging glass-works, for want of wood, the United States should establish theirs for her wood is in many places an encumbrance.

Mark Leavenworth, the New Haven entrepreneur who unsuccessfully attempted to establish the New Haven Glass Works in 1789 commented:

> Bottles were the logical product, for, he said, if they could be had at a reasonable price, the sale would be vastly extensive, and our farmers would be much benefited...our cider might be shipped to the West Indies and the Southern States to great advantage.

At about the same time Tench Coxe, a political economist and assistant secretary of the treasury under Alexander Hamilton, pointed out that "The manufacture of malt liquors for exportation actually was curtailed by an insufficient supply of the black bottles used as containers."

Containers for rum, gin, whiskey, porter, beer, and cider were particularly wanted because the consumption of alcohol was very high (about fifteen gallons per person per

Oil Painting, View of Wheeling *by Robert Hanna, c. 1845*

Figure 1.

year, compared to two and a half gallons in the 1970's). The third national census, in 1810, reported:

The quantity of ardent spirits annually distilled appears to equal the prodigious amount of 23,720,000 gallons! The extraction of brandy from peaches, of an alcoholic liquid from cider, and of whiskey from rye, and even maize, is carried to this alarming excess... Nor ought it to be concealed, that in a country where a gallon of this maddening stimulus can be bought for half a dollar, a gill may be obtained at retail for three cents and the seller at the same time double his money.

Americans love affair with drinking alcoholic beverages is perhaps best summed up by the following observation from *A Diary in America*, published in 1839 by Capt. Marryat, who toured America in the 1830's:

> They say that the English cannot settle anything properly without dinner. I am sure the Americans can fix nothing without a drink. If you meet, you drink; if you close a bargain, you drink; they quarrel in their drink, and they make it up with a drink. They drink because it is hot; they drink because it is cold. If successful in elections, they drink and rejoice; if not, they drink and swear; they begin to drink early in the morning, they leave off late at night; they commence it early in life, and they continue it, until they soon drop into the grave. To use their expression, the way they drink, is "quite a caution". As for water, what the man said, when asked to belong to the Temperance Society, appears to be the general opinion: "It's very good for navigation.

Much of this demand for bottles continued to be met by importations, especially in the eastern part of the country. Thomas Tisdale, a merchant in Hartford, Connecticut, advertised in the *Connecticut Currant* in 1790: "HALF-PINT Dram Bottles, suitable to carry the comfort of life into the field,...". The need for bottles was just as great in the Midwest - that area west of the Allegheny Mountains which served as a formidable barrier to the transport of glass from the east coast of which Pittsburgh and Wheeling were the primary and secondary centers of a steadily growing area of population and commerce. Rum, which had been the

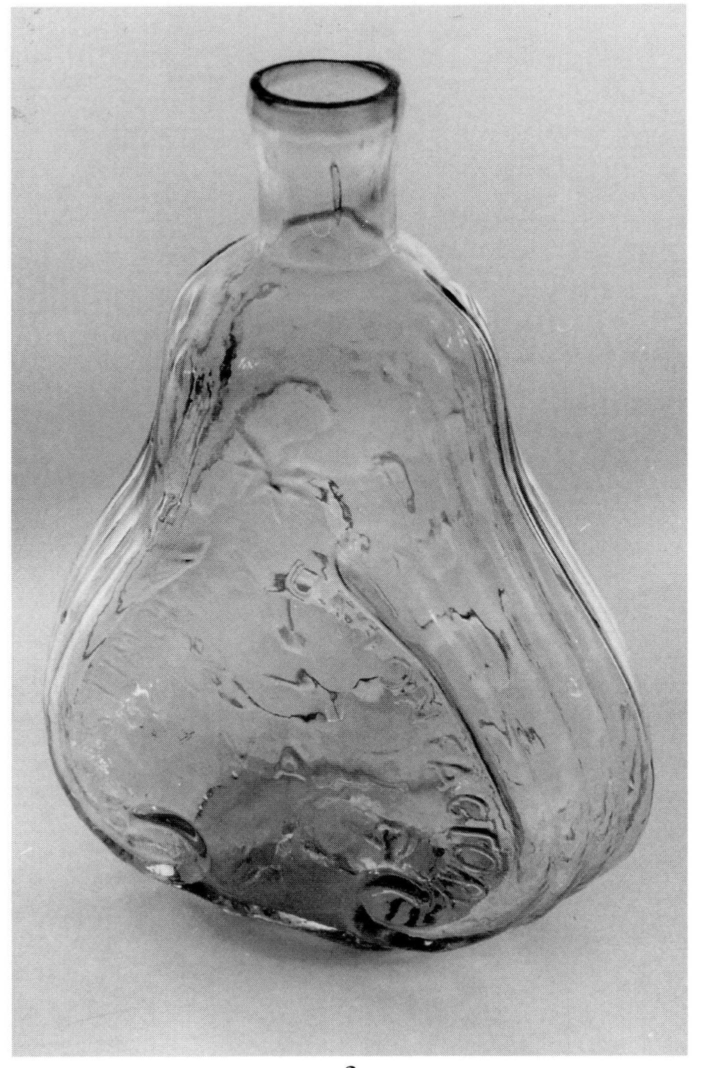

2.

most popular distilled beverage until the end of the Revolutionary War, gave way to whiskey. This was largely due to the settlement of western areas in Kentucky and elsewhere beyond the Allegheny Mountains where the rich soil of new farms produced abundant crops of rye and corn, and where every sixth farmer was a distiller. By 1791 there were, south of Pittsburgh, 272 stills in Washington County alone. The produce of these stills was more readily transported to Southern and Eastern markets than the grain itself: "One horse could carry the equivalent of 24 bushels of grain as whiskey," thus greatly reducing the cost of distribution and increasing profitability. Whiskey also became a form of monetary exchange, used even to pay taxes and the minister; and was widely used by almost everyone. "What a bank bill was at Philadelphia or a shilling piece at Lancaster, that was whiskey in the towns and villages that lay along the banks of the Monongahela River." "It was the circulating medium of the country."

Whiskey was also part of the daily routine of almost everyone, as the following observations indicate. A traveler sojourning in Pittsburgh wrote home that "Everyone, high and low, great and small, rich and poor, male and female, clergy and laity, makes free use of whiskey; it is as common a supply upon the sideboard as bread and meat." Joseph Weeks in his *Report on the Manufacture of Glass*, 1880 stated: "Mr. Isaac Craig (probably the son or grandson of Isaac Craig, who was with General O'Hara, one of the founders of the Pittsburgh Glass Works in 1798) writes me 'I recollect distinctly seeing both tumblers and decanters made of green glass. In old times decanters were used in every house, most commonly by the poorer families who could not afford cut glass. Whiskey was set out to every visitor in these decanters, before and after every meal...' " In the Midwest, as late as the 1860's, it was a breach of etiquette not to set out one of the long-necked green glass quart bottles when the minister called.

3.

4.

As noted above, imported bottles – primarily from England – filled some of the demand for bottles in the eastern part of the country, but the additional cost to transport them from the east coast across the Allegheny Mountains was prohibitive: Wagon freight of five to ten dollars per hundred pounds and poor road conditions limited shipments of fragile wares such as bottles and glass mainly to the summer months. (*Standard History of Pittsburgh, P. 74 Gallatin Papers).* Transportation from England to the east coast of the United States was actually less than from there to Pittsburgh or Wheeling. Faced with such costs and an abundance of readily available raw materials for glass making, it is little wonder that numerous glasshouses were soon erected in the Midwest to fill this need and demand.

Two glasshouses were founded in the closing years of the eighteenth century: The Geneva Glass Works (also called the Gallatin Glass Works) was founded in Geneva, Pennsylvania, about sixty miles south of Pittsburgh, in 1797 by Albert Gallatin and five glassblowers from Amelung's defunct New Bremen Glass Manufactory. It began production in 1798, and in the following year, Major Isaac Craig and General James O'Hara opened the Pittsburgh Glass Works in Pittsburgh. Both produced window glass and bottles, as well as hollow wares. The latter consisted of tumblers, decanters, bowls, jugs and other tablewares and accessories made from the same glass as their principal products, window glass and bottles. For a number of years previously, such wares were generally considered by authors as "offhand", or individual pieces made by the workers in their spare time for the use of their families and friends, but advertisements indicate hollow wares were a regular part of the production of most window and bottle glasshouses, as the following advertisement indicates:

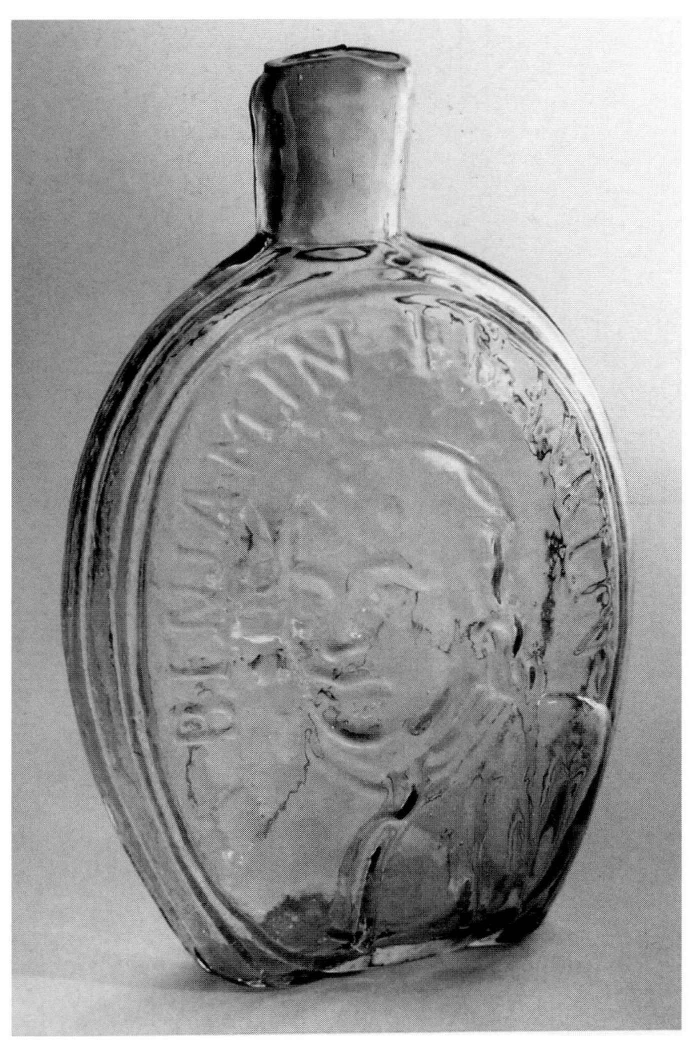

5.

GENEVA GLASS

The subscriber informs his friends and public generally that he has on hand a large assortment of Geneva Glass, consisting of the following articles, to wit:

10 by 12, 8 by 10, and 7 by 9, Window Glass

Gallon, half gallon, quart and pint bottles

Gallon, half gallon, quart and pint jars,

Pitchers assorted

Quart, pint, half pint and gill tumblers,

Quart, pint, half pint and gill decanters

Goblets, cream jugs, quart and pint mugs and

Bowls

All of which he will sell at the lowest Geneva prices, for cash or approved paper.

Pittsburgh, April 6, 1807. Thomas Cromwell.

Geneva glass was advertised for sale in Wheeling in 1807.

Bakewell's Pittsburgh Glass Works, founded in 1808 for the manufacture of flint glasswares, added green glass to its production in 1811, and made bottles and figured flasks at least until the 1840's. The Zanesville (Ohio) Glass Works, founded in 1815; the Birmingham Glass Works, founded in 1826, near Pittsburgh; and W. and C. Ihmsen's Pennsylvania Black Bottle Works, also located in Pittsburgh, were among other early bottle glass manufacturers in the Midwest. (Innes, *Pittsburgh Glass*, pp. 204-230; McKearin and Wilson, pp. 42-185.) Between 1800 and 1832, at least 102 attempts were made to establish new glass houses. Thirty-three of them were in the Midwest; by 1832 only 71 remained; in at least 39 of them bottles were made. Among them were five factories in what was then Virginia. The second of these was founded in 1820 by George Carruthers, a glass blower, and two other glassmen, Peter Yarnell and Thomas McGiffen, in Wheeling, (West) Virginia. After Carruthers failed in 1824, the glassworks was sold at public auction to Charles Knox and Redick McKee who named it the VIRGINIA GREEN GLASS WORKS, and operated it as Knox & McKee. The works employed 30 hands, and produced large quantities of window glass as well as green hollow ware, including gallon, half-gallon, and quart bottles and "innumerable" pints, oil and porter bottles. They also made at least three Figured Flasks including GI-69,GI-92, GI-130 all of which are rare, or extremely rare. (McKearin and Wilson p. 128)

On March 24, 1830, Knox & McKee leased the glassworks for three years to Ensell & Plunkett of Pittsburgh who operated the works until 1833, but then did not renew their lease, and in July, Knox & McKee sold a half interest in the Virginia Green Glass Works and a neighboring one they owned to Jesse Wheat and John Price. Called Wheat, Price & Co. this firm changed the name of the works to the Fairview Glass Works (see McKearin and Wilson, p. 129 and

6.

Catalogue No. 1). On January 31, 1834 John and Craig Ritchie and George Wilson bought the Fairview Glass Works and operated it successfully until the panic of 1837. The works was operated by several others afterwards, until they finally ceased operations about 1848, and in the following year the glassworks were torn down.

Other factories founded in Wheeling for the production of bottles and figured flasks are: The Union Glass Works established in 1849 by R. Knowles & Co.; (see Cat. No. 3); the glassworks established by Ensell & Plunkett about 1833, in North Wheeling; and the Wheeling Glass Works, North, – originally built in 1848 and operated by several firms until it was purchased in 1860 by George W. Robinson and his father and operated as "Geo. W. Robinson". (see Cat. Nos. 13 & 14).

At least two glasshouses were established in Wellsburg (formerly Charlestown) (West) Virginia. The first was erected in either 1813 or by 1815 by Isaac Duval, a glassblower, with two partners, also glassblowers. The works produced both flint and green glass, and from the latter undoubtedly made various midwestern types of pattern molded bottles and holloware, including –probably–some pattern molded in a "ten–diamond mold". Several advertisements indicate that the works were operated – at least – sporadically – even after Isaac Duval died in 1828. It is believed the works continued to operate until the late 1840's, but little is known about its operations, or products. (See McKearin and Wilson, pp. 114-115).

McCarty and Torreyson, two glassblowers who seem to have worked in Duval's factory, bought the works in 1842, and continued its operations. (See cat. nos. 4 & 5 and McKearin and Wilson, p. 169).

These glasshouses, and perhaps others of which we have yet no knowledge, undoubtedly produced vast quantities of black glass junk bottles suitable for bottling whiskey, beer, porter and cider, from deep green or amber bottled glass, as well as numerous forms of globular, club, and tapered, or decanter shaped, bottles of light green or aquamarine colored glass, and also many varieties of pocket flasks of both dark and light green glass. Many of the latter two groups were pattern molded – primarily with vertical or swirled ribbing, or a combination of the two. Though the bottle collection in the Oglebay Museum is not extensive, it contains representations of most of these types of bottles, as well as a good representation of figured flasks made in West Virginia factories. Except for the figured flasks which bear the names of the manufacturers, the origins of these containers still go unidentified. Although attempts have been made in the past to associate certain rib – counts with particular factories, and although Harry Hall White's excavations of some glasshouse sites have identified certain rib – counts with them, further studies have concluded that positive identification of origin by this means is largely invalid. This is primarily because of limited sources for such molds, and the fact that when the firm went out of business, its molds were sometimes acquired and used by another firm. Common usage of molds precludes precise identification of the origins of most of these vessels.

Although Wheeling finally succumbed in its competition with Pittsburgh to be the number one port on the Ohio River and the transportation center in the Ohio River valley, it nevertheless continued to grow in population, and as it did, its industry and commerce also developed. The manufacturing of flint glass was one of these industries whose products gained Wheeling a well deserved reputation (see chapter 2 for the history and development of the flint glass industry in Wheeling).

Fig. No. 1.

Figured Flask GI 116 Very Rare

Fairview Glass Works, Wheat, Price & Co., Wheeling (West) Virginia

1833-1834

Pint Ht. 6¾"

INSCRIPTIONS Obverse: "WHEAT, PRICE & CO. WHEELING VA.", the N in WHEELING reversed; Reverse: "FAIRVIEW" at top of glasshouse "WORKS" below.

Light bluish green glass. Blown in a full-size mold with an unidentified bust facing right on the obverse surrounded by the inscription and a view of a glasshouse with a tall smoking chimney on the reverse and the name of the works.

REMARKS: Wheat, Price & CO. was formed in July 1833 when Jesse Wheat and John Price purchased a one-half interest in the Virginia Green Glass Works and a neighboring glassworks from Knox & McKee. The name of the works was changed to the Fairview Glass Works. On January 31, 1834, John and Craig Ritchie and George Wilson bought the Fairview Glass Works which was successfully operated by Ritchie & Wilson until 1837. Since molds were expensive, it is possible Ritchie & Wilson may have continued to produce this flask after they took over the works. McKearin & Wilson, (AMERICAN BOTTLES AND FLASKS AND THEIR ORIGINS, p. 129, 506-507, 552-553).

7.

Fig. No. 2.

Figured Flask GIX-47 Extremely Rare

Union Glass Works, R. Knowles & Co., Wheeling (West) Virginia

1849-1850

Pint Ht. 6⅞"

INSCRIPTION; Obverse: within the scroll medallion "R. KNOWLES & Co." on the left side and "UNION FACTORY" on the right, with "SOUTH WHEELING in circular form surrounding "VA" in the center of the medallion.

Aquamarine. Blown in a full-size mold, the inscription on the obverse within a scroll medallion with a large 8-pointed star above; on the reverse, a large conventional modified, fleur-de-lis ornament, with a large 8-pointed star above.

REMARKS: Despite extensive production over a number of years, this is the only known marked flask from this glassworks. In 1849 R. Knowles & Co. was formed and the Union Glass Works erected at First and Mercer streets (now Twenty-fourth and Jacobs streets) in South Wheeling. Richard Knowles, and three other glassblowers – Cambern, Gorsell and McGranahan – practical glassmen, with Morgan Ott who provided the capital were the founders. Except for Knowles, the glassblowers withdrew in 1850 and A. E. Quarrier bought their interest, and the firm became Quarrier, Ott & Co. Its products were vials, bottles and every description of druggists' ware. An advertisement in the Wheeling Directory for 1851 offered:

"Union Glass Works – Quarrier, Ott & Co., Manufacturers of Vials, Bottles, etc., corner of First & Mercer St. Center Wheeling. Common vials, Prescriptions, Green Glass Jars, Acid bottles, Mineral & Soda Bottles, Patent Medicine Vials, Ink Bottles, Druggist's Packing Jars, Flasks, Cologne Bottles, etc." After the Civil War, Knowles and two sons moved to Glassport, Pa., and the factory was sold to the Ohio Glass Company, which continued in business for many years producing window and plate glass." (McKearin & Wilson, , pp. 168, 423, 628-629) (See also Fig. No. 13.)

Fig. No. 3.

Figured Flask GIX-48 Scarce

McCarty & Torreyson, Manufacturer, Wellsburg (formerly Charlestown), (West) Virginia.

1842-1845

Pint Ht. 7½"

INSCRIPTION "McCARTY & TORREYSON" in semicircle above "MANUFACTURERS" in straight line, with "WELLSBURG, VA." below in a semicircle.

Light bluish-green glass. Blown in a full-size mold of two vertical sections that opened diagonally leaving a diagonal mold seam on the base. Embossed with a large five-pointed star above MANUFACTURERS within which is a circle containing a small five-pointed star on the obverse; the reverse is decorated with a circular frame containing a large sunburst with 24 rays surrounding concentric rings in the center.

REMARKS: McCarty and Torreyson seem to have been part of a group of Irish glassblowers who became associated with the glassworks that had been established by Isaac Duval in 1813. By 1842 McCarty and Torreyson apparently bought the works and thereafter produced a wide variety of bottles and a number of figured flasks. This works also produced a quart flask like this one with the same markings (GI-49), and another similar quart flask, unmarked, and several Jenny Lind figured flasks (GI-108, GI-109 and GI-110) are also attributed to this factory because they are so similar to this flask (GI-48) and also to GI-49. It is not known how long this firm operated. See Fig. No. 4. (McKearin & Wilson, pp. 169, 423, 628-629).

Fig. No. 4.

Figured Flask Jenny Lind GI-108 Scarce

Attributed to McCarty & Torreyson, Wellsburg (formerly Charlestown (West) Virginia

Probably 1851-1855

Pint Ht. 7¼"

Aquamarine glass. Blown in a full-size mold of two vertical sections; obverse and reverse the same, decorated with a three-quarter bust of Jenny Lind facing left, wearing a broad plain bertha; below is a lyre with three strings; the obverse and reverse sides meet with the edges to form a 10-sided scalloped base. Rough pontil mark.

REMARKS: See Fig. No. 3. for attribution. (McKearin & Wilson, pp. 169, 423, 467, 550-551).

Fig No 5.

Figured Flask Franklin/Dyott GI-93 Extremely Rare

Wheeling Glass Works, Possibly Ensell & Plunkett, Wheeling (West) Virginia

Early 1830's; possibly 1830-1833

Pint Ht. 6¾"

INSCRIPTIONS Obverse: "BENJAMIN FRANKLIN" in semicircle above bust; Reverse: "WHEELING GLASS WORKS", the "S" in WORKS is small and faint.

Light Green. Blown in a full-size mold of two vertical sections with a three-quarter profile bust of Benjamin Franklin on the obverse and a three-quarter profile bust of Thomas W. Dyott on the reverse.

REMARKS: This is the only FRANKLIN flask produced in the Midwest; it resembles closely the three pint FRANKLIN-DYOTT flasks (GI-94, GI-95 and GI-96) produced by T. W. Dyott in his Philadelphia and Kensington glass factories, but the inscription WHEELING GLASS WORKS displaced Dyott's name. Helen McKearin believed this flask was brought out in the early 1830's, possibly by Ensell & Plunkett during their rental of the works established by Knox & McKee, who had called it the Virginia Green Glass Works, but no definite evidence as to the factory producing this flask has been found. (McKearin and Wilson, p. 456, pp. 548-549).

Fig. No. 6.

Figured Flask American Eagle GII-3 Rare

Probably Pittsburgh – Monongahela district

1825-1835

Pint Ht. 7"

Light green glass. Blown in a full-size mold of two vertical sections bearing an eagle on an oval cartouche facing rightt on each side with nine 6-pointed stars above eagle, an olive branch in its left talons and a laurel branch in its beak on the obverse; reverse is the same except eight of the stars are 5-pointed and one, the center star, is 6-pointed. On the obverse there is a vertical mark in the oval frame on which the eagle rests which may be from an accidental mark in the mold.

REMARKS: It is not known in which of the Monongahela and Early Pittsburgh district factories this flask was produced. It is closely related to five other figured flasks bearing an American eagle on each side (GII-1, GII-1a, GII-2, GII-4 and GII-5) all attributed to the same district. (McKearin and Wilson, pp. 557-559).

Fig. No. 7.

Figured Flask American eagle GII-24 Common

Midwestern, possibly Kentucky Glass Works, Louisville, Kentucky

1850-1855

Pint Ht. 6¾"

Aquamarine glass. Blown in a full-size mold of two vertical

sections with the same pattern on both sides: an American eagle with outstretched wings, head turned left, on an oval cartouche bearing an 8-pointed ornament, with a ribbon in its beak and 14 stars above, all surrounded by a pattern of ribs.

REMARKS: The Kentucky Glass Works was founded in 1850 and, like numerous glasshouses, underwent several changes in management between then and about 1855 when it became the Louisville Glass Works. According to two advertisements, its principal products were vials, demijohns, porter and other bottles; including mineral and wine bottles, pickle and other jars, and flasks. No marked flasks are known from the Kentucky Glass Works, but at least four others are attributed to that firm. (GII-22, GII-25, GII-26 and GII-27). (McKearin and Wilson, pp. 169-170 and 172 and pp. 562-563).

CONDITION: Base damaged.

8.

Fig. No. 8.

Figured Flask   Horse and Railroad Cart GV-5 Common

Probably Vernon Glass Works, Vernon, N.Y., or successor in Saratoga, N.Y.

1830-1845

Pint Ht. 6¾"

INSCRIPTIONS: on both sides: "SUCCESS TO THE RAILROAD", in an arch around the horse and cart on the railroad track.

Dark Green glass. Blown in a full-size mold of two vertical sections. Pontil mark on the base.

REMARKS: The Mt. Vernon Glass Works was established in Vernon, N.Y. in 1810 and removed to the Saratoga, N.Y. area in 1844-1845, where it was called Saratoga Mountain Glass Works. Fragments of this flask have been excavated at both these sites, the mold having been taken from Vernon to Saratoga, testifying to the long-term popularity of these railroad flasks. (McKearin and Wilson, pp. 95-98, pp 602-603).

Fig. No. 9.

Figured Flask   Washington   Sheaf of Rye   GI-58 Common

Possibly Dyottville Glass Works, Benners, Smith and Campbell or H.B. & J.M. Benners & Company., Kensington, near Philadelphia, Pa.

1850-1855

Pint Ht. 7½"

Aquamarine glass. Blown in a full-size mold of two vertical sections and a base plate to form the bottom of the flask; tooled sloping lip with a rounded collar below. Pontil mark. On the obverse is a classical profile bust of Washington facing left – on the reverse a sheaf of rye on a crossed rake and pitchfork.

REMARKS: The attribution of this flask to the Dyottville Glass Works is tentative, based upon flasks of this same type and form marked Dyottville. It is quite possible other glassworks copied this form, so this flask is termed a "Dyottville type". A quart flask bearing the same decorations (GI-57) was also made. (McKearin and Wilson, p. 88, 538-539).

Fig. No. 10.

Figured Flask   GXV-18   Rare

The Wheeling Glass Works, North, operated by Geo. W. Robinson

1867-68, and probably 1869

Quart   Ht. 8¾"

9.

INSCRIPTIONS: Obverse: "GEO. W. ROBINSON" in arc, "NO 75" in straight line below, and "MAIN ST W. VA" in reverse are below it. Reverse: plain.

Light aquamarine glass. Blown in a full-size mold of two vertical sections and a base plate that formed a circular, slight depression in the base, the vertical sections opening on the diagonal (McK base Type 22, McKearin and Wilson p 520). Neck tooled with an applied flat ring below a thickened plain lip (McK Neck Type 11, McKearin and Wilson p 518).

REMARKS: In 1860 George W. Robinson and his father purchased this works which had originallly been built in 1848 and had passed through several ownerships in the meantime. It was located at the foot of McLane Street and a warehouse was maintained at 75 Main Street. The Directory for 1867-1868 lists George W. Robinson as "Manufacturer of Window Glass, Druggist Glassware, Fruit Jars, Flasks and Bottles". The firm was last listed in the 1869 Directory, but the works was taken over by others and operated by various firms until the late 1920's. Five figured flasks are known to have been made by the George W. Robinson firm: this one, GXIII-26, GXIII-26A, GXV-19 and GXV-20. See Fig. No. 11. for a half-pint flask, GXV-20. (McKearin and Wilson, p. 180, pp. 660-661, pp. 674-675).

Fig. No. 11.

Figured Flask GXV-18 Rare

Wheeling Glass Works, North, operated by Geo. W. Robinson

1867-1868, and probably 1869

Quart Ht. 8⅝"

INSCRIPTION Same inscription and placement as on Fig. No. 10.

Light aquamarine glass. Blown in the same mold as Fig. No. 10.

REMARKS: See Fig. No. 10.

Fig. No. 12.

Figured Flask GXV-20 Rare

Wheeling Glass Works, North, operated by Geo. W. Robinson

1867-68, and probably 1869

Half-pint Ht. 6⅛"

INSCRIPTION Same inscription and placement as on Fig. No. 10.

Light aquamarine glass. Blown in the same type of mold as Fig. No. 10.

REMARKS: SEE Fig. No. 10.

Fig.. No. 13.

Figured Flask GXV-25 Scarce

Attributed to the Union Glass Works, Quarrier, Ott & Co., Wheeling, (West) Virginia

1855-1863 and possibly after 1863

Pint Ht. 7¼"

INSCRIPTIONS. Obverse: "WHEELING" in arc above "VA" all within a large oval frame with narrow molding; reverse: "OLD RYE" in a slight arc just within top of a large oval frame, as an obverse.

Deep aquamarine glass (unrecorded in this color in McKearin and Wilson). Blown in a full-size mold of two vertical sections and a base plate that formed an oval depression in the base (McK base Type 32, p. 520,

McKearin and Wilson). Neck with applied, tooled rounded ring below thickened plain lip (McK Neck finish Type 12, McKearin and Wilson, pp. 518-519).

REMARKS: Since West Virginia entered the Union June 1863, this flask was first made before that date, probably as noted above. For the Union Glass Works and Quarrier, Ott & Co., see Fig. No. 2., REMARKS: (McKearin and Wilson, pp. 168-169; 676-677).

Fig. No. 14.

Figured Flask GXV-25 Scarce

Attributed to the Union Glass Works, Quarrier, Ott & Co., Wheeling, (West) Virginia.

1855-1863, and possibly after 1863

Pint Ht. 7½"

10.

INSCRIPTIONS See Fig. No. 13

Deep olive green glass. Same as flask in Fig. No. 13, but with a longer neck.

REMARKS: See Fig. Nos. 13. and 2.

Fig.. No. 15.

Pocket Bottle

Midwest

1810-1830

Ht. 6½"

Light green glass. Patterned in an 18-rib dip mold, blown and tooled, ribs swirled to the left. Lip probably slightly tooled and fire-polished. Slight kick-up in base; rough pontil mark.

REMARKS: One of various types of pattern molded pocket bottles characteristic of midwestern glasshouses. (See McKearin and Wilson pp. 320-321, pp. 322-328).

CONDITION: Cracked on lower part of body.

Fig. No. 16.

Pocket Bottle

Midwest, perhaps Zanesville, Ohio

1815-1830

Ht. 5"

Deep brownish amber glass. Patterned in a 24-rib dip mold, blown and tooled, ribs swirled to the left; lip probably tooled and fire-polished. Rough pontil mark.

REMARKS: Another form and color typical of midwestern pocket bottles. (See McKearin and Wilson, pp 323-328, pp. 360-361, No. 1).

Fig. No. 17.

Pitkin-type Pocket Bottle

Midwest

1800-1825

Ht. 6¼"

Light green glass. Formed by the German half-post method; patterned first in a 32-rib dip mold, removed and twisted to the left, then reinserted in either the same mold or in one with 31 ribs and patterned with vertical ribbing creating a broken swirl pattern, blown and tooled. Lip fire-polished and possibly tooled. Slight kick-up in base; rough pontil mark.

REMARKS: The color of the glass, its thickness and bold structure with its bold ribbing (swirled and vertical) terminating at the same point on the shoulder are all characteristic of midwestern Pitkin-type bottles. Formerly in the collections of Dr. E. R. Eller, Pittsburgh, a noted early collector and dealer in midwestern glass. (McKearin and Wilson, pp. 316-317, pp. 322-328).

Fig. No. 18.

Pitkin-type Pocket Bottle

Midwest

1810-1830

Ht. 4½"

Medium green glass. Formed by the German half-post method; patterned in an 18-rib dip mold, blown and tooled, the ribs remaining vertical; applied gather tooled to form a rounded lip. Rough pontil mark.

REMARKS: The relatively small size and the rolled lip, or collar, are unusual features on this flask, or pocket bottle. (McKearin and Wilson, pp. 316-317, nos. 3 and 6, broken swirl patterned pocket bottles; pp. 322-333).

Fig. No. 19.

Pocket Bottle

Midwest

1815-1830

Ht. 5⅞"

Light green glass. Patterned in a dip mold with 18 vertical ribs, blown and tooled; lip probably tooled and fire-polished. Rough pontil mark.

REMARKS: Similar in form and ribbed decoration to a slightly larger pocket bottle shown in McKearin and Wilson pp. 362-363, No. 3, found years ago in a home in Ohio. (See also McKearin and Wilson pp. 322-328, pp. 342-353).

Fig. No. 20.

Pitkin-type Pocket Bottle

Midwest

1810-1830

Ht. 5½"

Medium green glass. Formed by the German half-post method; patterned in a dip mold with 10 vertical ribs, then twisted to the right to form swirled ribs and re-inserted in the same dip mold and pattered with 10 vertical ribs; ribbing extends to just below the top of the second gather, or post. Pattern is termed broken swirl. Blown and tooled to final form; lip tooled and fire-polished; rough pontil mark.

REMARKS: The color of the glass, the sturdy fabric, its rounded form and bold broken swirl ribbing are all characteristic of midwestern Pitkin-type pocket bottles. (See McKearin and Wilson pp. 316-317, 322-323).

BIBLIOGRAPHY

Innes, Lowell, *Pittsburgh Glass, 1797-1891: A History and Guide for Collectors,* Boston, Houghton Mifflin, 1976.

McKearin, George S. and Helen, *American Glass,* New York, Crown, 1941; rev. ed., 1948.

McKearin, Helen and Kenneth M. Wilson, *American Bottles and Flasks and Their Ancestry,* New York, Crown, 1978.

Print, View of Wheeling, Virginia, From the Railroad, *c. 1850.*

11 12 13 14

17
19
15
16
20
18

21 *. Wheeling Flint Glass Works of J. & C. Ritchie. Window Pane For Use on Steamboats, ca. 1833-36. Pressed lead-formula glass. This decorative pane is in the old standard window glass size of 5" x 7". Gift of Mr. Arthur C. Stifel.*

22

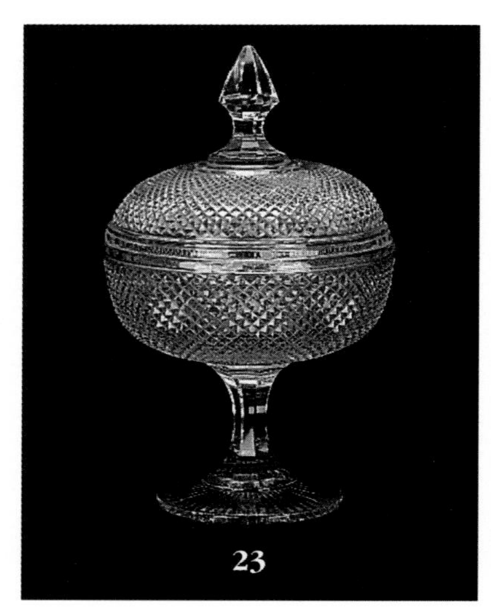

23

22. *North Wheeling Flint Glass Works, Sweeney Firm. Vase or Float Bowl, now commonly called the Sweeney Punch Bowl, ca. 1844-45.*

Blown and cut lead-formula glass, made in four sections, H. 5 Feet. Gift of Edward R. Sweeney (Michael Sweeney's grandson). Long prisms originally hung between each of the scallops and must have acted as a visual foil for the massive bowl and lid, which now look top heavy without them.

23. *North Wheeling Flint Glass Works, Sweeney Firm. Cut Diamond Comport with Cover, Star-bottom, ca. 1850-60. Blown and cut lead-formula glass, H. 13½ inches. Gift of Letitia Sweeney Ewing.*

Chapter Two

Wheeling Flint Glass Works (Ritchie) North Wheeling Flint Glass Works (Sweeney)

See Figures 28-29

Gary E. Baker

WHEELING FLINT GLASS WORKS.

PRICE CURRENT OF GLASS WARE MANUFACTURED BY

F. Plunket & Co. at their Glass Works,

WHEELING, VA.

TUMBLERS.

Item	Unit	Price
Quart Flint, strait or knob,	per doz.	$3 00
Pint do. do.	"	1 75
Quart do. puntied,	"	3 50
Pint do. do.	"	2 00
Third Quart, flint	"	1 25 to 1 75
Do. do. puntied	"	1 50 to 2 00
Half pint, tale taper	"	50
Do. No. 2	"	60
Do. No. 1	"	75
Do. Flint all shapes,	"	90
Do. Taper sham,	"	1 50
Third pint, do. do.	"	1 25
Do. Flint,	"	75
Do. light do.	"	60
Gill 50 cents, half gill,	"	30
Puntied Flint, half pint,	"	1 12½
Do. do. third pint	"	1 00
Heavy sheared, double flint, best ground, half pint,	"	1 75
Do. do. do do third pt.	"	1 50
Extra do. do. do flat and hollow half pint,	"	2 25
Do. do. do. do. third pt.	"	2 00
Taper sham, puntied half pint,	"	1 75
Do. do. do. third pint,	"	1 50
Best tale flat fluted, half pint,	"	2 00
Do. do. do. third pint	"	1 50
Double flint, 8 flute half pint,	"	3 50
Do. do. heavy long, 8 flute half pint,	"	4 50
Do. extra do. best Lima,	"	5 00
Mould flute do.	"	2 00 to 2 25
Best do. cut concave, &c. half pint	"	3 00 to 3 50
Do. assorted cut,	"	2 50 to 8 00

[illegible]

Item	Unit	Price
Plain pint,	"	2 00
Do. quart,	"	3 00
Do. 3 pint,	"	4 50
Do. half gallon,	"	6 00
Ringed Pint,	"	4 00
Do. quart,	"	6 00
Do. 3 pint,	"	8 00
Fluted quart,	per pair,	4 00 to 6 00
Do. 3 pint,	"	5 00 to 7 50
Fancy cut	"	5 00 to 15 00

CREAM JUGS.

Item	Unit	Price
Half pint, plain	per doz.	1 25
Do. footed,	"	2 00
Do. engraved,	"	2 00 to 2 50
Fancy cut,	each,	75 to 3 00

SUGARS AND COVERS.

Item	Unit	Price
Footed,	per doz.	3 00
Pressed foot, chevral arch rib,	"	4 00
Knob stem, do. do.	"	4 50
Do. engraved, do.	"	6 00

CELERY VASES.

Item	Unit	Price
Arch ribbed, knob stem,	"	4 00
Heavy plain or figured knob stem, round or pressed foot,	"	4 50 to 7 50
Engraved,	per pair,	1 50 to 2 50
Cut, fluted, &c.	"	3 00 to 10 00

CUT OVAL DISHES.

Item	Unit	Price
Various patterns and sizes,	"	5 00 to 13 00

LAMP CHIMNEYS.

Item	Unit	Price
Globe or thistle,	per doz.	2 50 to 3 00
French or straight,	"	2 00 to 2 25
Proof Vials,	"	1 00

MOLASSES CANS.

Item	Unit	Price
Glass stoppers, quart, plain	"	4 50
Do. do. pint,	"	2 50
Best, with cork tops, quarts	"	7 50
Do. do. pints,	"	4 50

DECANTERS.

Item	Unit	Price
Half pint and gill, common	"	62½
Globe or pear shape stoppered, quarts,	"	2 25
Do. do. do. pints,	"	1 50
Do. half pints,	"	1 00
Double ringed, mushroom stoppers, qt.	"	3 00
Do. do. do. do. pints,	"	2 00
Do. do do. half pints,	"	1 25
Triple ring, do. quart,	"	3 75
Do. do do. pint,	"	2 75
Double ring, engraved [illegible] qts.	"	6 00
Do. do. do. pints.	"	4 50
Triple ring, fluted top and bottom qts.	per pair	2 25
Do. do. do. pints	"	1 75
Best heavy fluted, cut stoppers, quarts,	"	4 00 to 6 00
do. do. do. pint,	"	3 00 to 4 00
Best do. fancy cut quart,	"	6 00 to 15 00
Do. do. do	"	4 00 to 10 00
Tavern decanters puntied, with mounted cork stoppers, [illegible] in neck, quarts,	per doz.	4 50 to 5 00
Do. do. pints,	"	3 50 to 4 00
Double ring quarts,	"	4 00 to 6 00
Do. do. pints	"	4 00 to 4 50
Triple ring quarts,	"	6 00 to 6 75
Do. do. pints,	"	4 50 to 5 25
Extra heavy quarts,	"	7 50
Do. do. pints,	"	6 00
Fluted top and bottom quarts	per pair,	3 00 to 4 00
Do. do. pints	"	[illegible]

[illegible]

Item	Unit	Price
Tale taper,	per doz.	75
Ring or knob stem, assorted,	"	90
Do. do. engraved,	"	1 25
Flint plain,	"	1 12½
Do. puntied,	"	1 25 to 1 50
Best flint flat fluted,	"	2 00 to 4 00
Do. do. cut fancy patterns,	"	2 25 to 7 50

CHAMPAIGNES.

Item	Unit	Price
Best plain puntied,	"	2 75 to 3 00
Do. do. fluted.	"	4 00 to 8 00

JELLY GLASSES.

Item	Unit	Price
Tale or common, plain,		90
Do. do. engraved,	"	1 50
Flint plain, per doz. 1 25 puntied,	"	1 50 to 1 75
Best flat fluted,	"	2 50 to 4 50
Fancy cut,	"	3 00 to 8 00

GOBLETS.

Item	Unit	Price
Arch. ribbed and ringed half pint,	"	1 50
Knob stem	"	2 00
Best do. plain or figured,	"	3 00
Fluted do. do.	"	4 00 to 8 00

LEMONADES.

Item	Unit	Price
Gill, strait or barrel,	"	1 00
Do. or do engraved,	"	1 50
Do. or do fluted,	"	2 50 to 4 00

EGG GLASSES.

Item	Unit	Price
Plain or pressed,	"	1 00

INK STANDS.

Item	Unit	Price
Cone or well,	"	50 to 75
Double inks, for red and black,	each	25 to 75

COMMON KNOBS AND PINS.

Item	Unit	Price
Plain	per dozen,	62½
Do. do. [illegible]	"	75
Do. do. [illegible]	"	90
Do. do. [illegible]	"	1 10
Do. do. [illegible]	"	1 20
Do. do. [illegible]	"	1 35
Do. do. [illegible]	"	1 50
Plain light, 1½ in. [illegible] in.	"	1 25
Cut, various patterns	"	2 50 to 4 50
Curtain pins, with [illegible] 3; 4 in. 4; 5 [illegible]		[illegible]

PRESSED [illegible]

Item	Unit	Price
Round or octagon [illegible]	"	[illegible]
Do. do. [illegible]	"	1 00 to [illegible]
Do. do. [illegible]	"	2 00 to 2 50
Do. do. [illegible]	"	1 25 to 1 50
Do. do. [illegible]	"	1 12½ to 1 50

PRESSED SAUCERS AND NAPPIES.

Item	Unit	Price
Round or octagon 8 inch,	"	4 50 to 5 00
Do. do. 7 "	"	2 50 to 3 00
Do. do. 6 "	"	1 50 to 1 75
Do. do. 5 "	"	1 12½ to 1 25

PRESSED DISHES.

Item	Unit	Price
Oval or octagon, [illegible] inch,	"	4 50 to 6 00
Do. do.	"	3 00 to 4 00
Do. do.	"	2 25 to 2 75

SALVERS OR JELLY STANDS

Item	Unit	Price
6 to 8 in each [illegible] to 62½; 9 to 10 in.	each,	75 to 1 00
11 to 12 in. " 1[illegible] 150; 13 to 14 in.	"	1 75 to 2 00

PRESSED SALTS.

Item	Unit	Price
Steam Boat, oval or square	per doz.	50 to 80
Heavy pillar, square or oval,	"	2 00 to 3 00
Cut salts,	per pr.	1 50 to 7 00

[illegible]

Item	Unit	Price
Heavy do.		75 to 1 50
Do. best plain		1 50 to 2 00
Do. cut,		5 00 to 8 00

L[illegible]

Item	Unit	Price
Do. cut	"	8 00 to 10 00
Pressed foot, tap[illegible]	per dz.	3 00 to 3 50
Do. heavy do	"	4 50 to 7 50
Do. cut,	per pr.	1 50 to 3 00
Segar, wine or [illegible]	per doz.	1 50 to 2 00
Socket or peg la[illegible]	"	150

LAN[illegible]

Item	Unit	Price
Barrel shape, tin [illegible]	each,	50 to 75
Signal, do.	"	75 to 1 00

CASTOR FRAMES.

Item	Unit	Price
Japanned, 3 to 5 glass,	"	75 to 1 00
Britania, 4 to 6 do.	"	1 50 to 2 00
Best metal Japan, 4 to 5 do.	"	1 50 to 1 75
Wood or paper, 3 to 6 do.	"	1 50 to 3 00
Do. Cut Bottles,	"	3 00 to 8 00

CASTOR BOTTLES.

Item	Unit	Price
Peppers, with plated tops,	per doz.	1 00 to 1 62½
Vinegars and stoppers,	"	87½ to 1 50
Mustards and glass tops,	"	1 25 to 1 62½
Cut assorted,	"	6 00 to 7 00

CUP PLATES.

Item	Unit	Price
3 inch cable edge	"	25
3 " scolloped assorted patterns,	"	28
3½ " do. do. do.	"	33
3¾ " do. do. do.	"	37½

APOTHECARIES' SHOP FURNITURE.

Item	Unit	Price
Specie Jars—lackered covers.		
Two gallon,	per doz.	10 00
Six quart,	"	8 00
Gallon,	"	6 00
Three quart,	"	5 00
Half gallon,	"	4 00
Quart,	"	2 75
Pint,	"	1 75
Half Pint,	"	1 25
Specie Jars & Covers—squat shape.		
Gallon,	"	6 50
Three quart,	"	5 50
Half gallon,	per doz.	4 50
Quart,	"	3 00
Pint,	"	2 00
Tinctures—with ground stoppers.		
Two gallon,	"	12 00
Six quart,	"	9 00
Gallon,	"	7 00
Half gallon,	"	5 00
Quart,	"	3 00
Pint,	"	2 00
Half pint,	"	1 50
Four ounce,	"	1 25
Salt mouths—with ground stoppers.		
Two gallon,	per doz.	13 50
Six quart,	"	10 50
Gallon	"	8 50
Three quart,	"	7 00
Half gallon,	"	5 50
Quart,	"	3 50
Pint, per doz. 2 25; half pint,	"	1 50
Four ounce,	"	1 50
Shew Globes—with globe stoppers.		
Two gallon,	each	1 50
Six quart,	"	1 25
Gallon,	each,	1 00
Half gallon,	"	75
Quart,	"	50
Breast pipes,	per doz.	3 00
Nipple shells,	"	90
Cupping glasses,	"	1 00
Nurse bottles,	"	3 00
Funnels, gill to quart,	"	1 25 to 2 25
Graduated measures,	each	1 00 to 1 50
Mortars and pestles, quart to half pint,	"	1 25 to 2 25
Pungents, assorted,	per doz.	1 00 to 1 37½

F. PLUNKET & Co. are now carrying on an extensive manufacture of CUT GLASS, of the *most splendid and new patterns*, which is unrivaled by any other factory in the splendor of the Glass and the beauty of the patterns.

Wheeling Oct. 12. 1837

Broadside Price List of the Wheeling Flint Glass Works issued by F. Plunkett & Co., dated October 12, 1837. This extensive wholesale price list is the single most important paper document for the study of the flint glass industry in Wheeling. Original now in the Rieger Collection at Bethany College, Bethany, West Virginia.

THE WHEELING FLINT GLASS WORKS AND THE NORTH WHEELING FLINT GLASS WORKS

By Gary E. Baker

Only ordinary green glass was produced in Wheeling between 1820 and 1829, the year that Ritchie & Wheat opened the Wheeling Flint Glass Works. In the ensuing years before the Civil War, a bewildering number of firms would make flint glass, but only two major flint glass factories would be in operation at any one time. This chapter deals with the two factories that have left us well documented tablewares from the ante-bellum period: the Wheeling Flint Glass Works (1829 - ca.1839) begun by Ritchie & Wheat, but eventually operated by Plunkett & Miller; and the North Wheeling Flint Glass Works (1835 - ca.1868) begun by M. & R.H. Sweeney & Co. and operated throughout its history by partnerships that included one or more members of the Sweeney family.

The term "flint glass" in the period before the Civil War was applied to all colorless glass with lead content whether it was worked into the finest cut tablewares, cheap tale glasses, or simple pharmaceutical vials. The flint glassmaker's ideal for fine wares was colorless glass of great clarity. Ironically, glass that approached this standard of perfect whiteness was often called "glass of good color." However, even under ideal conditions a glass pot yielded glass of varying qualities. Glass was a commodity too valuable for a business to waste. As long as it could be worked into a salable product the material was used. Thus even if a factory made luxury glass of the highest quality, it also made common and even poor wares. The Wheeling wares that can be identified today are largely luxury glasses made for use on the factory owners' tables. They are not broadly representative, but rather show the Wheeling factories at their best.

THE WHEELING FLINT GLASS WORKS

On November 11, 1829, the Wheeling Compiler announced the first production of flint glass in Wheeling:

> **FLINT GLASS**
>
> This elegant article is now manufactured in great perfection in this place. Messrs. Ritchie & Wheat have commenced operations at their works on an extensive scale. The furnace contains eight crucibles, each capable of holding eight hundred pounds of glass. All the materials are prepared by themselves. We ask the attention of the public to their advertisement in this paper, and hope their enterprise will be liberally rewarded.

The partners in this new venture were: John Ritchie, an entrepreneur (the son of Scottish immigrant Craig Ritchie, Sr. who was a successful merchant in Cannonsburg, Pennsylvania); Jesse Wheat, a practical glassman; and James M. Thompson, probably an investor. In their advertisement Ritchie & Wheat stated that they were, "ready to receive orders for any kind of Cut, Pressed, or Plain GLASSWARE," and warranted the quality of their glass "to be equal to any in the Western Country, and the prices as low." They closed by emphasizing their ability to produce high-style luxury wares and their willingness to satisfy the taste of their patrons:

> Having workmen of the first skill and taste, we are enabled to furnish setts of CUT GLASS, OF THE NEWEST & most BEAUTIFUL PATTERNS / Setts cut to any pattern that may be desired. Orders from a distance thankfully received and promptly executed.

Two travelers have left us their impressions of the fledgling flint glass factory and its products during its first months of operation. Benjamin L. C. Wailes, a Mississippi planter, who visited the factory on December 15, 1829, noted in his journal:

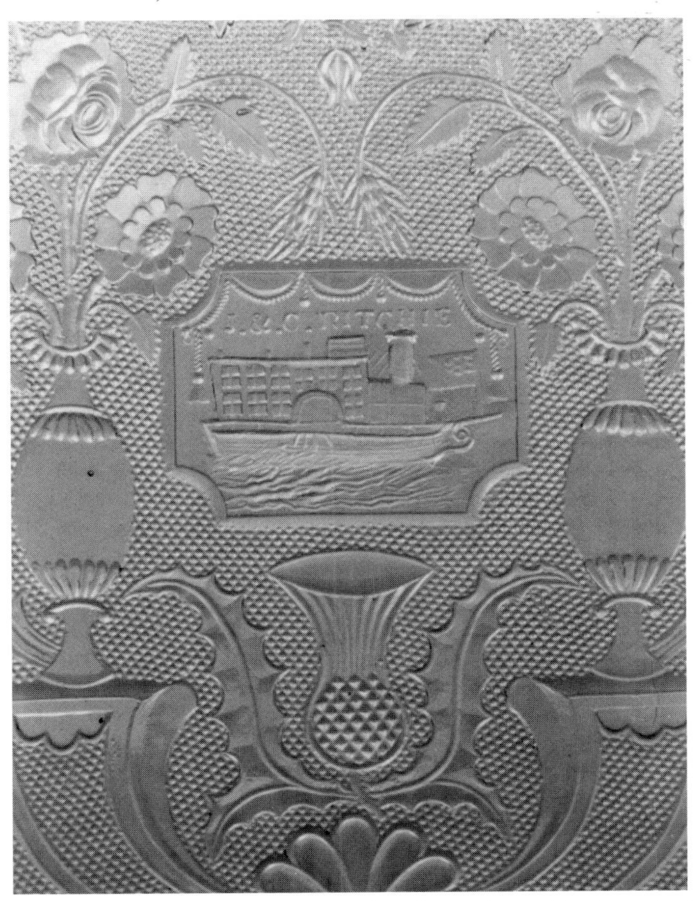

24. *Wheeling Flint Glass Works of J. & C. Ritchie. Detail of Window Pane For Use on Steamboats, ca.1833-36. Pressed lead-formula glass. This decorative pane is in the old standard window glass size of 5" x 7". Gift of Mr. Arthur C. Stifel.*

The furnace is in the shape of a cone (in the center of a large room) & has a chimney on top. It has eight arches in the side in which the crucibles of composition is placed, and under each is a place for the coal. The arches are closed until the necessary heat is obtained...

This glass is formed from stone brought down the Allegheny {sic} River....The stone is ground to powder in a stone channel by a large Iron-bound stone wheel, exactly in the manner that bark is ground for tanning. It is sifted very fine. A certain quantity of Red Lead & Potash being required to be added to the stone, a furnace for preparing the first & a large boiler for the latter is erected in the establishment. The common lead is placed in the furnace & kept at a proper temperature for ten or twelve hours, washed, & c., returned to the furnace & burnt to a handsome red color...the sand or ground stone is all baked in a furnace prepared for the crucibles.

Wailes also observed the blowing of tumblers and vials (staple items in any flint glass factory) , and the cutting of glassware with equipment "driven by a very small & neat steam engine."

25. *Wheeling Flint Glass Works, Ritchie Firm. Champagne Flute, Cut Six-flute with Knob Stems, ca. 1836-37. Blown and cut lead-formula glass, H.6¾" Museum Purchase, Ex-collection Philadelphia Museum of Art. These glasses were probably part of wedding gift sent to William Ritchie by his brother Craig Ritchie, Jr. in January 1837.*

26. *Wheeling Flint Glass Works, Ritchie Firm. Champagne Flute, Cut Six-flute with Fluted Stem, ca. 1835-37. Blown and cut lead-formula glass, H. 6⅞" Gift of Mrs. George Claypool. Fluted stems are one of several stem types that may have been called "figured" in the F. Plunkett & Co. Price List.*

The other traveler, an English woman, named Frances Trollope, was soon to achieve notoriety for her dislike of things American. In March 1830, she found Wheeling a flourishing town and visited its four-month-old flint glass factory. Trollope gave her opinion of its products in her famous book, Domestic Manners of the Americans:

We were told by the workmen that the articles finished there were equal to any in the world; but my eyes refused their assent. The cutting was very good, though by no means equal to what we see in daily use in London; but the chief inferiority is in the material, which is never altogether free from colour. I had observed this also in the glass of the Pittsburgh manufactory, the labour bestowed on it always appearing greater than the glass deserved. They told us also, that they were rapidly improving in the art, and I have no doubt that this was true.

The firm of Ritchie & Wheat was short-lived, lasting only from 1829 until November 1831, when Wheat bought Thompson's share and Ritchie in turn bought out Wheat. Ritchie did so with what he thought was an understanding that Wheat would continue at the works for a year at the annual salary of $500,

...directing and superintending the mixing of all the glass to be made at said works...& of managing and superintending all the operations of said works, and during the continuance of said service would teach and import to the said John all the art and mystery he possessed in the making of good flint glass, and all his skill and knowledge in the conduct and management of said works.

According to John Ritchie, Jesse Wheat left his service on December 10, 1831, and "unlawfully absented himself interested in a certain other flint glass works," in fact, the newly-formed rival firm of Wheat, Price & Co., which would first advertise its glass in August 1832. Ritchie sued Wheat for $3,000 in damages as a result of the incident, claiming that his business had suffered due to Wheat's absence. Depositions are preserved in the suit papers of the Ohio County Court (now at West Virginia University.) In 1833, the case was decided in Wheat's favor..

Four partners constituted the firm of Wheat, Price & Co.: Jesse Wheat, John H. Price, Charles D. Knox, and Redick McKee (who was ironically married to John Ritchie's sister, Eliza). Only Jesse Wheat is known to have been a practical glassman. The others seem to have been investors, although the commission merchants, Knox & McKee owned the Virginia Green Glass Works and had operated that factory before leasing it to the firm of Encell & Plunkett in July 1830. By August 1832, Wheat, Price & Co. had built and put into "complete operation" a flint glass works on land adjacent to the Virginia Green Glass Works. The factory complex fronted on Sixth Street (present-day Jacob Street) and was bounded by Zane and Clay Streets (present-day 17th and 18th Streets respectively). The firm's advertisement in the Western Virginia Times, stated that they were:

> prepared to execute ... orders for all the latest and most approved shapes and patterns, also: Fine cut Glass in Sets, Apothecaries' Shop Furniture, Lamps, Shades, Curtain Pins, Vials, Knobs, &c. &c. ... From the long experience of our senior partner, in this business, and the superior arrangements of the Establishment, we flatter ourselves that our WARE will be found, at least, equal in Colour, Shape and Weight, to any made in America.

After Wheat's departure, Ritchie apparently continued alone for a time. In his lawsuit Ritchie claimed that due to Wheat's absence he had "necessarily been put to great inconvenience, loss of time," and materials "in acquiring and procuring the necessary skill & knowledge in the business" and that he had "hitherto been prevented from making glass in the same quantity & of the same quality as he otherwise would." On March 22, 1833, perhaps in need of greater capital, John Ritchie sold his brother, Craig Ritchie, Jr., a half share in the flint glass works for $8,500 and took him into partnership; the resulting firm was called J. & C. Ritchie.

The operations of the two rival flint glassmakers at this juncture were small in scale as was typical of young glass factories in the Ohio Valley. When "A List of the Manufactories of the Town of Wheeling and Its Immediate Vicinity" was compiled in November 1833, J. & C. Ritchie employed 41 hands (six of whom worked in the cutting shop) and made an annual product valued at $22,000. At the same time, Wheat, Price, & Co. employed 48 hands (eight of whom worked in the cutting shop) and made an annual product valued at $30,000.

On January 31, 1834, John and Craig Ritchie expanded their growing business by buying out Wheat, Price, & Co. for $27,000 to be paid with interest in five equal annual installments, the first due on April 1, 1835. The Ritchies moved their operations to the factory complex built by Wheat, Price, & Co., renaming it the Wheeling Flint Glass Works. This brought together under one ownership the machinery, tools, and materials of the former rivals. The deed specifically stated that "moulds and presses" were included. To be paid for separately "at a fair evaluation" were:

> Cullet, boxes for packing glass, boards, sand & sand stone, clay, ashes, salts, salt petre, manganese, arsenic, lead, knobs, spindles, pepper tops, lamp tubes, jar tops, dray, cart and horses.

John and Craig Ritchie probably further enlarged this factory. In an advertisement dated March 13, 1835, published in the Wheeling Tri-Weekly Gazette, they announced that having put their "new and extensive works into operation" they were:

> now able to fill orders to a very large amount of CUT, PRESSED, AND FLINT GLASSWARE, together with chemical and philosophical apparatus of every description; apothecary's shop furniture, glass knobs, &c. &c.

They concluded with the less than modest claim that:

> Their apartment of fine cut glass is the most extensive in the western country, and is not exceeded by any in splendor of the glass, the beauty of patterns, and the style of the workmanship. Splendid sets put up to order.

In an advertisement dated October 9, 1835, appearing in the same newspaper, J. & C. Ritchie sought "8 or 10 boys of steady habits to whom a very favorable opportunity will be given to learn the glass cutting business."

By December 1836, the brothers had taken George W. Wilson as a partner. The firm of Ritchies & Wilson, in addition to flint glass, made crown window glass (in the green glass works adjacent to their flint glass works.) In December 1836, the firm's flint glass factory employed 55 hands and yielded an annual product valued at $75,000; its crown glass works employed 41 hands and yielded an annual product valued at $87,000.

Not surprisingly, Ritchies & Wilson forsook flint glass for crown glass manufacture during the next year, apparently leasing their flint factory first to F. Plunkett & Co. and then to Plunkett & Miller, who, in April 1838, advertised themselves as the "successors of Ritchies & Wilson in the manufacture of Flint Glass." Francis Plunkett and Horace Milton

27. *Wheeling Flint Glass Works, Ritchie Firm. Cream Jug, Fluted Top and Bottom, ca. 1835-37. Blown and cut lead formula glass with hollow handle, H. 5" Gift of Mrs. George Claypool.*

Miller probably rented the Ritchie factory until 1839 when they built their own factory in what is today South Wheeling. They failed in the Depression and in 1845 their vacant factory was rented by the bank to the new flint glassmakers, Barnes, Hobbs, & Co. (the progenitor of the great J. H. Hobbs, Brockunier & Co. which continued on the site throughout its existence.) Under the new management this new factory would eventually be called the South Wheeling Glass Works.

Both of the Ritchie brothers suffered losses in the Depression. John, who was declared an insolvent debtor, tried his hand as a merchant in New Orleans, but finally moved to the Texas frontier where he and his wife Ellen apparently lived out their lives in obscurity. Craig Ritchie, Jr., moved back to his hometown of Canonsburg, Pennsylvania, and became a merchant; most of the surviving glass associated with the Ritchie firms descended in his family.

Although no glass objects can be associated with Francis Plunkett today, his legacy is great. Plunkett's firm issued the only flint glass price list that has survived from a Wheeling maker of the ante-bellum period, a broadside entitled "WHEELING FLINT GLASS WORKS. PRICE CURRENT OF GLASS WARE MANUFACTURED BY F. Plunkett & Co. at their Glass Works, WHEELING, VA." and dated October 12, 1837 [page 24]. This extensive wholesale price list , arguably the single most important paper document for the study of Wheeling-made flint glass, broadly represents the types of wares made in Wheeling in the mid-1830s. It includes: tablewares ranging from costly fancy-cut pitchers to the cheapest tumblers; lighting devices — lamp goods and candlesticks; knobs and curtain pins (now called curtain tiebacks); and apothecary wares ranging from show globes to jars and cupping glasses. The list is especially useful in the study of flint glass taxonomy and the economics of the trade.

Patron taste and pocketbook governed the creation of flint glass objects, and must have played a significant role in the production of luxury tablewares, which were offered in a wide range of prices according to the elaborateness of the cutting. Engraved decoration was less expensive than cut. The finest, and hence, the most costly types of objects (with the notable exception of drinking vessels) were generally sold in pairs. Ordinary wares were sold by the dozen.

This hierarchy is readily seen in the prices of quart decanters: "fancy cut" sold for $6.00 to $15.00 per pair; "Best heavy fluted, cut stoppers" for $4.00 to $6.00 per pair; "Fluted top and bottom" sold for S3.00 to $4.00 per pair; "engraved or lettered" sold for $6.00 per dozen; the cheapest plain blown with stoppers sold for only $2.25 per dozen. Prices for quart decanters also varied with hot-applied decoration, weight of glass, and stopper type. "Triple ring" [referring to rings on the neck], sold for $3.75 per dozen, "Double ringed" for $3.00; both types were offered with "mushroom stoppers." "Tavern decanters puntied, with mounted cork stoppers, plain neck" were obviously made of heavier glass and so sold for $4.50 to $5.00 per dozen.

The firm offered pressed tablewares in a variety of sizes that included: plates, round or octagonal; saucers and nappies [i.e. bowls], round or octagonal; dishes, oval or octagonal; salts, oval or square; and cup plates with cable or scalloped edges in assorted patterns. Notably absent from the list are forms that would have required complex molds to produce, such as pressed cream jugs or sugar bowls. A simple pressed foot was optional on blown sugar bowls and celery vases. The "Mould Flute" tumblers could conceivably have been pressed, but more likely were blown molded, as references to molded tumblers occur on other lists that antedate the invention of mechanical pressing. Pressed egg glasses (offered at the same price as plain blown) were apparently the only pressed stemware available. The common knobs and curtain pins were undoubtedly pressed.

DOCUMENTED RITCHIE PRODUCTS

The cut glass objects at Oglebay Institute, that are documented by descent in the Ritchie family, parallel fashionable British glass of the 1830's. All, except one, are in the broad flute style. The stemware is cut with six flutes — the height of chaste, Greek-revival simplicity and the most expensive type of broad-flute cutting available. Cutting a disarmingly simple six flute vessel required a larger blank

28. *Wheeling Flint Glass Works, Ritchie Firm. Salt and Stand, Cut Diamond Pattern, ca. 1833-37. Blown and cut lead-formula glass, Overall H. 3".*

and greater precision than cutting a vessel with more flutes. The most tightly documented objects at Oglebay Institute are the pair of champagne flutes with "knob" (or knop) stems [Fig. 25] that were purchased from the Philadelphia Museum of Art in 1951. These flutes were part of a group of glass (sadly all long since deaccessioned) that had been donated to that Museum's predecessor, the Pennsylvania Museum, in 1906 by Henrietta and Craig D. Ritchie — the daughter and nephew of Craig Ritchie, Jr.. Craig D. Ritchie gave the Pennsylvania Museum two six-flute decanters and 11 six-flute champagne glasses that he stated (in correspondence now preserved at the Philadelphia Museum of Art) were part of "a very large present of glass — decanters, tumblers, wines, bowls &c." sent to his father William Ritchie in Philadelphia by his Uncle Craig on the occasion of William's second marriage in January of 1837. Craig D. then "a lad of seven years" remembered seeing the glass unpacked.

F. Plunkett & Co., later that year offered fluted champagnes that wholesaled for $4.00 to $8.00 per dozen suggesting a wide range of options. This pair of six-flute champagne glasses must have been some of the best that the Wheeling Flint Glass Factory made. The simple round knop at the center of their stems is a feature that was found on other glasses in the 1906 Ritchie gift including a celery vase and a punch bowl that had belonged to Craig Ritchie, Jr. "Knob" stems were specifically listed by Plunkett as an option on sugar bowls, celery vases, goblets, and wine glasses. Another six-flute champagne [Fig. 26], donated to Oglebay Institute by Charlotte Claypool, a great-granddaughter of Craig Ritchie, Jr., in 1950, was undoubtedly still more expensive, because its stem is also fluted.

The cream jug [Fig. 27], also a Claypool gift was probably intermediate in price. It is "fluted top and bottom" with a few simple cuts on its neck that vaguely suggest expensive British step-cutting. By using a hollow handle with a rigaree terminal the makers increased the handle's light refractivity without subjecting the jug to the stress of cutting in this delicate area.

The salt and stand [Figs. 28 & 29], donated by Mrs. Claypool, is an unusual survival in American glass. Both its form and its elaborately cut shallow diamonds have close parallels in British glass. That such a form was made in Wheeling during the 1830's is suggested by the survival of a pair of Sweeney stands for salts, and by the F. Plunkett price list, which offered cut salts ranging in price from $1.50 to $7.00 per pair. A salt and stand was the most expensive type of cut salt that was offered for sale by the London glassmaker Apsley Pellatt in the early 1840's.

Although the Ritchies' production of pressed glass must have been extensive, the only pressed glass object that we can be certain was made by them is the splendid "lacy" pressed glass window pane marked "J. & C. RITCHIE" [Figs. 21 & 24]. These panes were probably intended for use on steamboats, but those that have survived were put to use on land by builders and cabinetmakers. The Pittsburgh flint glass manufacturer, Bakewells & Co., which produced similar marked panes, advertised "pressed Panes for steam boats" in the mid-1830's. The elaborate and fanciful decoration of the Ritchie window pane, with its pair of eccentric neo classical vases and profusion of flora immediately calls to mind the fancy painted chairs of the period. The elongated octagon on which the charmingly naive sidewheel steamboat appears is a neoclassical shape that had long been popular in so-called medallion back windsor chairs. Although parallels have drawn between the Ritchie pane and six-inch octagonal plates decorated with a steamboat [Fig. 30], it does not necessarily follow that these objects were made in the same factory. Indeed the mold work in the octagonal plates is rather more sophisticated. The steamboat is incised into the underside of the glass rather than raised on it, and the four anthemia are rendered in a tighter, more archaeologically correct manner than the single floppy anthemion on the Ritchie pane. The octagonal plate could have easily have been made by one of the Pittsburgh factories, such as Bakewell; a mold (now at the

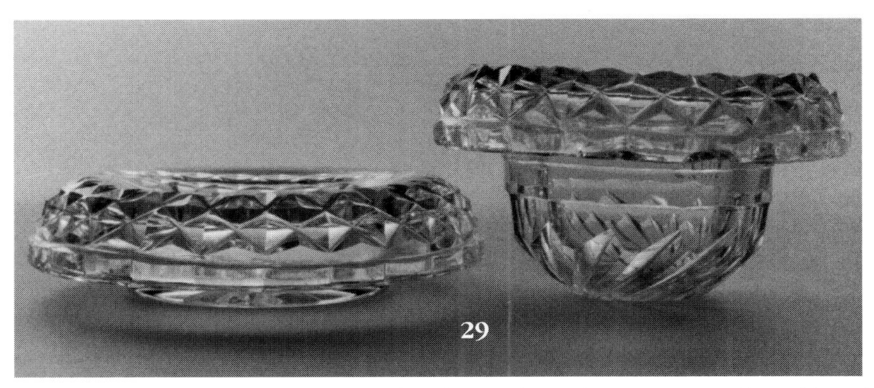

29. *Salt dish taken out of stand to better show the cutting and profiles of both elements. Gift of Mrs. George Claypool. Mrs. Claypool recalled this object being used for salt on her grandmother's table during her childhood.*

30. *Upper Ohio Valley, Possibly Bakewells & Anderson, Pittsburgh. Six-inch Octagonal Plate with Steamboat, ca. 1835-40. Pressed lead-formula glass, 6¼" across. Museum Purchase. Six-inch octagonal plates were among the pressed glass forms listed by F. Plunkett & Co. Pressed plates were undoubtedly made by both the Ritchie & Sweeney firms. Although this plate has sometimes been attributed to the Ritchie firm because the steamboat is similar to that found on the J. & C. Ritchie pane, the steamboats are actually rendered differently (see text for discussion).*

Corning Museum of Glass) for making a pressed glass image of Bakewell & Anderson's factory rendered that factory as a similar incised image on the glass. We are less certain about the attribution of a set of seven pressed six-flute tumblers [Fig. 31] that also descended in Craig Ritchie's family. These tumblers are of a type made before 1860, but if they were indeed made by the Ritchie firm, they are the earliest identifiable pressed tumblers made in Wheeling. Since tumblers like these were inexpensive and widely available they could easily have been acquired by Craig after he left the flint glass business.

THE NORTH WHEELING FLINT GLASS WORKS

The Sweeneys, Wheeling's most successful flint glass manufacturers, founded the North Wheeling Flint Glass Works in 1835. Members of the Sweeney family were partners in the firms which successively operated the North Wheeling Flint Glass Works from 1835 until about 1868: M. & R. H. Sweeney & Co. (1835-45); M. & T. Sweeney (1845-48); Sweeneys & Bell (1848-51); T. Sweeney & Son (1852-63); Sweeney, Bell & Co. (1863-67); and Sweeney, McCluney & Co. (1867- ca. 1868). The original firm of M. & R. H. Sweeney & Co. began modestly, but by 1838 its annual product value was nearly equal to that of the Wheeling Flint Glass Works.

M. & R. H. Sweeney & Co. had its origin in a family-run iron foundry. On September 6, 1830, members of the Pittsburgh iron firm of Cuthbert & Co., which included the brothers Thomas and Campbell Sweeney, purchased from the Wheeling Manufacturing Co. a brick workshop and foundry located on the bank of the Ohio River at Wheeling's northern extreme and the right to mine coal in the hillside nearby. On March 1, 1833, Thomas and Campbell Sweeney bought this foundry from the other partners for $13,000. The resulting firm of T. & C. Sweeney, however, was soon dissolved by Campbell's death later that spring. Thus in 1833, Thomas Sweeney, who had served an apprenticeship as an iron molder and had been employed in that trade in Pittsburgh, became the sole proprietor of an iron foundry. Two years later, presumably using profits from his iron foundry as a source of capital for expansion, Thomas entered the flint glass manufacturing business with his brothers, Michael and Robert Henry, forming the firm of M. & R. H. Sweeney & Co. The three brothers were the last surviving of eight sons born to protestant Irish immigrants Thomas and Sarah Ann Campbell Sweeney. Thomas was born in Ireland in 1806, his younger brothers in the United States. Their father died shortly after moving the family to Pittsburgh in about 1816 and the brothers grew to adulthood in that city.

The brothers announced the opening of their glass factory with the following advertisement in the Wheeling Tri-Weekly Times:

> North Wheeling Flint Glass Works.
> THE GLASS WORKS lately erected by the undersigned adjoining the Wheeling Foundry, are now in full operation and we are prepared to fill all orders that we may be favored with. One of the firm has had fifteen years practical experience in the business. We therefore feel confident in saying that our glass shall be equal in excellence of materials, transparency and beauty of color, in variety of patterns and in cheapness of price, to any manufactured in this place, or else where.
>
> We only ask those disposed to purchase to give us a fair trial to confirm our statements.
>
> All orders in our line of business shall be punctually attended to.
>
> Wheeling, Nov. 10, 1835. M. & R. H. Sweeney & Co.

Although Thomas Sweeney was not himself a practical glassman, he would remain the central figure in the partnerships operating the North Wheeling Flint Glass Works for the next 28 years. Michael Sweeney provided the glass expertise; Michael had served an apprenticeship as a glass blower at the factory of Pittsburgh's preeminent flint glass manufacturer, Benjamin Bakewell. Michael Sweeney's presence at this very important factory during the 1820's must have had a lasting impact on him. There he would have witnessed Bakewell's pioneering efforts in the manufacture of pressed glass and he would have been keenly aware of the fame that Bakewell had achieved with its luxury glasses through presentations, important commissions, and participation in fairs. Bakewell had presented cut glass to

Presidents Madison and Monroe, the Marquis de Lafayette, and New York Governor DeWitt Clinton, and had made glassware for the White House for both the Monroe and Jackson administrations. Finally, Bakewell's glassware had been awarded first prize (a silver medal) in 1825 by the Franklin Institute of Philadelphia at its second annual fair. The Bakewell factory not only gave Michael Sweeney practical experience, but in its achievements provided a model which his own firm would later emulate.

Thomas and Robert H. Sweeney probably served as general business managers at the Wheeling firm keeping an eye on the firm's bookkeepers, tending to sales, and overseeing the operation of the firm's glass store. Thomas Sweeney's ownership of the foundry property may well have put him in the position of a senior partner even though his first name was not represented in the firm's name. Michael and Robert did not buy shares in the glass works property until September 1843. However, Thomas Sweeney's business practices have made his exact role difficult to document. In 1869, he would testify under oath:

> I have been in the habit almost during my entire business life of transacting my business without written contracts. I do not believe that I have had a dozen such papers in business of forty years.

Lasting a decade, M. & R. H. Sweeney & Co. was the longest lived of any glassmaking partnership that operated in Wheeling during the ante-bellum period. Although technically dissolved by Robert H. Sweeney's death on March 28, 1845, the firm in a sense continued until 1848, because the survivors carried on the business as M. & T. Sweeney without taking on additional partners. During the first year of production the Sweeneys' glass works employed 55 hands, consumed 110,000 bushels of coal, and yielded a product valued at $35,000. This is considerably less than Ritchies & Wilson, who, in the same year, produced flint glass worth $75,000, employing an equal number of hands and consuming an equal amount of coal. The difference no doubt reflects the usual difficulties of operating a new glass works, such as improper furnace construction or the frequent bursting of glass pots. Another factor may have been the production ratio of expensive cut wares to plain blown and pressed wares. Both firms advertised cut glass, but one would expect the longer established firm to have built a larger trade in this luxury item. A labor intensive "cold working" process, cutting would have greatly added to the product value without significantly increasing coal consumption. Conversely, the production of a larger volume of pressed and plain blown wares would have involved a larger volume of hot work, significantly increasing the consumption of coal without a corresponding increase in product value.

Late in 1838, when the 1839 Wheeling directory was compiled, M. & R. H. Sweeney & Co. reported the same coal consumption that it had in 1836 and employed 60 hands, but yielded an annual product valued at $70,000. This increase in product value without an increase in coal consumption suggests a more efficient use of fuel and labor, and perhaps indicates the increased production of cut wares. In the 1839 Wheeling directory, J. B. Bowen wrote:

> The flint glass works of Messrs. M. & R. H. Sweeney & Co., with cutting or grinding establishment appended, turn out glassware exceedingly transparent, and manufacture articles of the best materials and workmanship. They are made to every pattern and receive every variety of beautiful finish, cut, pressed, and plain ...

Yet a more convincing indication of the growing prestige of the firm and its reputation for high quality luxury wares is the fact that, in July of 1838, they filled an order from the eminent Whig statesman, Henry Clay, for an extensive cut glass beverage service in the stylish six-flute pattern at the cost of $125. While the best flat-fluted wine glasses in the F. Plunkett price list had wholesaled at from $2 to $4 per dozen, Clay's six-flute wine glasses cost $7 per dozen.

The relative prosperity of 1838 was but a brief respite from the Depression of 1837. Late in 1839, the economy took another turn for the worse. M. & R. H. Sweeney Co. was the only Wheeling glassmaker to survive. During 1840-41, their factory seems to have operated in a diminished capacity and may have even been shut down a portion of that time. Michael and Thomas Sweeney later recalled that they "worked" their "hands but half time".

Why did M. & R. H. Sweeney & Co. succeed where Plunkett & Miller failed? It was probably a matter of timing. The Sweeneys built their factory in 1835 near the peak of the country's prosperity; Plunkett & Miller built their extensive new factory in 1839. Thus when

31

31. *Probably Upper Ohio Valley, Possibly Wheeling Area. Pressed Six-flute Tumblers (two of seven) Late 1830's - ca. 1860. Pressed lead-formula glass, H. 2¼" Gift of Mrs. George Claypool. Pressed six-flute tumblers like these must have been staple items of production in most American flint glass factories during the 1840's and 1850's. The presence of a pontil mark on the bottom of these tumblers suggests a pre-1860 date.*

32. *North Wheeling Flint Glass Works, Sweeney Firm. Candlesticks, Fluted, with Metal Sockets, ca. 1835-45. Blown and cut lead-formula glass, with pewter sockets, H. 9½". Gift of Letitia Sweeney Ewing.*

glass sales fell off, Plunkett & Miller had hardly begun to pay off the debts incurred in the construction of their factory. The Sweeney firm was probably free of heavy debt.

Prosperity did not fully return to the glass industry until the mid-forties. In February 1842, M. & R. H. Sweeney & Co. advertised that their glass works was "in complete repair" and "in full operation again." They reassured customers by stating that they hoped "their long and successful experience (one of the firm having been engaged in the business more than twenty years)" would "be a sufficient guaranty of their capacity to fill all orders on them." On March 18, the Wheeling Times and Advertiser noted the problems that had beset the flint glass industry and lauded the Sweeneys' efforts in surmounting them:

> CUT GLASS — We are much pleased to perceive, as we do by their advertisement, that Messrs. M. & R. H. Sweeney & Co. have again set their Flint Glass establishment in operation, and are now manufacturing on their former extensive scale, cut, pressed and plain glass of every description. The stock of Glass ware, of this kind, purchased by families and merchants in the west, from two to ten years since, was very large, and always beyond demand; but within two years scarcely any purchases have been made, the establishments for its manufacture have been closed or faintly dragging along a weary existence. In the meantime, the stock in consumption has been diminished, and we now flatter ourselves, that the demand must increase, and we shall be surprised, if those establishments that now go into operation do not meet with prompt & steady sales. The establishment we have named, Messrs. Sweeney & Co. as we perceive, is one of those that have adopted the true policy. They have cut close, and are determined to manufacture as low as possible and sell at the least possible price; lower than any manufactures of the same description in the west. Already has this house supplied a number of Western Merchants with fine stock this spring, and we have heard several of them speak in the highest terms, both of the beauty of their articles and price. For a supply of this article of Western manufacture there cannot be the slightest occasion for any man going beyond Wheeling. If they do they will fare worse.

With domestic competition recovering from the Depression and foreign competition recently curtailed by the Tariff of 1842, the Sweeney firm made a bid for a broader market opening stores in Pittsburgh and St. Louis and seeking to publicize their wares by entering them in industrial fairs of national stature and by presenting specimens as gifts to Henry Clay.

During the period from 1842 through 1845, the firm produced extraordinary large-scale objects of cut glass that were obviously calculated to flaunt the firm's technical virtuosity and win prizes at industrial fairs. In 1842, the firm entered the annual fair of the Franklin Institute in Philadelphia. Although they won no award, the judges' manuscript notes described their entry as a "Cut glass bowl ... finished in a superior manner, and nearly equal in colour to the best offered."

The firm persevered. On September 1, 1843, a journalist from the Wheeling Times and Advertiser visited their glass store and saw what he thought was "the finest specimen of Cut Glass" he had ever seen:

> a FLOAT BOWL, measuring about two feet at the top, and of the purest glass, the richest cutting and finest polish...of princely dimensions and appearance....

M. and R. H. Sweeney and Company probably entered this and other objects in the Fair of the Mechanic's Institute at St. Louis, where in November they "took the premium awarded for the purest cut glass."

Between 1844 and 1845, the firm produced three multiple section covered urn-shaped vases or float bowls of cut glass, ranging in size from approximately three feet six inches to five feet one inch in height. The smallest of the three had been completed by October 1844, when the Wheeling Times and Advertiser reported that the Sweeneys had manufactured a set of glassware "intended for exhibition at the institute in Philadelphia...the most conspicuous article" of which "was a float bowl ... that Victoria might covet." The judges of the Fourteenth Exhibition of the Franklin Institute held that year awarded the firm a silver medal, the first premium, for its lot of flint glass

> comprising one very large and beautiful covered bowl, fruit bowls, celleries, pitchers, decanters, tumblers, and wine and jelly glasses, all richly cut. This glass is of uniform quality throughout, remarkably clear and brilliant,and will compare favorable with the best ever brought to these exhibitions.

The Sweeneys' only competitor, The Boston and Sandwich Glass Company, received a silver medal for colored glass. According to the judges,

> The samples furnished by the Messrs. Sweeny [sic], prove that the difficulty heretofore experienced in producing good color and brilliance in the article, west of the mountains, has been overcome; and that they are now prepared to furnish the best and purest flint glass.

In November, the Sweeneys triumphantly displayed the covered bowl or vase, and other glass from the prize-winning lot in their recently established Pittsburgh warehouse, where the vase created a minor sensation! The Pittsburgh Gazette, which proclaimed the great cut glass vase "unequaled by anything of similar description ever made in the United States or perhaps the World," gave the vase's weight as 92 pounds, its height as three feet six inches, and its diameter as 18 inches.

By the end of November, some of Pittsburgh's Whigs had attempted to buy the vase from the Sweeneys so that they could present it to Henry Clay, who had just lost the 1844 presidential election, "as a token of their respect, and admiration of his brilliant services in the cause of Protection." In a letter sent from Wheeling on November 25, 1844, the Sweeneys replied:

> Sir — We ourselves design on having the honor of presenting the "Vase" to Mr. Clay, and consequently it is not for sale.

Giving the vase to Clay was an astute move, because the Sweeneys had every reason to believe that the news of the gift would be linked with that of their prize medal and that the story would be spread across the nation via Whig newspapers. (Clay prized the vase, and it evidently served as a font for his baptism in the parlor of his home several years later. It survived into this century, but was destroyed by fire.) To ensure additional publicity, the firm also presented "a pair of splendid cut glass salt sellers" from their prize-winning lot to the editor of the Pittsburgh Gazette who wrote of them: "The material is very white, beautiful and clear as crystal."

Two vases, yet larger than the one presented to Clay, were made in 1845. The costly production of two vases was probably necessitated that year by the overlapping schedules of the two nationally important exhibitions for which they were intended. The Fair of the American Institute in New York ran from October 7 through 23 and the Exhibition of the Franklin Institute in Philadelphia ran from October 21 through November 1. In May, one of the completed vases was shown at the Sweeneys' Wheeling store before being shipped to Pittsburgh "and thence to New York, for exhibition." The Wheeling Times and Advertiser, in an article entitled "Splendid Glass," described the vessel in detail:

> It is in the form of a float bowl; the whole of which is of the purest cut glass five feet and a half inch high. It is in four pieces - the stand is conical 25 inches, with flutes four and a half inches at bottom; upon which rests a cylinder one foot eight inches in diameter. On this hangs eighteen brilliant drops. On these rest the bowl, which is sixteen inches high and about eighteen in diameter. The cover is twenty-one inches high and beautiful in the extreme, forming in all the most perfect specimen of glass ever manufactured. The whole weights 202 pounds.

The article identified the glass cutter as Mr. Westwater. This was probably William Westwater (born in Scotland about 1811) who was listed in the 1850 Census as a glass cutter living in the same city ward as the Sweeney factory, and was possibly the same William Westwater who had been listed as a glass cutter in New York City directories in the mid-1830's. It would later be stated in the press that the vase cost $2,000 to make.

That November the firm was richly rewarded for its effort and expense when its displays of glassware were awarded gold medals by both the American Institute in New York and the Franklin Institute in Philadelphia. The latter awarded its gold medal by a special vote of the judges for its normal first prize was a silver medal. The Franklin Institute's judges called the large vase "a triumph in American art" without "equal for size and beauty in any country" and declared the display "the best lot of flint glass ever made in this country." (The surviving Sweeney vase [Fig. 22] now at Oglebay Institute was placed in a glass and granite vitrine on top of Michael Sweeney's grave in Greenwood Cemetery in the late 1870's and remained there until it was donated to the Institute in 1948. It originally had 17 prisms, but the non-lead formula glass prisms retrieved from the cemetery at that time seem to be late 19th century replacements.)

Although the vase was copiously described in 19th century newspapers, the firm's other tablewares were not. We do know from newspapers that these displays included a fairly full range of cut tablewares and pressed glass. The Sweeneys undoubtedly made substantial quantities of pressed glass by the 1840's. In 1843, the Sweeneys' St. Louis store advertised glass for sale in a wide range of forms that included pressed tumblers, dishes, stemware and candlesticks. So perhaps they were then producing pressed forms as ambitious as stemware and candlesticks. From their advertising we not only learn some of the forms that they were offering for sale, but have evidence that they were probably making substantial quantities of pressed glass that included stemware.

On January 1, 1848, the firm of M. & T. Sweeney was dissolved by mutual consent of the partners. Michael Sweeney, the practical glassman, retired from the firm to enter the iron industry in which his brother Thomas had made so much money. Michael would eventually suffer enormous loses in this and would finally return to the glass industry in Wheeling in 1859. The new firm of Sweeneys & Bell was comprised of Thomas Sweeney, Andrew J. Sweeney (Thomas's eldest son, a machinist, who would eventually be granted Wheeling's first glass patent), and

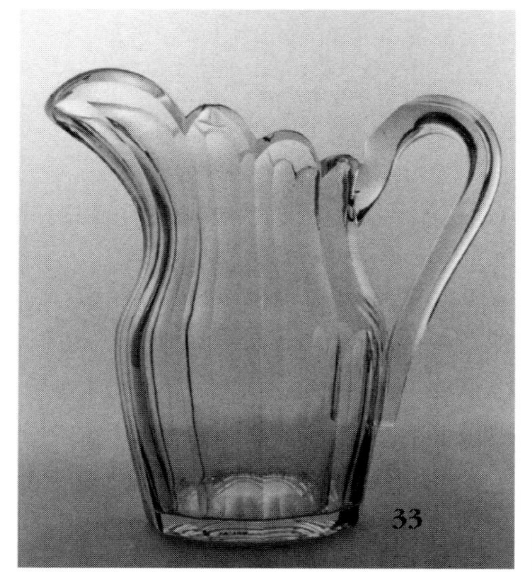

33. *North Wheeling Flint Glass Works, Sweeney Firm. Quart Pitcher, Fluted and Scalloped, ca. 1835-45. Blown and cut lead-formula glass with solid handle, H. 8½" Gift of Letitia Sweeney Ewing. The cutting on this pitcher shows an awareness of London fashions. Compare this object with illustrations of pitchers made by Apsley Pellatt at about the same time.*

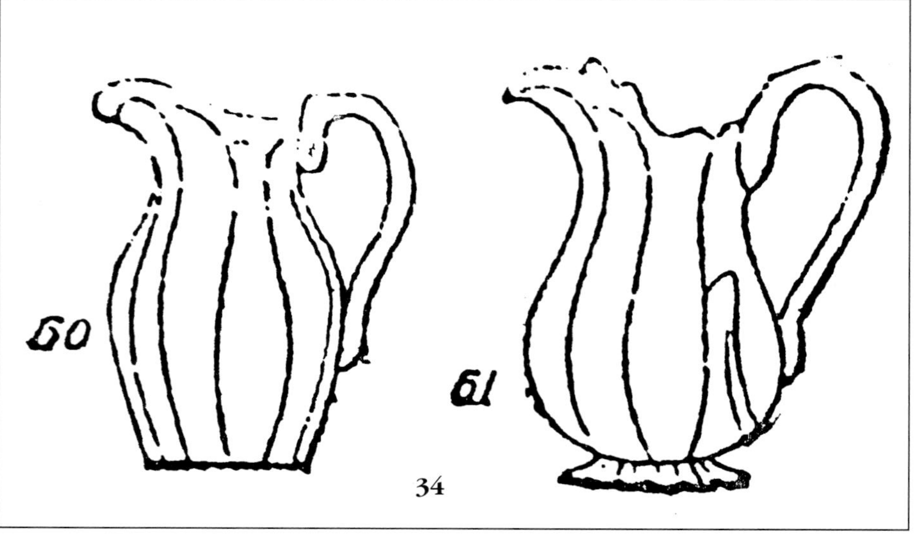

34. *Apsley Pellatt, Falcon Glass Works, London, England. Cut pitchers as illustrated in advertisements, ca. 1838-42. These pitchers or "water jugs" first appeared in an advertisement in the serial publication of Charles Dickens'* Nicholas Nickleby *in November 1838, but were reused in price lists into the early 1840's.*

Joseph R. Bell, the late firm's bookkeeper. Thomas, the senior partner held a half share and each of the new partners held a quarter share. The manuscript returns for manufacturers in the 1850 United States Census show that Sweeneys & Bell then employed substantially more hands and produced an annual product of greater value than that of the famous Pittsburgh firm of Bakewell, Pears & Co. Sweeneys & Bell employed 131 workers and produced an annual product valued at $100,000. With a staff of 90 Bakewell produced an annual product valued at $70,000.

Sweeneys & Bell suffered heavy losses when the cutting, grinding, and packing rooms of its glass factory were destroyed by fire on January 29, 1851. The fire was later said to have prevented the firm from entering its glass in the first World's Fair held in London that year. Joseph Bell withdrew from the partnership on December 31, 1851, and the firm then became T. Sweeney & Son.

The new firm soon recovered from the fire. In October, 1853, T. Sweeney and Son was awarded a gold medal for its glass at the Sixth Annual Exhibition of the Maryland Institute held in Baltimore. The Institute's published list, which is unusually detailed, gives us a broader understanding of the types of fine wares made by the firm in the late 1840's and early 1850's. It is reprinted here in full:

> 2 Best cut hollow side Goblets, 3 Best cut hollow side Champagnes, 11 Best cut hollow side Wines, 12 Best cut Kossuth Wines, 6 Best cut Kossuth Champagnes, 6 Best cut Kossuth Goblets, 3 Best cut Bowls, 2 Best cut Pitchers, 1 Best cut Scolloped Salt, 1 sett cut Washington Decanters, l pair cut Diamond Wine Decanters, 3 pair cut Ashburton Wine Decanters, 1 pair cut Washington Wine Decanters, 1 pair cut Washington Celeries, 1 cut & scolloped Salt, Star-bottom, 1 Large Cut Glass Vase — worth $2000, all manufactured and deposited by Thomas Sweeney & Son, Wheeling Va.

It is evident from this list that the Sweeney firm made many objects cut in patterns other than the broad flute style now popularly associated with Wheeling work, and that at least some of these were in patterns fashionable nationally. To be sure, fluted wares were included in the Baltimore display, most notably the great vase that was once again "trotted out." The judges of the Maryland Institute praised the Sweeney products: "All this glass is very perfect, both as regards the shape, cutting, and quality of the glass. The cut glass vase is a very rich and very superior specimen of glass cutting, and possesses a very high degree of excellence..."

The manuscript returns for manufacturers in the 1860 United States Census showed little change in size: T. Sweeney and Son employed 125 persons and produced an annual product valued at $100,000. Other major flint glassmakers had grown. By way of comparison the rival Wheeling firm of Hobbs & Barnes reported an annual product valued at $120,000 and Bakewell, Pears & Co. of Pittsburgh reported $130,000. T. Sweeney & Son had crested.

The Civil War brought problems for state, family, and factory. Wheeling became the first capital of the pro-Union Restored Government of Virginia and then, in 1863, the capital of the newly formed State of West Virginia. Wartime demand made the Sweeney iron foundry very profitable. At the same time, the war posed difficulties for the flint glass factory — much of its former market lay behind enemy lines. Not surprisingly T. Sweeney & Son ceased flint glass manufacture in November of 1863. Ironically, Joseph Bell, by this time a successful iron and nail manufacturer in his own right, rented the old North Wheeling Flint Glass Works from the father and son who had been his partners more than a decade earlier, and operated it with two other partners, Michael Sweeney and James McCluney (former bookkeeper for T. Sweeney & Son.) Being good businessmen they chose a firm name that enabled them to capitalize on the goodwill of the earlier firms that had occupied the factory – Sweeney, Bell & Co. Advertising suggests that the new firm may have experimented with the use of non-lead glass formulas, but the exact nature of these efforts cannot now be determined. At Joseph Bell's retirement in 1867, the firm became Sweeney, McCluney & Co. That firm concentrated its efforts on a new factory in Martins Ferry, Ohio, called the Excelsior Works. When its lease of the North Wheeling Flint Glass Works expired in 1868 glass production in that factory ceased.

The panic of 1873 brought financial embarrassment to both Michael and Thomas Sweeney, and caused Andrew J. Sweeney difficulties. Michael died of an apparent heart attack in 1875, while trying to salvage his business. Within two years the great urn-shaped vase was appropriately placed on his grave. Thomas retired from active business and lived out his long life in Wheeling. Andrew was a successful steamboat builder at the time of his death in 1893.

DOCUMENTED SWEENEY PRODUCTS

With the exception of the great Sweeney Vase that stood on Michael Sweeney's grave for over seven decades, all of the tightly documented glass objects associated with the North Wheeling Flint Glass Works were given to Oglebay Institute by descendants of either Thomas Sweeney, or his eldest son, Andrew J. Sweeney, who entered the firm in 1848 at the age 21. After Thomas Sweeney's death in May 1890, his personal glassware was apparently divided among several of his children. Most of the glass at Oglebay Institute that once belonged to Thomas came into the collection in 1937 initially as a loan from his youngest child, Letitia Sweeney Ewing (b. 1876); additional objects have since been donated by her son, Robert W. Ewing. Another major group was donated in the 1950's by Thomas's grandson, Julian McFerran Sweeney (b. 1878), son of John F. Sweeney (1851-95). Some of Andrew J. Sweeney's glassware (which may have included a share of his father's) came to Oglebay Institute in the early 1950's as gifts and bequests of Andrew's maiden granddaughters, Eleanor M. and Kate Lukens Sweeney.

Only the Sweeney Vase can be dated with absolute precision. Obviously the family's glassware was neither made nor acquired all at once, but rather intermittently during the course of Thomas Sweeney's long tenure at the North Wheeling Flint Glass Works. Much of the glass cut in the broad flute style must have been made in the factory's earliest years (although that style probably remained popular for some time.) The handsome pair of heavy cut candlesticks with inverted baluster stems [Fig. 32] probably date to the factory's first decade. The shape and central placement of the knop in the stem (a feature popular during the 1820's and 1830's) is seen in other Wheeling work from the 1830's including the pair of Ritchie champagne flutes discussed earlier. Comparable baluster-form candlesticks with similarly shaped candle sockets (but with a straight shaft connecting the elements rather than a knop) were once in Craig Ritchie's family. The protective pewter inserts, called "metal sockets" on the F. Plunkett & Co. Price List, were in widespread use during this period.

The elegant broad-flute quart pitcher [Fig. 33] must also date from the firm's first decade. Similar pitchers were made by the Ritchie firm as well. In fact, both firms were merely following London fashion, as can be seen from the illustrations of quart water jugs [Fig. 34] that London glassmaker Apsley Pellatt offered for sale between 1838 and 1842. The Sweeney firm evidently continued to make some objects with scalloped rims as late as 1853 for it included two different cut "Scolloped" salts in its gold-medal-winning display that year at the Maryland Institute. One of these salts had a "Star-bottom" (a feature that today is commonly called a rayed base).

The gifts of several of Thomas Sweeney's descendants have reunited a pair of celery vases with matching drinking goblet, champagne, wine glass, and tumbler [Fig. 35-39] – elements from what must have originally been a much more extensive service. All have star-bottoms. The celeries, which in their massiveness call to mind the Sweeney Vase, have scalloped rims. They are essentially cut in a pattern that was imitated in pressed glass in the 1850's which is today called Bigler by pattern glass collectors.

Portions of yet another cut service, ca. 1845-60. [Fig. 40-44] descended largely in the family of Andrew Sweeney and so may have been his originally (although he could have inherited them since the matching quart decanter came from one of Andrew's nephews). It consists of a quart and pint decanter, and matching goblets and champagne (or wine) glasses. The cutting on the body of these glasses resembles two patterns that are well-known through their pressed versions: Ashburton and old Argus. The 19th century illustration that most closely resembles this pattern, however, is of an ale glass labeled "Con(cave). Ash(burton)," which appears in a catalogue issued by the Pittsburgh firm of Bakewell, Pears & Co. in the 1870's. In that illustration there is a band of horizontal ovals dividing at mid-section the flutes with each oval centered on the corners of flutes. In the old Argus pattern, as illustrated in the 1859/60 and 1864 McKee catalogues the horizontal ovals are in line with flutes below and ovals above. So perhaps Concave Ashburton is the original name for this pattern. Since the Sweeney firm exhibited "3 pair cut Ashburton Wine Decanters," at the Maryland Institute in 1853, these glasses may represent the Sweeney's version of the well-known Ashburton pattern.

The beautifully cut fine-diamond pattern covered comport, with star bottom, ca. 1850-60 [Fig. 23] donated by Mrs. Ewing is one of the firm's masterpieces. The eight-sided

35-39. *North Wheeling Flint Glass Works, Sweeney Firm. Celery Vase and Matching Drinking Vessels, ca. 1840-55. Cut with "Star Bottoms" in pattern similar to Bigler. Blown and cut lead-formula glass, Celery Vase H.10¼". Gifts of Letitia Ewing, Robert W. Ewing, and Julian McFerran Sweeney.*

finial and stem call to mind the broad flute style, but the proportions suggest a later date. In the early 1850's, diamond pattern cutting, a perennial favorite, again became popular. Glass with diamonds in a variety of sizes was exhibited by numerous glassmakers at the 1851 World's Fair; the Brooklyn Flint Glass Co. (the only American glassmaker to be awarded a gold medal at that fair showed a decanter heavily ornamented with fine diamond cutting.) The diamond cutting of the Ritchie salt and stand is essentially in Georgian taste. Fine diamond cutting, like that seen in the Sweeney covered comport, evidently appealed to the mid-Victorian desire for elaboration and refinement for this type of cutting was widely imitated in pressed glass. The New England Co., for example, showed "130 pieces pressed sharp diamond-pattern glass ware, consisting of bowls, tumblers, goblets, champagne, wine, and jelly glasses," at the New York Crystal Palace in 1853. T. Sweeney & Son evidently kept pace for they exhibited "1 pair cut Diamond Wine Decanters," at the Maryland Institute held in the same year.

The fact that so many of the Sweeney firm's cut glass objects are related in design to pressed pattern glass suggests that the firm was cutting glass in patterns that were nationally, and even internationally popular. We may never know which of the cut patterns, if any that they originated. One thing, however, remains certain about the surviving objects. They are high-style wares of exceptional quality that were made for national market. In gazing upon them now we easily understand how their makers achieved some measure of fame in 19th-century America.

Select Bibliography

Full citations for much of the information given above are contained in Gary Everett Baker, "The Flint Glass Industry in Wheeling, West Virginia: 1829-1865" (M.A thesis, University of Delaware, 1986). My thesis also contains an extensive checklist of individuals connected with the glass industry in Wheeling prior to 1865 that was derived from city directories and census records.

Bakewell, Pears & Co., *Bakewell, Pears & Co. Glass Catalogue,* reprint. Pittsburgh: Thomas C. Pears III, 1977.

Innes, Lowell. *Pittsburgh Glass: 1797-1891.* Boston: Houghton Mifflin Co., 1976.

Lee, Ruth Webb. *Early American Pressed Glass.* 35th ed. Wellesley Hills, Massachusetts: Lee Publications, 1960.

M'Kee and Brothers. *M'Kee Victorian Glass: Five Complete Glass Catalogs from 1859/60 to 1871.* New York: Corning Museum of Glass and Dover Publications, Inc. 1981.

Moore, John Hebron, ed. "A Glimpse of Industrial Wheeling in 1829: A Selection from the Journal of B. L. C. Wailes of Natchez." *West Virginia History* (January 1959): 126-9.

Rose, James H. "Wheeling Lacy Glass." *Antiques* (June 1956): 526-7.

Sweeney, Tom. *Flight to Erin.* New York: The Exposition Press, 1948.

Wakefield, Hugh. *Nineteenth Centruy British Glass,* 2nd ed. London: Faber and Faber, 1982.

Warren, Phelps. *Irish Glass,* 2nd ed. London: Faber and Faber, 1981.

Warren, Phelps. "Apsley Pellatt's Table Glass, 1840-1864" *Journal of Glass Studies,* (1984), 120-35.

Watkins, Lura W. "Pressed Glass of the New England Glass Company - an Early Catalogue at the Corning Museum." *Journal of Glass Studies,* (1970): 149-64.

Wilson, Kenneth M. *New England Glass and Glassmaking.* New York: Thomas Y. Crowell Co., 1972.

40.-44. *North Wheeling Flint Glass Works, Sweeney Firm. Quart and Pint Decanters with Matching Stem Ware, ca. 1845-60. Cut in a Pattern similar to Ashburton and early Argus, perhaps called "Concave Ashburton." Blown and cut lead-formula glass, Quart Decanter H. 13¾". Gifts of Julian McFerran Sweeney, Eleanor Sweeney, Kate Lukens Sweeney, and Mrs. Wilmont L. Harris. Note the rim of the quart decanter originally matched flaring rim of the pint, but has since been ground down to remove chips. The tumbler is cut in yet another pattern that has parallels in pressed glass; it calls to mind several patterns including Bigler. Gift of Mary Sweeny.*

The Sweeney Vase (Punch Bowl) as it looked on Michael Sweeney's grave. The Vase is now displayed at the Oglebay Institute Glass Museum inside a reproduction of the granite monument. The original monument can still be seen in Wheeling's Greenwood Cemetery.

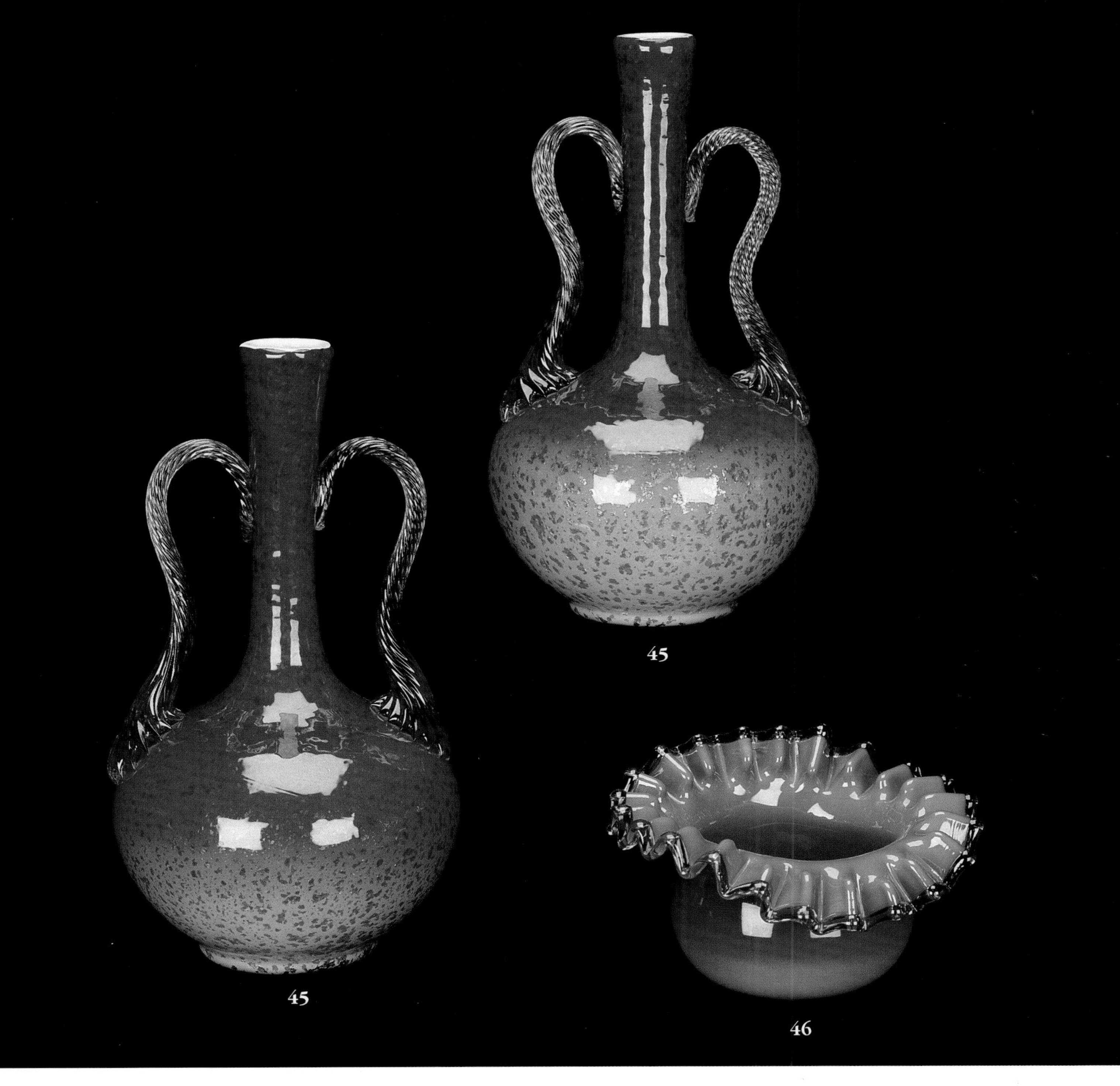

***45**. Very rare pair of spangled Peachblow Vases with applied reeded and starred handles. 10½" tall.* ***46**. Peachblow Vase with lavender interior and ruffled top with amber edging. This is the only known example of Wheeling peachblow where the inner lining is any color but white.*

47. Hanging lamp with a Hobnail pattern shade in Gold Ruby. This piece rests on a brass frame on which cut prisms are attached. ***48.*** *Hobnail pattern lighting shades, also in Gold Ruby.*

Chapter Three

Glassmaking in South Wheeling 1845-1893 (Hobbs, Brockunier and related firms)

49. Footed Cake Plate. Although Oglebay Institute has no catalogue showing this pattern, this identical hand appears on the arms of a Hobbs, Brockunier chandelier located in Wheeling. Recently, a shard of this hand also was found on the former site of the factory. A similar, but not identical, hand was made as a novelty salt shaker by the Central Glass Company.

Jane Shadel Spillman
James S. Measell
Holly H. McCluskey

GLASSMAKING IN SOUTH WHEELING 1845-1893

HOBBS, BROCKUNIER AND RELATED FIRMS

By Jane Shadel Spillman, James Measell and Holly McCluskey

One of the largest and most innovative glass companies in America was located in South Wheeling. Hobbs, Brockunier is remembered for its versatility, making everything from fine cut lead crystal and pressed tableware to colorful art glass. At this Wheeling firm in 1864, William Leighton, Sr., a partner and chemist in the company, developed and perfected a lime glass formula that could be worked in a mechanical press.

By 1879, J. H. Hobbs, Brockunier and Company was among the largest glass houses in America. In that same year, the publication *A History of the Panhandle: West Virginia* described the glassmaking establishment as follows:

> In February, 1863, the present firm of J. H. Hobbs, Brockunier and Co., was formed, consisting of J. L. Hobbs, John H. Hobbs, and Charles W. Brockunier. This firm was not only destined to become famous for the variety, quality and beauty of its pressed ware, and the richness of its cut, engraved and blown ware; but also for almost completely revolutionizing the character of glass and the method and appliances of finishing it. The works cover an area of several acres. It has an extensive cutting department, engraving room, mould making department and all the conveniences and appurtenances of a complete and well arranged works. Its production now consists of all articles of glass for table use, engraved, cut and etched; bar goods, lamps, chandeliers and epergnes. Its wares are sold in every state in the Union, and Cuba, South America, Australia and Europe.

The factory bounded by 36th, 37th, Wetzel and McColloch streets in South Wheeling was among the foremost in America, especially during the 1870s and 1880s, when its production of pressed and blown glass rivalled that of factories in New England and Pittsburgh. The plant included much of the best glasshouse technology available, such as Gill patent furnaces and improved pots purchased from Dixon and Woods, a prominent Pittsburgh supplier.

Personnel

In 1845, John L. Hobbs and James B. Barnes, former employees of the New England Glass Company in East Cambridge, Massachusetts, came to Wheeling. They leased and later purchased the idle glasshouse known as the South Wheeling Glass Works. The enterprise soon began to prosper. The project was apparently the brainchild of Barnes who, with his son James F. Barnes, owned more than half the stock and who made the first trip to Wheeling in 1843 or 1844. An engineer, Barnes was credited by Deming Jarves with the successful design and construction of the New England's furnaces. Hobbs was foreman of the New England's glass cutting shop and also principal salesman, according to *A History of the Panhandle*. The qualifications of the younger Barnes are not recorded, but he was probably trained in the glass business since it was common for sons to follow fathers. James B. Barnes died in 1849, and the firm's name was changed from Barnes, Hobbs and Company to Hobbs, Barnes and Company. This reflected alterations in the partnership shares as well as the entry of Hobbs' son, John Henry Hobbs, into the business.

The Barnes family had marriage ties to Thomas Leighton's family. Leighton was the superintendent of the East Cambridge firm and his son John married James Barnes' daughter, Jane. In 1863, William Leighton, another son of Thomas Leighton, joined the Wheeling venture. A chemist and glass blower, Leighton returned to Cambridge in 1868, but his son, William Leighton, Jr., left the New England Glass Company and took his father's place in Wheeling. The Leightons were tireless experimenters with glass formulas and manufacturing methods. Much of the later success of the firm in producing pressed tablewares and fancy colored glass was due to them.

In 1863, James F. Barnes retired. John H. Hobbs, who then controlled the company, took in two new partners—William Leighton and Charles W. Brockunier (the bookkeeper for the firm). From 1863-1881, the glasshouse was known as J. H. Hobbs, Brockunier and Company, although local citizens continued to call it the South Wheeling Glass Works.

In addition to the various partners, the plant was, at different times, home to a number of glassworkers who went on to make names for themselves in the American glass tableware industry, whether by owning and operating their own plants or by holding significant managerial positions. Among them were the following men: Andrew Baggs, Percy J. Beaumont, Charles N. Brady, Peter Cassell, Jacob Crimmel, William K. Elson, John Henderson, Otto Jaeger, Nicholas Kopp, James Leasure, Charles W. Leighton, Harry Northwood, John Oesterling, J. E. Radcliff, James B. Russell, William F. Russell, and Charles Voitle.

Cut Glass

An early announcement in the *Wheeling Times and Advertiser* was headlined "PLAIN, PRESSED AND CUT FLINT GLASS," so it is obvious that one of the firm's intentions was to produce cut glass. At first, Barnes, Hobbs probably produced a general line of "white" or flint glass, including commercial containers, apothecary's wares, bar wares, and, after kerosene lighting became popular, lamps and lamp chimneys. The *History of the Panhandle* account, which was probably based on interviews with one or both

50.-52. *Three Caster sets, about 1870-1890. Colorless non-lead glass, mold-blown and engraved. The engraved floral and leaf patterns on these sets are similar, although the silver-plated holders are not alike. The engraved patterns are typical of the 1870's and 1880's and are related to the designs in the Hobbs engraving pattern book in the Mansion Museum collection.*

of the Hobbs men, lists solar chimneys, jars, vials, tumblers, salts, cologne bottles, pungents, tinctures and lard oil lamps as products of the first year.

A Barnes, Hobbs and Co. tradecard, now in the Corning Museum's Rakow Library, says they "would inform their friends and public that they are now prepared to execute orders for FLINT AND FANCY COLORED GLASS in all the varieties of CUT, PLAIN, MOULDED AND FIRE POLISHED." The 1851 *Directory of the City of Wheeling & Ohio County* shows "Jno. L. Hobbs, Jas. F. Barnes, Jno. H. Hobbs/HOBBS, BARNES & CO." and lists the same products as does the pre-1849 tradecard. Also from this time period is a drawing of the factory, which descended in the Barnes family; this shows a multi-storied building with a stepped gable and one chimney, indicating a medium-sized company. By 1857, an article in the *Wheeling Intelligencer* mentions three furnaces and a cutting room.

U. S. Census records for 1850, and the 1851 *City Directory*, researched by Gary Baker, list eight glass cutters living in South Wheeling who were probably employed at the South Wheeling Glass Works of Hobbs, Barnes & Company which was a mile away from any other factory. One of these cutters, George Birch, was profiled in the *History of the Panhandle.* The article indicates that he was trained at the New York firm of Jackson and Baggott, one of the leading cutting firms in the United States in the 1820s. He must have been a tableware cutter, and his presence among a staff of eight suggests that more cut glass was made at Hobbs, Barnes in the 1850s than can now be identified. Four of the original eight cutters were gone by the 1860 U. S. Census, but they had been replaced by four others, leaving a constant number of glass cutters in South Wheeling. Cut glass was surely a standard product at the Hobbs factory. The 1860 Census reported an annual product of $120,000 for Hobbs, Barnes & Company. In its first fifteen years, it had grown tremendously, but it was to double in output during the next twenty years.

The younger Barnes sold his share of the firm to John H. Hobbs and John L. Hobbs in 1861. The influence of the elder Hobbs, who was a master glass cutter, eventually led the company into more extensive production of cut glass in the late 1860s and the 1870s. By this time, the other Wheeling cutting firms had closed, and Hobbs presumably had a market free from local competition as well as employees who were experienced glass cutters. Because there are no extant catalogues for these years of the company, it is impossible to know exactly what was produced; the earliest evidence for the production of engraved glass are the blown bells which were made for the 1860 presidential election. These are relatively simple and inexpensive and would not require a highly skilled engraver.

The firm also was producing engraved graduates and other laboratory wares, part of a line of apothecary shop glassware and a staple of many glass factories. The company needed engravers to produce these, and the same workmen could have engraved the bells [Fig. 64].

By the 1870s, the Hobbs company had built additional buildings and was producing quantities of cut and engraved glass. *Crockery and Glass Journal* (August 26, 1875) mentioned that the company was operating three furnaces and went on to discuss other particulars: "The rooms intended for new wash and selecting rooms are about completed. The addition to their cutting shop was put into operation last week. Their cutting shop is the largest one in the West, and one of the largest in the country." In the 1860s and 1870s, only a few plants in New England and New York were producing cut glass. The Pittsburgh output was almost entirely pressed glass, so the Hobbs cutting shop would not have needed to be particularly extensive in order to be the largest in the West.

Surprisingly, the Hobbs exhibit at the Philadelphia Centennial in 1876 displayed as much cut glass as pressed ware. The Oglebay Institute collection has several pieces which were probably shown there, including two pitchers and a footed tumbler [Figs. 58-60]. The exhibit was described at some length in the *Wheeling Intelligencer* on April 10, 1876:

> We had the opportunity of seeing on Saturday the cut and engraved glass ware selected from the manufactures for exhibition at Philadelphia by Messrs. J. H. Hobbs, Brockunier & Co.... We noticed among their regular manufactures ... a "bubble tumbler"... so light that when filled to one-sixteenth of an inch of its edge with water, it will float in water; and yet these fragilities are elaborately decorated by the cutter and engraver. In the great variety of richly cut, engraved, obscured or frosted, and embossed ware, we noticed more particularly the rich cutting and engraving on three of the leading shapes. Of these, one comprises what is known to the trade as the No. 58 or "Mitchell" shape cut, what is technically termed the "Strawberry Diamond Pattern."... This pattern is carried throughout on smaller bowls, celery glasses, pitchers, dishes (cushion shape) finger bowls, decanters, nappies with and without handles, goblets, champagne, claret, wine and cordial glasses, and other table ware... The second we note is what is known to the trade as the No. 86 shape... Here we have a bowl 9 1/2 inches high and 10 inches in diameter at its edge. The edge has 16 OG scallops;...grooves are cut to near the bottom...the panels formed by the grooves are filled with "sharp" or "silver" diamonds and the scallops are filled in with "mitre" fans. The whole effect is very rich;...The third set is a combination of prisms and concaves. The decanters of this set are of the No. 49 shape; the goblets, wines etc, are of the No. 5 shape; the dishes are oval shape...The engraved ware is not only very beautiful, but the engraving is exquisite, among which is a celery glass engraved with moss rose, vines and flowers; two glasses, one with a charioteer, horse and chariot, another a rampant goat and prostrate beer drinker; a goblet with the representation of the "vintage", a Fifth Avenue pitcher with the full monogram of the firm "J.H.H.B. & Co." elegantly engraved on it;.....

This article describes clearly three patterns of cut tableware of different shapes, and it shows that Hobbs was producing a fairly complete line of tableware. The three patterns—strawberry diamonds, silver diamonds, and prism cutting—were typical of the period and not particularly ornate or innovative. The "obscured or frosted ware" was probably acid-etched or sandblasted or both. These techniques were relatively new in the 1870s. Etching was popular in England during the 1860s, and sandblasting was first demonstrated at the Vienna World's Fair in 1873. An article from an unknown publication (preserved in the Thomas Gaffield scrapbooks at MIT) describes the Hobbs, Brockunier exhibit and credits the firm with "as fine engraved work as any factory west of the Allegheny mountains."

In spite of the firm's extensive display of cut and engraved glass, the original commendation given to Hobbs, Brockunier was for "Lime glass table-wares, lamps, etc., pressed and cut, of very good quality, also some bone-glass ware. Forms rather heavy, cutting moderately good, prices low."

In the mid-1870s, the company patented glass chandeliers which were mostly pressed, but had some cut elements. An ad in *Crockery and Glass Journal* (January 16, 1879) mentions that the South Wheeling Glass Works of J. H. Hobbs, Brockunier and Company are manufacturers of "Flint & Fancy Colored Glassware, Cut and Engraved Goods, and Glass Chandeliers." During the same year, Hobbs, Brockunier purchased a new gas furnace which was a great innovation, and three separate articles in the same trade paper describe its installation and the effect upon business. In a lengthy article in *Crockery and Glass Journal* (September 18, 1879) it was mentioned that the new furnace was then the largest in this country, if not the world. The following week, the *Journal* interviewed William Leighton, Jr., about its capabitlites, and reported as follows:

53.-57. ***53.****Goblet, about 1865-1885. (Ht. 6¼", D. 3½"). Colorless non-lead glass, pressed and engraved with flowers and the initials "EJG" for Elisabeth Jane Good.* ***54.*** *Decanter, about 1860-1880 (Ht. with stopper 13⁷⁄₁₆", D. 4"). Colorless lead glass, blown, and engraved with ferns and the inscription, "R.C. to P.B."; polished pontil mark on base, blown stopper engraved to match. This is probably a typical example of Hobbs tablewares from 1855-1880, and is said to have been a wedding present.* ***55.*** *Carafe, about 1860-1880 (Ht. 6", D. 4¼"). Colorless lead glass, blown and cut in a pattern of vertical ribbing and horizontal bands, cut star on base.* ***56.*** *Bowl about 1875-1885 (D. 4½", Ht. 2½"). Colorless lead glass, blown and cut with interlocking mitre cuts across the base, and panels of silver diamonds separating polished areas with cut facets. The design on this bowl is unusual in its combination of elements. It came to the Mansion Museum from a member of the Hobbs family.* ***57.*** *Egg Cup, about 1865-1880 (Ht. 3¹³⁄₁₆", D. 2½"). Colorless non-lead glass, pressed and cut with stars in a pattern numbered "135" and illustrated in a pattern book used by a Hobbs salesman and now owned by the Mansion Museum.*

> The factory it is claimed, is the largest in the United States. It includes three large furnaces working up about sixty tons of glass weekly, employs three hundred and thirty hands, most of them skilled laborers, has the largest cutting-shop in the country, and last year did a business of over $300,000...Of the variety and extent of the products of the South Wheeling Works, I can only speak generally...I have called it a tableware factory because the larger part of its manufacture is intended for table use, but its patents reach from glass chandeliers to glass coffins and monuments, and are sufficient to light the way into the world as well as to provide a decent exit from it.

It is difficult to make comparisons with other glass companies on the basis of the statistics given, but $300,000 worth of business and 330 employees certainly made Hobbs larger than the New England Glass Company or the Bakewell firm in Pittsburgh, two of the oldest and most prominent glass tableware makers in the country. The New England Glass Company had been much larger in mid-century, but most of the Eastern firms were having problems in the 1870s. Cut and engraved wares were an Eastern specialty at this time, and the New England glass companies exhibited mostly cut glass at the Centennial, while the Pittsburgh companies exhibited only pressed glass. The financial figure given is apparently not for the cut and engraved glass, but the entire output of the firm, and much of it was pressed glass tableware. It seems plain from these articles that Hobbs had turned from making primarily apothecary's and bar wares (some of which were engraved or cut) in the 1860s to making primarily lighting and tablewares, both pressed and cut or engraved.

On April 7, 1881, a notice in the *American Pottery and Glassware Reporter* revealed that "the employees of the cutting department at Hobbs, Brockunier and Co.'s glass works were discharged on Friday last, and the work will now be done by contract, with an entire change of hands." Labor problems were endemic in the glass industry at this

58.-60. 58. *Footed tumbler, about 1876 (Ht. 6 9/16"). Colorless lead glass, blown, with sheared rim and applied stem and foot, polished pontil mark and cut lines on base. Copper-wheel engraved with a male classical figure driving a one horse chariot, ferns engraved on the reverse. Bands of engraved lattice-like decoration at top and bottom frame the scene. This glass is presumably the glass described in the 1876 Centennial article as having a "charioteer, horse and chariot".* ***59.*** *Pitcher, about 1876 (Ht. 9 3/4"; W. 4 1/2"). Colorless lead glass, blown, tooled with applied handle and foot, cut and engraved decoration of roses and thistles in one medallion and lilies of the valley on the opposite side in another. The medallions are surrounded by engraved ferns and a shield engraved under the spout with a monogram JHHB with the letters superimposed on each other. This piece came from the executor of Charles W. Brockunier's estate and is probably the "Fifth Avenue pitcher, with the full monogram of the firm, J.H.H.B. Co. engraved on it" shown in Philadelphia. It may be the work of Otto Jaeger, a European engraver who worked for the company in the 1870's and early 1880's.* ***60.*** *Pitcher, about 1876 (Ht. 10 1/8", W. 4 3/4"). Colorless lead glass, blown, tooled, with applied handle and foot, cut in a pattern of diamonds in panels with fans above; foot cut into scallops, cut star underneath. This helmet shape was apparently called "Fifth Avenue" by Hobbs; the diamond pattern cut on it was made by many companies from the mid-1830's until the 1880's. This combination of motifs matches the second cut pattern described in the Centennial article above, with a scalloped edge, panels of "sharp or silver diamonds" and the scallops filled with fans, and it may have been shown in Philadelphia, especially since the piece came to the Mansion Museum from a member of the Brockunier family. The helmet shape of both these pitchers is an unusual one in American cut glass although some pressed patterns use it.*

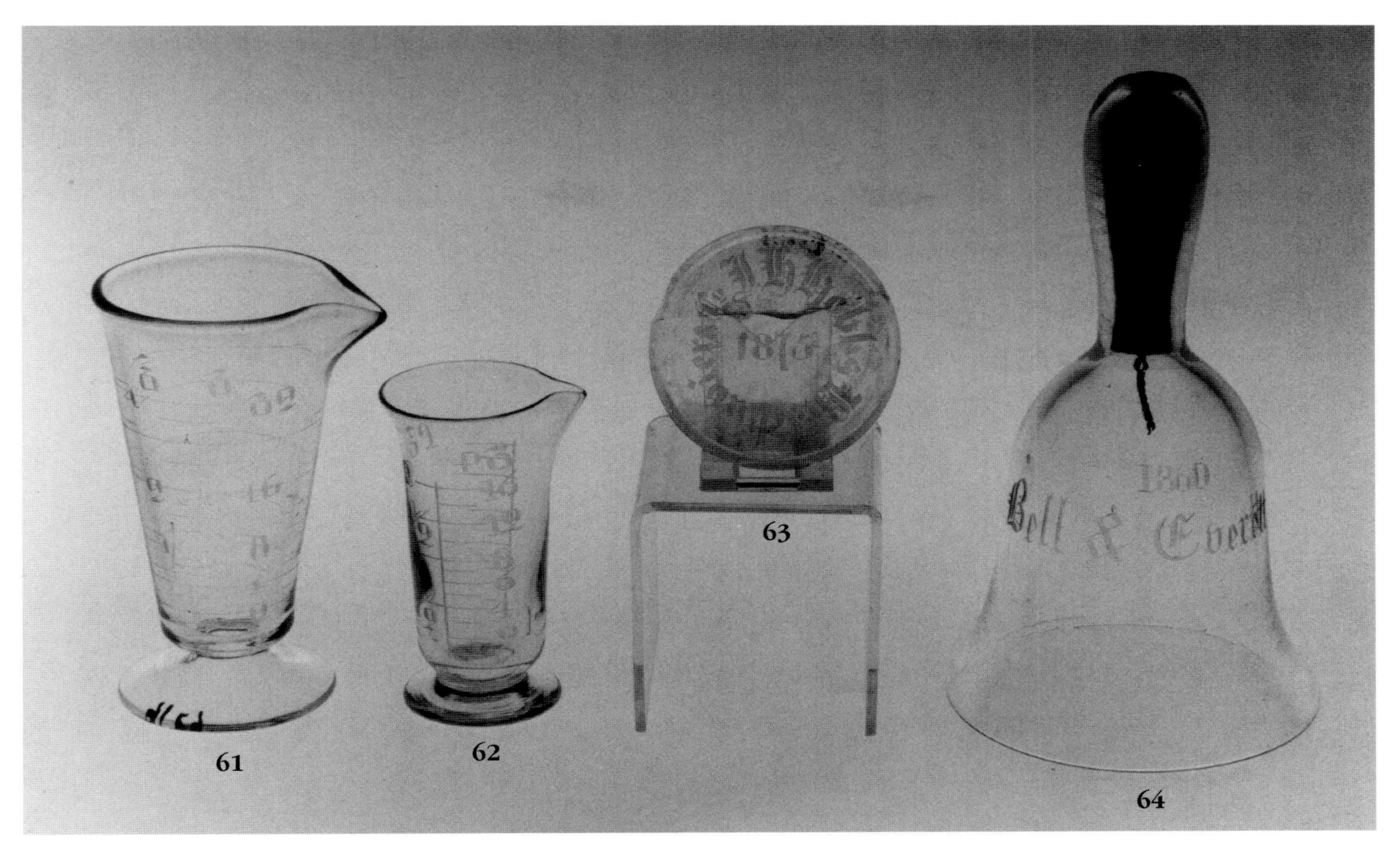

61.-64. 61.-62. *Two blown and engraved graduates, probably about 1850-1880 (Ht. 5¼", D. 3"; 88.6: Ht. 4⅛", D. 2½"). These simple blown and tooled pieces are probably typical of Hobbs's products in the 1850's and 1860's. The graduates were shaped in a mold, tooled and have applied feet. The measuring lines are engraved.* ***63.*** *Plaque, engraved "J. H. Hobbs, Brockunier Co/1875" (D. 3"). This was found in the cornerstone of the Old Capitol Building in Wheeling where it was presumably placed when the stone was laid.* ***64.*** *Blown glass bell engraved "1860/Bell & Everett" (Dia. 4½"). Abraham Lincoln's principal opponent in the Presidential election of that year was Stephen A. Douglas, nominated by the Democrats, but the Democratic vote was split because the southern conservative wing of the party nominated Senator John Bell of Tennessee. Bell was extremely popular in the south and siphoned off enough of Douglas' support to permit Lincoln's win. The colorless lead glass is of an excellent quality, better than the typical glass used for commercial purposes like the graduates. The handle of the bell has been filled with plaster of paris to hold the clapper. This descended in the Brockunier family.*

time, and the mass firing probably followed an attempt by a fledgling glass workers' union to organize the cutters.

The factory was damaged by fire in February, 1882, but the cutting room and packing shop escaped unharmed, and, by mid-March, the newspapers reported that one furnace was operating and the cutting shop was running full-time. At the West Virginia State Fair on Wheeling Island in September of that year, engraved glass with flora and fauna was exhibited to great praise. These were the work of Harry Northwood and Otto Jaeger, both Hobbs employees at the time.

The Oglebay Institute collection includes an undated engraving pattern book (probably from the 1870s), which was used by the firm's chief salesman, A. G. Frohme. It has an entwined "AGF" monogram on the cover which is similar to the one on the pitcher exhibited at the Centennial, and it includes a variety of simple floral and leaf patterns to be engraved on tableware as well as sample inscriptions for bar and bitters bottles, an overall star pattern and one for engraving measurements on graduates. Much of this type of engraving was done on pressed tablewares, since similar patterns are found in factory catalogues from several Pittsburgh producers of such wares.

The production of cut and engraved glass was apparently phased out by the mid-1880s. In spite of the three stylishly cut patterns shown in 1876, it is likely that the minor lines of cutting and engraving, maintained perhaps for prestige, were but a small part of the company's business. Similarly, the Franklin Flint Glass Works in Philadelphia owned by the Gillinders was a company famous for its pressed glass in the 1870s and 1880s, but it was also one which demonstrated cutting and engraving at the Philadelphia Centennial, exhibiting several elaborately engraved pieces. For both of these firms, cutting and engraving were probably techniques done more for "show" than for financial reasons. If this were not the case, more identifiable examples of Hobbs cut and engraved glass would probably be in existence today.

Chandeliers

As indicated in the previous section, ornate chandeliers were an important part of Hobbs, Brockunier's production from the late 1870s through the 1880s. These chandeliers were covered by several patents issued in 1876-78. A catalogue (now in the Oglebay Institute collection) devoted to these chandeliers explains the fixtures: "these goods are all constructed of Iron Gas Pipe, plated or tinned, and put together in a strong and workmanlike manner. The covering is made of heavy moulded and cut ornamental glass, and the whole complete makes the strongest and most durable fixture made."

The major sections were made as pressed glassware, and some segments were fashioned into elbows while the glass was still in a malleable state. The globes were blown glass, and most were decorated with acid-etching to create a frosted finish that diffused the light without glare; some featured additional etched effects, generally in geometric or floral motifs. Although the major portion of each chandelier was manufactured in South Wheeling, some of the prisms and decorative chains were imported. The journal *Scientific American* (May 24, 1879) reported that "Wheeling manufacturers make the beautiful glass chandeliers which have become so fashionable of late, but they import the cut glass pendants from Switzerland, where the peasants make them by hand cheaper than they can be made by machinery in this country. Many of these chandeliers are sent to London, so the pendants make two voyages across the ocean."

The catalogue shows a variety of "gas and coal oil glass fixtures" and sixteen different "patent pressed chandeliers" available with 6, 8, 12, 16, 24 and 32 lights. It goes on to claim that Hobbs firm's chandeliers have six advantages over similar gilt or bronze fixtures, namely "Cheapness, Beauty, Cleanliness, Economy of Light, Harmony of Effect and Cheerfulness." Many older residences in the Upper Ohio Valley still have a Hobbs chandelier, now electrified, hanging in a front hall, dining room or parlor. The Oglebay Institute Mansion Museum has three chandeliers on display.

Pressed Ware

From the late 1860s through the early 1890s, the South Wheeling Glass Works produced a great variety and huge volume of pressed tableware for the American and European markets. Undoubtedly, the success of Hobbs, Brockunier's pressed glassware came from William Leighton, Sr.'s development of lime glass, a new, non-lead glass formula that could be used in a mechanical press. An account in *History of the Panhandle* describes the company's attempts to produce this new glass:

> [In 1863] John L. Hobbs became convinced that the glass of the future would be a glass in the manufacture of which one of the principal ingredients to be used would be lime, and that lead would be discontinued. He caused material to be purchased, and, in spite of several unsuccessful experiments he was not discouraged in eventually attaining success.... In the fall of 1863, William Leighton, Sr., was admitted into the firm, and took charge of the manufacturing department. He entered readily into the prospect of finding a glass pure in color and durable without lead being a component part of its composition. After numerous experiments, sand, (from Berkshire County, Massachusetts) Spanish whiting or chalk, bicarbonate of soda, with the other usual ingredients, were found to make a brilliant and durable glass. Every glass works at this time, East and West, of any importance, was making lead glass, and today the same works are making the soda-lime glass....

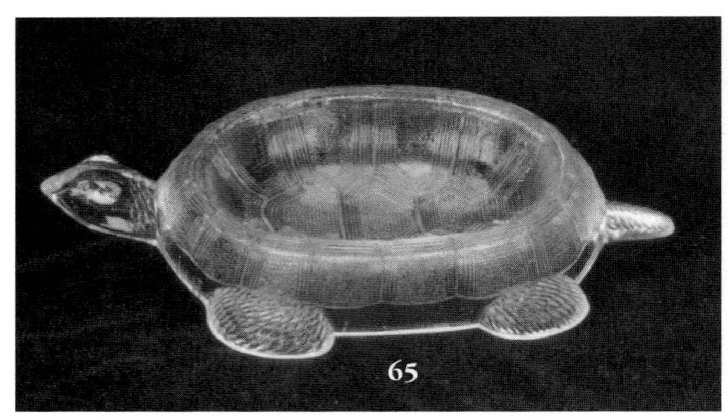

65. *Turtle-Shaped Dish, made in colorless glass. This design was patented by William Leighton, Jr. on June 15, 1875.*

This colorless, non-lead formula cost less than a quarter as much as the traditional lead glass previously used in pressing, and it worked as well or better in a mould than the lead formulas. Leighton's invention in 1864 revolutionized the American glass industry, and it did much to ensure the Wheeling-based company's financial success.

66. *Pair of colorless, pressed candlesticks in Hobbs No. 3 pattern.*

An assortment of Hobbs pressed pattern ware:
67.-71. *Hobbs Centennial pattern:* ***67.*** *Water Pitcher,* ***68.*** *Creamer,* ***69.*** *Covered Compote,* ***70.*** *Covered Pickle or Marmalade Jar,* ***71.*** *Covered Sugar.*
72. *Beer Mug designed by George B. Fowle for the American Centennial and patented April 11, 1876,* ***73.*** *Goat's Head pattern Spooner,* ***74.*** *Centennial pattern Bread Plate,* ***75.*** *Goat's Head Spooner with frosted finish on foot,* ***76.*** *Centennial Celery Vase.*
77.-82. *Further examples of the Centennial pattern:* ***77.*** *Base of a Butter Dish,* ***78.*** *and* ***79.*** *small Sugar and Creamer,* ***80.*** *Salt,* ***81.*** *Covered Butter Dish with frosted finish on feet,* ***82.*** *Oval Covered Relish.*

Hobbs pressed ware in opal (or milk glass):
***83.** and **84.** Sawtooth pattern Spooner and Creamer, **85.** Blackberry pattern Celery Vase, **86.** Paneled Wheat pattern covered Sugar Bowl with Spooner Rim, **87.** Crucifix Candlestick - similar to but not made by Hobbs, Brockunier.*
***88.** and **89.** Blackberry pattern Sugar (missing lid) and Creamer, **90.** and **91.** Grape with Overlapping Foliage pattern Spooner and Creamer, **92.** and **93.** Paneled Wheat pattern Sugar and Creamer.*
***94.** Blackberry pattern Double Egg Cup, **95.** Blackberry pattern Master Salt, **96.** Blackberry pattern Dish, **97.-98.** No. 330 Hobbs Block pattern Spooner and two Salt Shakers.*

In the late 1860s and throughout the 1870s, the firm made pressed wares in crystal and opal (pronounced o-pal), an opaque white glass often called "milk glass" by collectors today. Among the earliest patterns were "Grape with Overlapping Foliage" [Figs. 90 - 91] and "Blackberry" [Figs. 85,88-89,94-96]. The designs for these were registered by John H. Hobbs and William Leighton, Jr. on February 1, 1870 (#3,828 and #3,829, respectively). On February 28, 1871, Hobbs registered the design for "Paneled Wheat" [Figs. 86, 92-93]. Naturalistic designs, featuring birds, fruit and flowers were quite popular at this time.

For the nation's 100th birthday in 1876, the firm produced a line of pressed tableware which they called Centennial, known as Viking or Bearded Man today. The design was officially registered to John H. Hobbs on November 21, 1876 (#9,647). The head of a bearded Viking appears on the feet of most pieces, as well as on the spouts of pitchers and creamers and the finials of covered articles [Figs. 67-71, 74, 76-82]. On January 8, 1878, Hobbs registered the design for Goat's head (#10,392) [Figs. 73 and 75]. Both patterns were produced in colorless or frosted glass. Interestingly, John Hobbs' inspiration for these two designs came from the same source. According to Eason Eige (NEAGC *Bulletin*, summer, 1991), Hobbs copied both the Viking and the Goat's Head from silverplate patterns made by the American Sterling Company which were first patented by James Stimpson in 1854.

The Oglebay Institute collection contains two pressed celery holders in the firm's No. 77 pattern [Fig. 102], a plain line of stemware first made in the 1870s which remained in production for well over a decade. The celery holders are engraved with the name "McNell" (a prominent Wheeling attorney). A similarly engraved oval dish [Fig. 104] was part of the company's No. 53 line, and two covered apothecary jars [Fig. 103] were likely made at the same time. The set was a wedding gift to the McNells, who were married in 1880.

Pressed glass of exceptional quality often rivalled cut glass in terms of brilliance and attractiveness. Hobbs, Brockunier's most popular imitation cut design was their pattern No. 101 [Figs. 105-125, 188, 195]. The company called this "Hob Diamond and Star," but it is known today as Daisy and Button. The No. 101 line was intended to be utilitarian rather than decorative. A catalogue from the late 1880s shows Daisy and Button in a four piece table set (butter dish, creamer, spooner and covered sugar bowl), cruet set, a variety of bowls, tankards, plates and nappies as well as such novelties as the "toy tumbler," and a yacht-shaped salt, pickle and celery. The most decorative piece of No. 101 was the "hanging canoe," [Fig. 119] shown in the catalogue page as dangling from an elegant cord and tassel.

Hobbs, Brockunier's No. 101 was available in five regular production colors: crystal, old gold [amber], sapphire, marine green and canary as well as amberina, a special color. Amberina was a heat-sensitive glass that displayed a range of color from ruby to amber which had been patented by the New England Glass Company in 1883. In 1886, under a contractual agreement with the New England Glass Co., Hobbs, Brockunier produced Amberina, using the patented name, in its No. 101 line only [Figs. 119-125]. An advertisement placed by Hobbs in the *Glass Factory Directory* for 1886 states "Licensed manufacturers of the celebrated AMBERINA ware in PRESSED SHAPES."

Another imitation-cut line was Hobbs, Brockunier's pattern No. 102 (U. S. design patent #16,994), designed by William Leighton, Jr., and patented Nov. 23, 1886 [Fig. 126]. Leighton described this as a "series of Maltese crosses, a series of angular ribs between the crosses, and a series of fan-like figures." *Pottery and Glassware Reporter* (August 26, 1886) remarked that "this is very beautiful ware and difficult to tell from cut." Although usually found in crystal glass, it is also listed in catalogues as available in old gold, sapphire and canary. Pieces in crystal may be decorated with bright yellow stain; this was called decoration No. 9 by the company.

The Oglebay Institute collection has several pressed dishes or bowls embellished with what collectors call Tree of Life [Figs. 127-131]. Some of these are shown in the firm's advertsing in the early 1880s, along with the No. 98 leaf.

The No. 330 line was introduced in 1889. Now known simply as "Hobbs Block," this was an extensive line of tableware which included the typical berry set, table set and water set as well as many sizes of bowls and other utilitarian objects [Figs. 132-143]. Articles are usually found in crystal glass which has been treated with hydrofluoric acid to create a frosted, satin-like finish; the typical amber stain decoration provides a pleasing contrast. This treatment is known as Frances Ware and was applied to several other patterns as well. Some opal articles were also made using moulds from the No. 330 line [Figs. 97-98]. The Fenton Art Glass Company of Williamstown, WV, used this line as the inspiration for a similar pattern made in the mid-1950s in various opaque colors.

Decorating also played a prominent role in three pressed lines in crystal glass which debuted in early 1889. These were No. 334 Crystalina, No. 335 (now called Hexagon Block) and No. 337. No. 334 can be found with either gold edge or ruby edge, as can No. 337. No. 335 (Hexagon Block) was available with ruby stain [Figs. 147, 150, 152] and with ruby stain and engraving. By the spring of 1889, *Pottery and Glassware Reporter* (April 10, 1890) said the company "can't make and ship pressed goods fast enough" and mentioned "very large sales" for the No. 334 and No. 335 lines.

No. 339, which today's collectors call Leaf and Flower, was introduced in early 1891 [Figs. 148-149, 151, 153]. It was available in crystal as well as a dark amber stain (decoration No. 25) or a bright yellow stain (decoration No. 30). This was an extensive line of tableware and other utilitarian pieces.

Blown Ware

Many collectors associate Hobbs, Brockunier with their blown-moulded lines and free-blown pieces. Produced mostly in the 1880s, this glassware was available in a variety of colors and decorative effects that appealed to 19th century Victorian tastes.

One of the company's earliest endeavors into so-called "fancy glass" was what the firm marketed as "Craquelle" [Figs. 154-158]. In an article for *The Magazine ANTIQUES* (March 1975), Robert DiBartolomeo explained how this was made:

> In October 1882, C. W. Brockunier concluded an

interview with a local reporter by speaking about the "ornamental tableware" which the company then made as its "specialty." Brockunier declared that he was very happy to learn that "some of the famous crackle [sic] ware manufactured at the South Wheeling Works" was being sold in Philadelphia as "extra fine imported glassware." What had begun as an experiment early in the year was now the specialty of the glasshouse. The "crackle" was what the company called "Craquelle," a frosted ware produced by rolling "an inflated gather over a marver that had been previously covered with fragments of pounded glass." The pulverized bits stuck to the gather, which was reheated and formed into the finished article.

Another special decorative glass was Hobbs, Brockunier's "spangled ware," which was patented by William Leighton, Jr., on January 29, 1884. These are multi-layered, mould-blown articles in which tiny mica flecks are trapped between layers of glass, giving a metallic sheen to the pieces [Figs. 159-164].

In early 1885, *Pottery and Glassware Reporter* (January 22, 1885) credited Hobbs, Brockunier with "some of the choicest ware ever made or put on the American market." This ware surely included items in ruby glass made from glass batches containing gold dissolved in a mixture of strong acids called aqua regia. These articles are eagerly collected today.

The article in *Pottery and Glassware Reporter* went on to mention several specific colors, namely Rubina and Rubina Verde, and it paid tribute to the Wheeling-based company's "large force of highly skilled artisans, capable of work rivalling in beauty and exquisite workmanship the old world's best productions." A similar color from this same period was called "Ruby Amber."

These three are heat-sensitive glass formulas. Re-heating blown items (in an auxiliary furnace called a glory hole) produces ruby color on crystal [Figs. 198-199] and ruby on greenish-yellow [Figs. 177-186, 188-189], respectively. In like manner, the Ruby Amber color was obtained by re-heating items in canary glass [Figs. 171-174, 176, 192].

The Rubina, Rubina Verde and Ruby Amber colors were used for many pieces of blown glassware made by Hobbs, Brockunier. Among these were individually-numbered articles in the No. 300-series and a line dubbed No. 331 [Fig. 198].

99.-101. *Three Blown Molasses Cans:* ***100.*** *and* ***101.*** *are examples of the Hobnail pattern. They were found along with other cargo when the Wheeling-built Steamboat* Bertrand *was excavated in 1968-69.*

One of the most impressive items in the Oglebay Institute collection is a No. 101 covered cheese dish in a ruby/blue color combination, called Bluerina [Fig. 195]. A heat-sensitive glass, it is reminiscent of British glassmaker Thomas Webb's "Alexandrite" ware.

The short No. 205 and No. 206 lines consisted of blown ware in opaque glass with edges of contrasting colors. Several of the No. 205 and No. 206 flat bottom bowls feature tight crimping effects that are found as a finishing technique on other Hobbs pieces [Fig. 280].

The most popular design in Hobbs' blown-moulded ware was their No. 323 line; collectors call it simply "Hobnail" today. Trade journals such as *Pottery and Glassware Reporter* (May 6, 1886) mention both the names "Pineapple" and "Dewdrop" in discussing these wares in their own time, and it is possible that these terms were the original company names for this product. An article from *Pottery and Glassware Reporter* (November 25, 1886) described the line's popularity this way:

> Hobbs, Brockunier and Company, South Wheeling, are running their big establishment on full, the demand being very good with them, especially in their superb lines of fancy and art glass. The demand is very large for their 323, or Pineapple in opalescent and parti [sic] ruby colors. The Coral and Peach blow also continue in active request. Their entire plant is supplied with natural gas by the Manufacturer's Gas Company, of which Mr. Charles W. Brockunier is president. The specialties above noted are not to be exceeded in attracting universal attention. The delicacy and fine shading of the different tints are exquisite to behold and seem to have about reached the limit of perfection. In general lines the firm is doing a very fair trade also, though the active season is drawing to a close.

The Oglebay Institute collection includes numerous pieces in Hobnail. Colors range from crystal and other transparent colors (canary, old gold and sapphire) to the heat-sensitive: ruby, Rubina and Rubina Verde [Figs. 47-48, 204-227, 259-262, 271]. Some articles were treated with acid to impart a frosted, satin finish [Figs. 228-230].

Opalescent colors, also achieved through a heat sensitive process wherein the glass strikes white upon reheating, were also made [Figs. 83-98]. Milk glass, called opal in the 19th century, was also used by the company to make blown-moulded molasses cans, as they were called, in both hobnail and plain styles [Figs. 99-101]. These have applied handles, also of opal glass, along with pewter or tin tops.

Among the best-known Hobbs, Brockunier products in Hobnail is Frances Ware. This began as a crystal glass, and it was treated with acid to obtain a satin finish except for the topmost edges or upper portions. These areas were given an amber stain [Figs. 232-240]. Although it is not certain which "Frances" inspired the name of this line, Kyle Husfloen, editor of the *Antique Trader Weekly*, offered this explanation in the June/July, 1990, issue of *Glass Collector's Digest*:

> Although I haven't actually seen the fact verified, I have always felt that the name "Frances Ware" was derived from the first name of the popular First Lady of the late 1880s, Frances Folsom Cleveland, the young wife of President Grover Cleveland, the only American President married in the White House. Mrs. Cleveland, only 21 when she married the 49-year old President, became a popular image in this country and her pretty face and figure were quite often used as a promotional gimmick by numerous American firms.

Frances Ware was popular for some time and appears in several original catalogues.

The characteristic Frances Ware treatment also was applied to another line of blown ware, No. 326. This line also was made in a number of other colors. An article in *Pottery and Glassware Reporter* (January 17, 1889) mentioned "ten effects, namely, crystal, crystal opalescent, sapphire, ruby, these four colors in satin finish, decorated No. 7 and Frances." Decoration No. 7 was an amber stain applied to crystal pieces, while the term Frances Ware was reserved for amber stain on crystal pieces which had been satin-finished with acid. Collectors often call the No. 326 Frances Ware pieces "Sateena Swirl"[Figs. 145-146].

Opalescent glass also was a staple of production at the South Wheeling Glass Works during the 1880s. The number 325 line featured a white opalescent swirl on crystal, ruby and sapphire pieces [Figs. 243, 246, 253, 255, 258, 264, 265-267]. No. 323 Hobnail also was available in opalescent.

One opalescent pattern featuring a patriotic theme is called Stars and Stripes today. This appears in a Hobbs catalogue as their No. 293 line, and it was offered in ruby opalescent [Figs. 248 and 254], crystal opalescent and sapphire opalescent. This type of ware also was made by the Beaumont Glass Co. in Martins Ferry, Ohio during the 1890s, and more recently, by the Fenton Art Glass Company for the Metropolitan Museum of Art.

Among Oglebay Institute's more interesting blown-moulded items are four glass bells [Figs. 268-271]. While these novelties cannot definitely be attributed to Hobbs, Brockunier, the three ruby pieces do resemble the Wheeling firm's Coin Spot; No. 207 swirl; and Hobnail respectively. All four bells have similarly-shaped handles.

The No. 230 Neapolitan line was introduced in mid-1887, and the trade publication *Pottery and Glassware Reporter* mentioned "fancy colors." An original catalogue shows these articles in acid-finished rubina glass. The Oglebay Institute collection has several examples from this line, including two vases in frosted ruby, each with different crimping at the top [Figs. 277, 282-283]. Figure 283 is hand-painted. No. 230 also was made in ruby glass [Figs. 272-276]. These mould-blown articles required careful finishing by skilled workers who applied and shaped the decorative

102.-104. *McNell table set, 1880 (Ht. 8¾", D. 4½"). Colorless, non-lead glass, pressed and engraved "McNell". The set consists of two celery vases, two compotes(not shown), two jars and an oval bowl. The shape is pattern No. 77 in a Hobbs catalogue of the 1880's. The set was a wedding gift to Mr. and Mrs. Frank McNell in 1880. McNell was a Wheeling attorney.*

feet, attached a rosette to the underside and, when necessary, fashioned a pouring lip and applied a handle of crystal glass.

One vase in the Neapolitan line is particularly important [Fig. 282]. This piece was actually an invitation issued to President and Mrs. Grover Cleveland to visit Wheeling. It was signed by members of the Wheeling Chamber of Commerce, including Charles Brockunier, and dated August 1887. Unfortunately, neither the beauty of the vase nor the good will of the Chamber encouraged the President to take a trip to Wheeling that summer. On August 31, 1887, a local newspaper reported that he and his wife would not make the visit.

Wheeling Peachblow

Wheeling Peachblow is certainly Hobbs, Brockunier's most famous fancy glass. Originally called Coral Ware by the company, this is a heat-sensitive colored glass that shades from a rich ruby to yellow-green. Coral Ware was developed in 1885 to compete with the English "Peach Glass," another heat-sensitive ware that was being exported to America by Thomas Webb. After an interview with Charles W. Brockunier, the *Wheeling Intelligencer* (September 14, 1886) explained what happened: "When Mr. Thomas Webb of England made his first shipment of coral or peachblow to New York, Mr. William Leighton, Jr. secured a piece of the ware and before the second shipment the always enterprizing [sic] firm [Hobbs, Brockunier] was turning out the same ware."

Apparently the new line met with immediate success. Both the local newspapers and the glass trade publications mention a great demand for Coral Ware. For example, *Pottery and Glassware Reporter* (November 26, 1885) had this to say:

> Hobbs, Brockunier and Co., Wheeling, are now running all three of their furnaces full time. They have a big trade and are behind with orders in many cases. Among their latest novelties is the Coral Ware, which for elegance of shape and beauty of coloring cannot be excelled anywhere. They have a line of pitchers in this ware of exquisite finish, the color rivalling the bloom on the peach.

The "peachblow" name associated with this glass today originated on March 8, 1886, when the widow of shipping magnate Charles Morgan auctioned her art collection for charity. One item in the sale, an antique Chinese porcelain vase, sold for $18,000. This was an immense sum of money in those days, and news of the sale shocked the art world. The color of the vase was described as "peachblow."

Almost immediately the word "peachblow" became associated with opulence and wealth. Enterprising American businesses could not let such an opportunity pass, and soon all manner of "peachblow" ceramics, glass and even cosmetics were made and sold. An article in *Pottery and Glassware Reporter* (April 29, 1886), headlined "THE CRAZE FOR PEACH BLOWS," discussed the peachblow phenomenon:

> A new craze in glassware has been developed. As might have been expected, it is anything in 'peach-blow' color, caused by the public interest aroused in the celebrated vase from the Morgan collection. On the counters and shelves of glassware dealers are beginning to be seen all shades of the 'peach-blow,' and it is prophesied that it will spread over nearly every article of ornamental crockery.

Peachblow lines were offered by three American glass companies—the Mt. Washington Glass Co. of New Bedford, Mass.; the New England Glass Co. of Cambridge, Mass.; and Hobbs, Brockunier. The Wheeling firm simply changed the name of its Coral ware to Peachblow.

Wheeling Peachblow always has an inner lining, typically white or opal. The exterior is deep ruby, shading to yellow-green. Peachblow has two finishes, shiny and matte or flat. The shiny is a natural finish, while the matte results from treating the piece with acid.

The archetype of the Peachblow line is the vase on the dragon stand [Fig. 285]. This is a facsimile of the porcelain piece that sold in 1886, and therefore it is called the Morgan Vase. Other shapes in Wheeling Peachblow range from utilitarian pieces such as salt shakers and cruets to decorative vases. Many shapes in Peachblow were used in other lines, such as the No. 91 and No. 301 blown jugs.

One extremely rare piece is the small, round vase with the purple lining [Fig. 46]. This is the only known example of Wheeling Peachblow where the lining is other than opal glass.

Lamps

Lamps and lighting fixtures were a staple of the South Wheeling Glass Works production line from the Civil War era until the factory closed in the early 1890s. Original catalogues show a wide variety of styles, colors and patterns available in lamps and shades. Lamps ranged from small fairy lamps in old gold, crystal and sapphire colors to hand lamps with opalescent fonts and crystal bases. The larger stand lamps, made with crystal or opalescent fonts, have opal or crystal bases.

On May 24, 1870, John H. Hobbs patented a brass connector for stand lamps [Figs. 316-317]. Although the connector can be one distinguishing characteristic in identifying a Hobbs lamp, it cannot be used in dating a piece. The company's patent lasted for over twenty years, and the connector was in use until the early 1890s.

Lamps in the Oglebay Institute collection date to the 1880s and early 1890s [Figs. 314-319]. The collection also has several lamp shades, all in ruby glass [Figs. 47-48, 320]. Hobbs, Brockunier's catalogues included dozens of shades ranging from 4 to 14 inches in diameter. As with the lamps, these were produced in a wide variety of patterns and colors.

Combination and Closure

The partnership of Hobbs, Brockunier and Company officially expired on December 31, 1887. Charles W. Brockunier and William Leighton, Jr., left the firm to pursue other interests. In 1888, John H. Hobbs, the third stockholder in the firm, reorganized the glasshouse as the Hobbs Glass Company and remained as general superintendent. From 1888 to 1891, the company produced a variety of lamps and tableware much as they had done in the past. In fact, one Hobbs Glass Company catalogue belonging to Oglebay Institute features several pages under the heading "Hobbs, Brockunier and Company," a clear indication that many of the same lines were still available.

In March 1891, the company's stockholders decided to join the newly-formed United States Glass Company. Headquartered in Pittsburgh, this conglomerate brought together more than a dozen heretofore separate enterprises located in Ohio, Pennsylvania and West Virginia.

The major goals of the cartel were simple: (1) maintain control of prices; (2) effect economics of scale relative to raw materials and freight rates; and (3) operate with non-union labor as much as possible. The United States Glass Company identified each of the factories under its aegis with a capital letter. The Hobbs Glass Company became "Factory H," and its day-to-day operations continued much as before. Within a few months, several key managers decided to leave the United States Glass Company and to associate themselves with independent concerns, such as the Elson Glass Company in Martins Ferry.

The directors of the United States Glass Company decided to concentrate the firm's operations in its Pittsburgh-area plants, and, after closing two factories in Findlay, Ohio, they later decided to build a large, modern plant at Gas City, Indiana, where the town offered all manner of inducements such as free natural gas, tax abatements, etc. Furnaces at the Wheeling-based Factory H were shut down in the fall of 1893 (*China, Glass and Lamps*, October 11, 1893). Salesman A. G. Frohme was directed to sell off the glassware stored in the plant. This was accomplished in about eight months (*China, Glass and Lamps*, May 23, 1894).

Despite several attempts to revive and/or sell the plant during the late 1890s, it remained idle until the Wheeling Board of Trade forged a deal with Harry Northwood in 1902. The plant was renovated and reopened as H. Northwood and Company. Ironically, Northwood had begun his career as a glass etcher at Hobbs-Brockunier in the early 1880s.

References

Baker, Gary Everett. "Hobbs, Brockunier & Co.'s. Glass Factory Burned." *Glass Club Bulletin* of the National Early American Glass Club, No. 153 (Fall, 1987), pp. 14-16.

J. Stanley Brothers File, Rakow Library, Corning Museum of Glass, Corning, New York.

DiBartolomeo, Robert E. "Wheeling Peachblow: The Glass Made from Gold." From lecture notes at Oglebay Institute Mansion Museum.

Eige, Eason. *A Century of Glassmaking in West Virginia.* Huntington Galleries (now Huntington Museum of Art), 1980.

Hajdamach, Charles R. *British Glass: 1800-1914* Suffolk: Antique Collectors' Club Ltd., 1991.

Jefferson, Josephine. *Wheeling Glass.* Columbus: Heer Printing Company, 1947.

J. H. Newton et al., *History of the Pan-Handle; West Virginia.* Wheeling: Caldwell, 1879.

Revi, A. C. *American Pressed Glass and Figure Bottles.* London: Thomas Nelson and Sons, 1964.

Welker, John W. and Elizabeth F. *Pressed Glass in America: Encyclopedia of the First Hundred Years, 1825-1925.* Antique Acres Press, 1985.

Examples of Hobbs No. 101 Daisy and Button pattern:
105. *8½" Square Bowl in Crystal with Amber decoration,* ***106.*** *Canary Star Bowl,* ***107.*** *Bowl in Old Gold.*
108. *and* ***109.*** *Canoes,* ***110.*** *Canary Cruet with Cut Stopper,* ***111.*** *Old Gold Toy Tumbler,* ***112.*** *Old Gold Star Nappy,* ***113.*** *5" Bowl,* ***114.*** *7" Canary Plate for Butter.*
115. *Finger Bowl,* ***116.-117.*** *Two examples of 4½" Square Nappy, one in Sapphire Blue,* ***118.*** *Yacht Celery.*

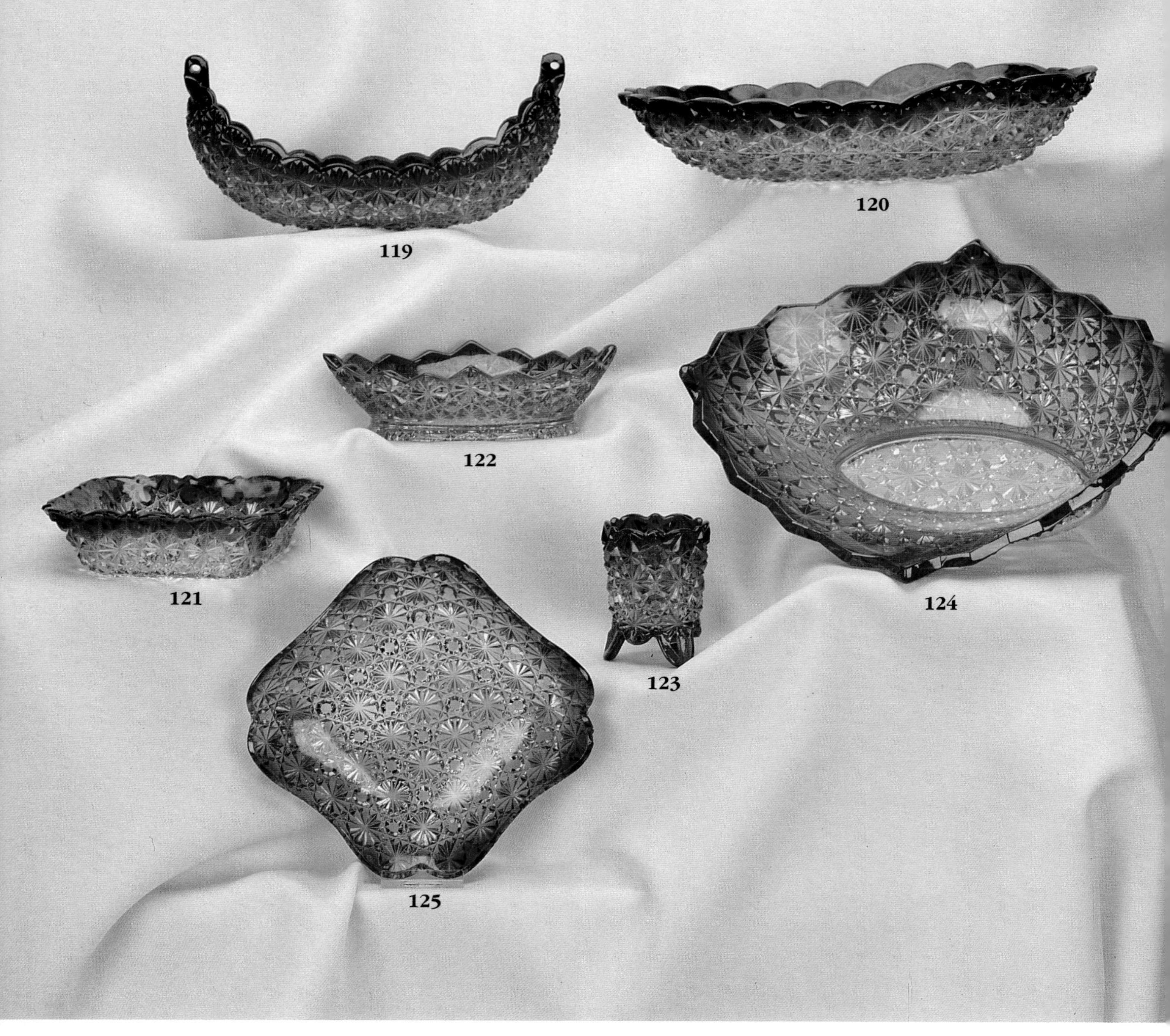

All of these pressed items in Amberina are from the firm's No. 101 line:
***119.** Hanging Canoe, **120.** 10" Oval Bowl.*
***121.** 4½" Nappy, **122.** 6 " Nappy, **123.** Toy Tumbler, **124.** 10" Bowl.*
***125.** Ice Cream Saucer.*

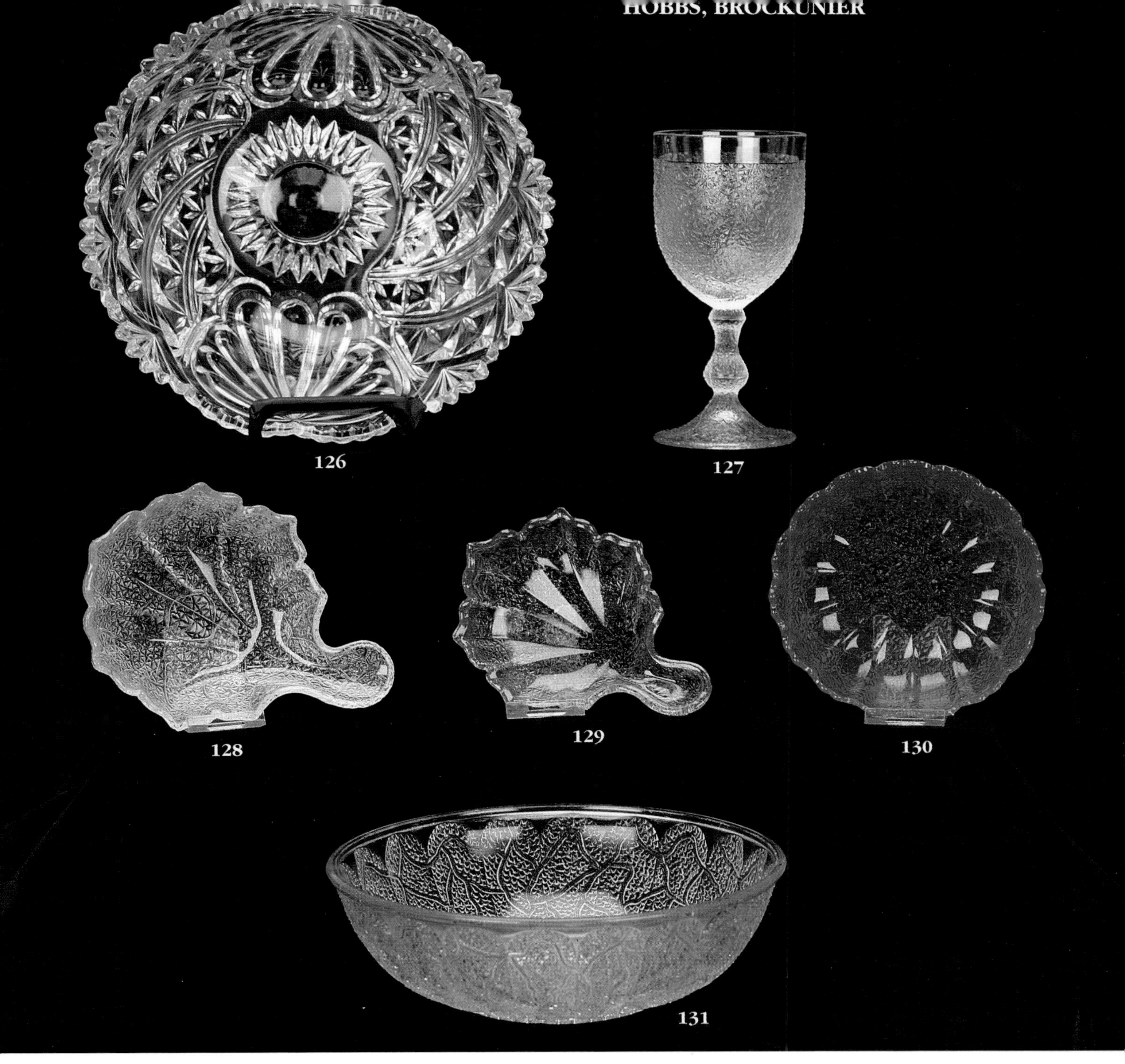

126. *Hobbs No. 102 Bowl in undecorated Crystal,* ***127.*** *Crystal Goblet embellished with Tree of Life.*
A Study in Hobbs Tree of Life decoration: ***128.*** *and* ***129.*** *No. 90 Leaf Dishes, 5" and 4½", respectively,* ***130.*** *No. 98 Nappy in Sapphire Blue.* ***131.*** *8½" Round Bowl (not Hobbs, Brockunier).*

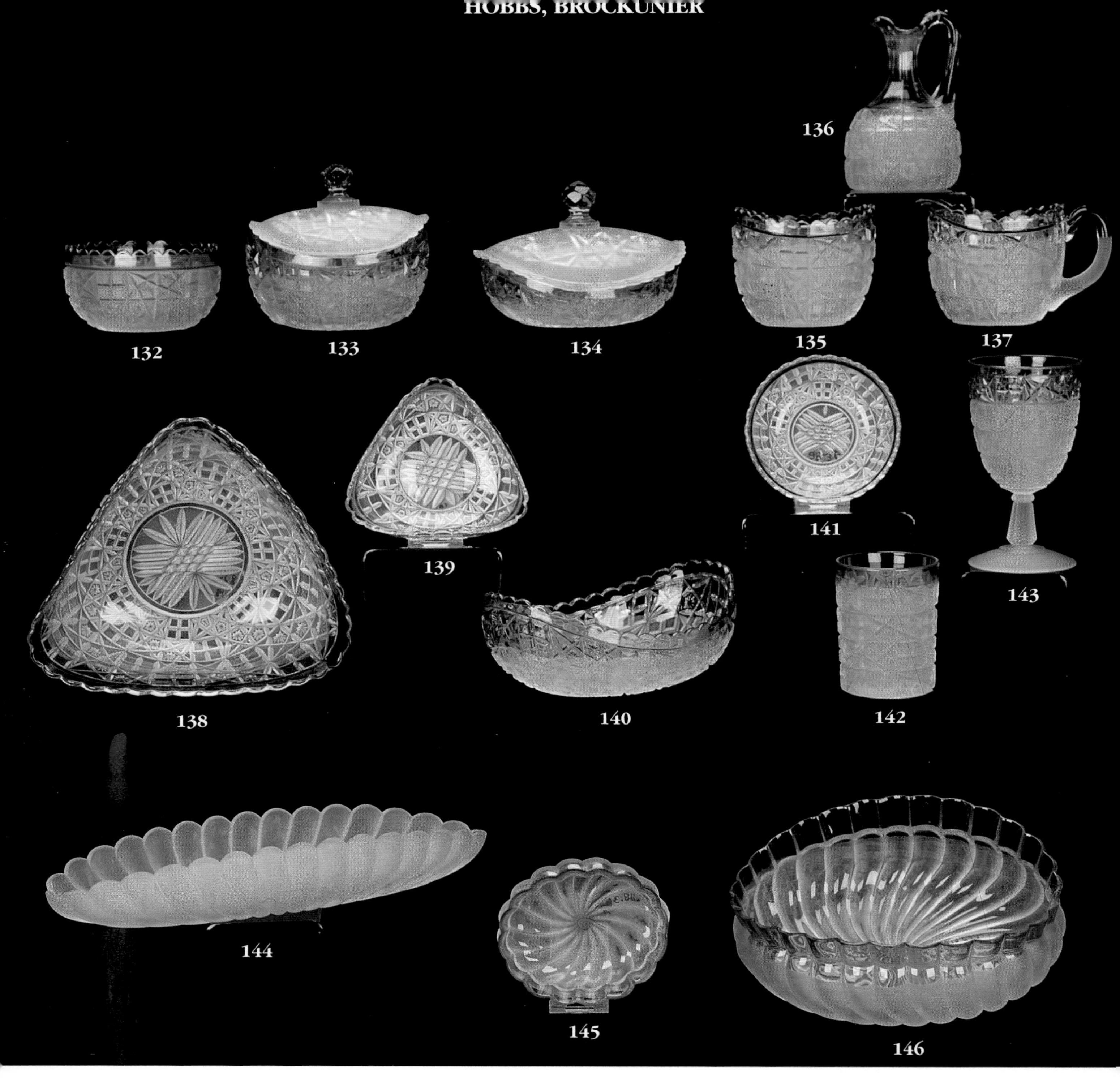

132.-143. *Frances Ware in the No. 330 pattern, known as Hobbs Block:* ***132.*** *Finger Bowl,* ***133.*** *Covered Sugar,* ***134.*** *Covered Butter,* ***135.*** *Spooner,* ***136.*** *Cruet (missing stopper),* ***137.*** *Creamer.*

138. *and* ***139.*** *Bowls, 9" and 4½" respectively,* ***140.*** *Oval Dish,* ***141.*** *Round Nappy,* ***142****. Tumbler,* ***143.*** *Goblet.*

144*. Hobbs No. 326 Celery Boat in frosted finish,* ***145.-146.*** *Nappy and Bowl in No. 326 pattern decorated in Frances Ware.*

HOBBS, BROCKUNIER

Hobbs pressed patterns of the late 1880's and early 1890's: ***147.*** *No. 335 Hexagon Block Tankard embellished with ruby stain and engraving,* ***148.*** *No. 339 Leaf and Flower Basket Celery, undecorated,* ***149.*** *No. 339 Tankard, with frosted finish and dark amber stain called Decoration No. 25. Height 12¾".*
150. *No. 335 Berry Bowl with ruby stain and engraving,* ***151.*** *No. 339 9" Berry Bowl with Decoration No. 25.*
152. *No. 335 Nappy with ruby stain and engraving,* ***153.*** *No. 339 Salt or Pepper, with Decoration No. 25, missing top.*

A collection of crackled glass:
154. *Blown Pitcher (probably not Hobbs, Brockunier),* ***155.*** *Hobbs Craquelle Pitcher in Amber,* $9\frac{1}{16}$*".*
156. *Hobbs Craquelle No. 302 Ice Cream Dish,* ***157.*** *and* ***158.*** *Hobbs Craquelle Pitchers.*

160

161

159

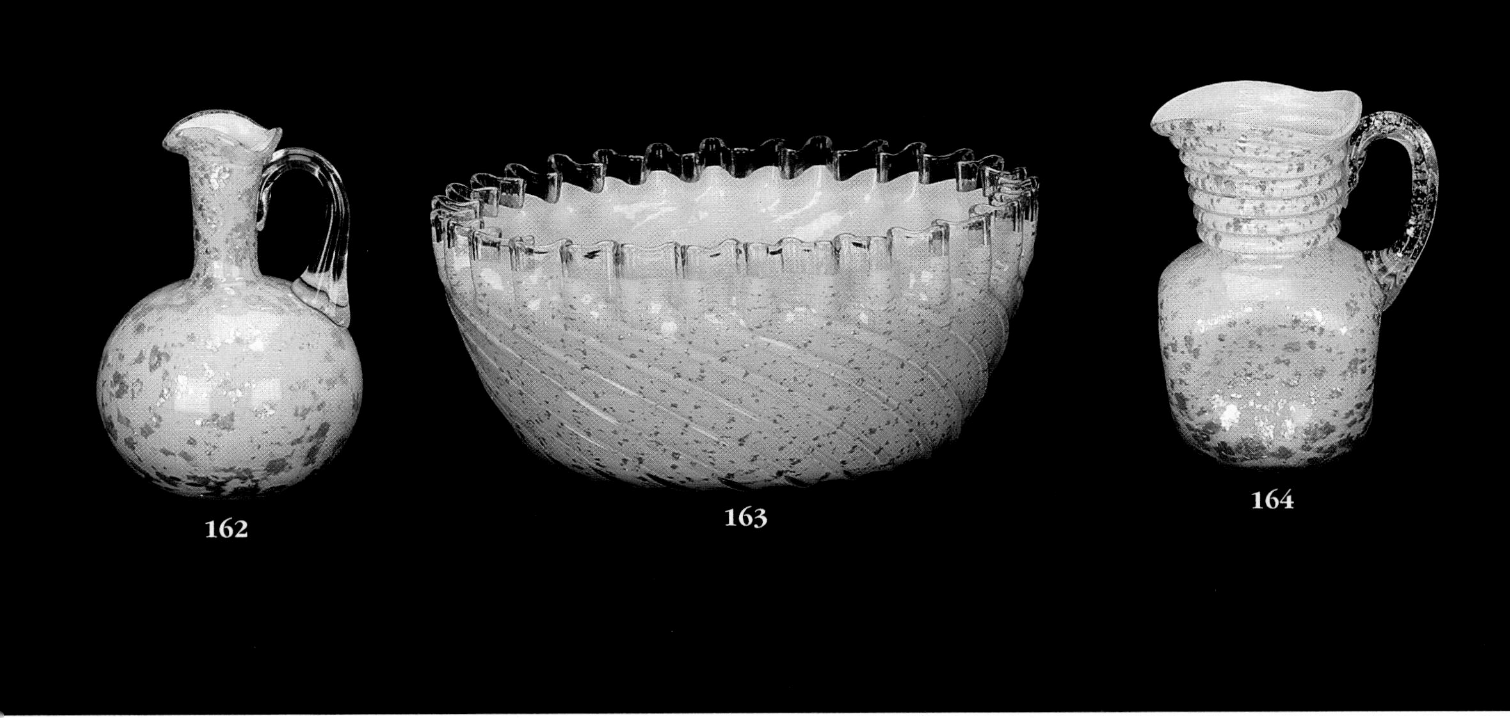

159.-161. *Three examples of Hobbs No. 315 Spangled Ware Jugs.*
162. *and* ***164.*** *Hobbs Spangled Ware Cruet (missing stopper) and Creamer,* ***163.*** *Bowl with ruffled top (probably not Hobbs, Brockunier).*

Hobbs, Brockunier's Ruby Glass in the company's Polka Dot pattern. This mould-blown process that produced a pattern of circular shapes is sometimes referred to as Inverted Thumbprint today.

165. *Pitcher with Ruffled Top. Height 8½".*

166. *No. 101 Polka Dot Cheese and Cover.*

167. *No. 236 Tumbler,* ***168.*** *No. 93 Finger Bowl,* ***169.*** *No. 306 Oil (stopper probably not original),* ***170.*** *No. 319 Jug or Creamer.*

171. *Ruby Amber Dish.*
172. *No. 319 Jug in Ruby Amber,* ***173.*** *Ruby Amber Bowl with handles.*
174. *Ruby Amber Bowl with Ruffled Edge,* ***175.*** *No. 93 Finger Bowl in Amber,* ***176.*** *Ruby Amber Pitcher.*

A collection of Rubina Verde:
***177.** No. 323 Hobnail Witchball, with chain, **178.-179.** No. 323 Tumbler and Jug, **180.** Small Bottle with stopper, **181.** Cruet.*
***182.** No. 304 8" Bowl, **183.** No. 236 Tumbler, **184.** and **185.** No. 319 Jugs.*
***186**. No. 93 Finger Bowl, **187.** No. 314 Spooner in Canary, **188.** No. 101 Polka Dot Cheese and Cover.*

A colorful assortment of Hobbs No. 507 Custard Cups (R to L starting at the top):
189. *Rubina Verde in Polka Dot pattern,* ***190.*** *Ruby,* ***191.*** *Amber in Polka Dot,* ***192.*** *Ruby Amber in Polka Dot,* ***193.*** *Crystal Opalescent in Polka Dot,* ***194.*** *Sapphire Opalescent in Polka Dot.*

195

195. *No. 101 Polka Dot Cheese and Cover in the rare Bluerina color. The Daisy and Button underplate is Crystal. Height 5½".*

196. *Pair of Hobbs Ruby Vases with Opal Ruffled Edges, Height 9½".* ***197.*** *Ruby Bowl.*
198. *No. 331 Creamer in Rubina,* ***199***. *No. 319– "O" Jug or Creamer in Rubina, Polka Dot pattern,* ***200.*** *No. 96 Finger Bowl in Ruby,* ***201.*** *Ruby Bowl with Crystal Edge.*

202.-203. *Hobbs No. 333 Water or Lemonade Jugs in Ruby Opalescent and Crystal Opalescent, Height 8½",* ***204****. No. 323 Hobnail Jug, Ruby Opalescent.*
205.-206. *No. 323 Hobnail Witchballs in Ruby Opalescent and Crystal Opalescent,* ***207.*** *No. 323 "O" size Jug or creamer in Ruby Opalescent,* ***208.*** *No. 323 Jug, with flared-out rim in Ruby Opalescent. Note the wide band of opalescence on the neck of this piece.*
209. *Hobbs No. 326 Cruet in Ruby Opalescent,* ***210.*** *No. 323 Hobnail 4½" Square Nappy in Ruby Opalescent,* ***211.*** *No. 323 Tumbler in Ruby Opalescent,* ***212.*** *No. 323 Finger Bowl, Ruby Opalescent.*

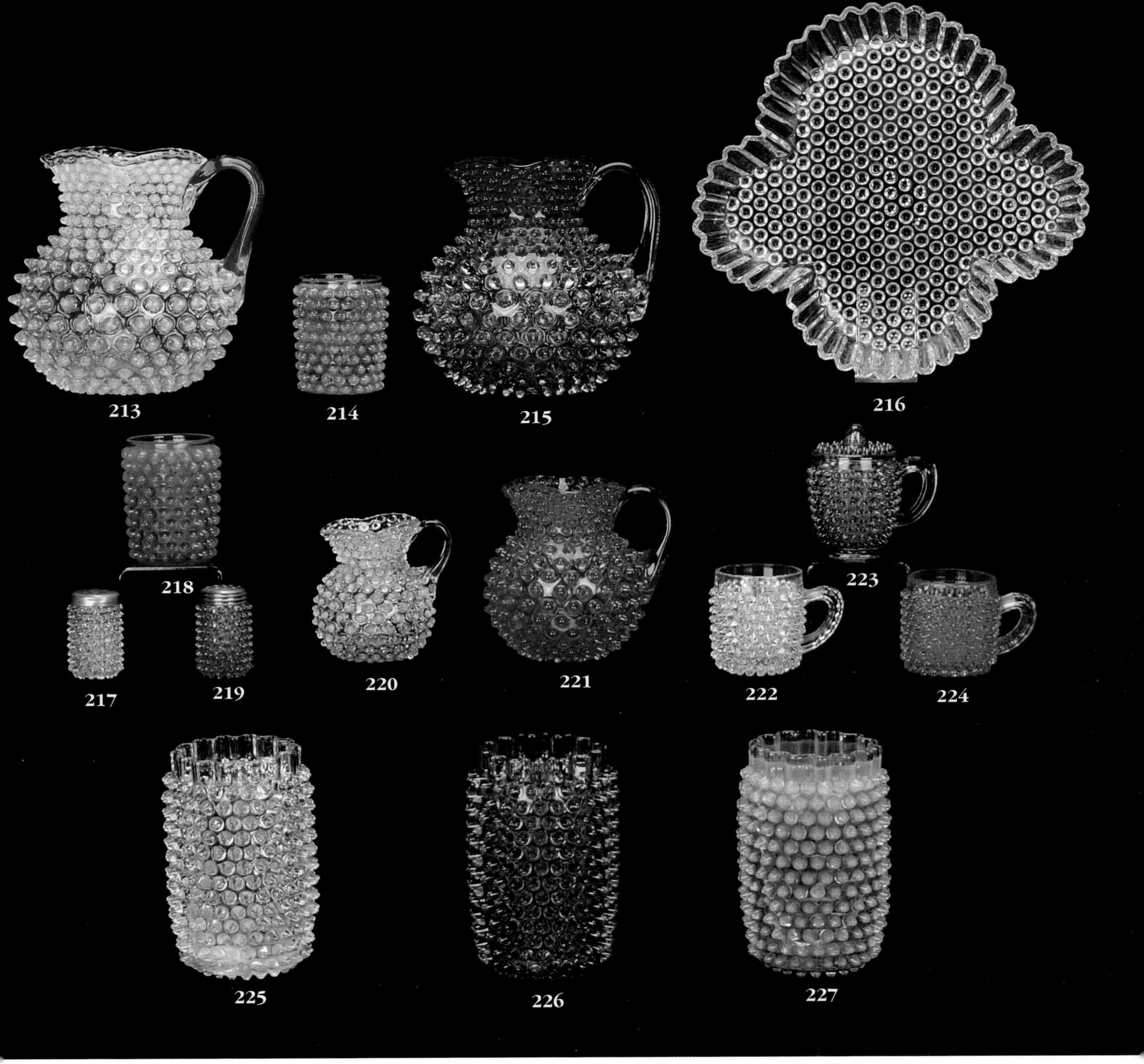

213 214 215 216

217 218 219 220 221 222 223 224

225 226 227

An impressive array of Hobbs No. 323 Hobnail line in a variety of colors:
213. *Canary Opalescent Jug,* ***214.*** *Ruby Opalescent Tumbler,* ***215.*** *Ruby Jug,* ***216.*** *Crystal Cloverleaf Tray.*
217. *and* ***219.*** *Salt or Pepper Shakers in Crystal and Sapphire,* ***218.*** *Sapphire Opalescent Tumbler,* ***220.*** *"O" size Jug or Creamer in Crystal Opalescent,* ***221.*** *"1" Jug in Sapphire,* ***222.*** *and* ***224.*** *Mugs in Crystal and Sapphire,* ***223.*** *Mustard Pot or Condiment Dish in Old Gold.*
225.-227. *Three Celery Vases in Crystal, Old Gold and Ruby Opalescent.*

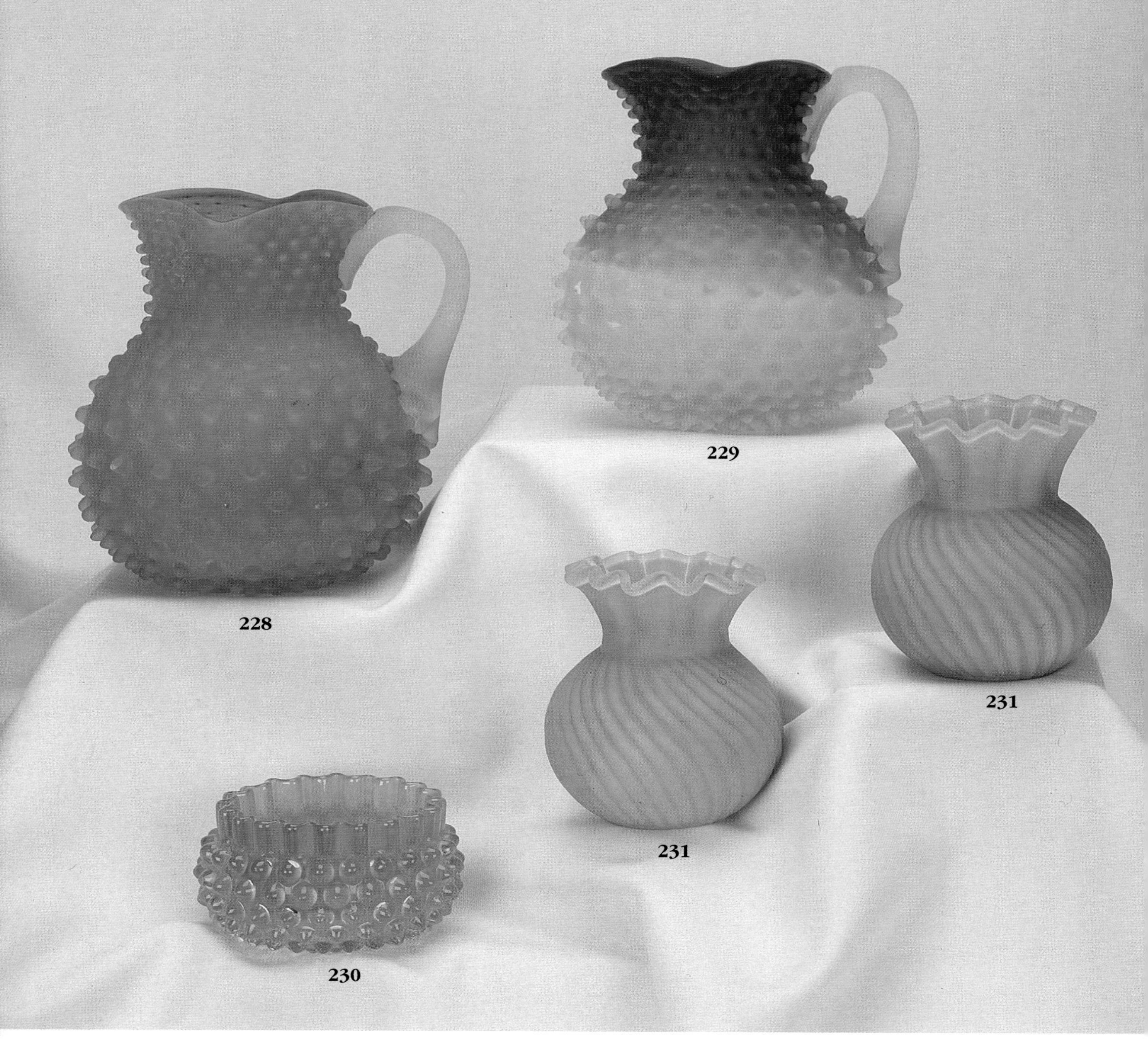

228.-229. *No. 323 Hobnail Pitchers in Frosted Ruby Opalescent and Frosted Rubina.*
230. *No. 323 Finger Bowl in Frosted Ruby Opalescent.* ***231*** *. Pair of Vases, possibly from Hobbs Neapolitan line.*

All of these items are Hobbs celebrated Frances Ware decoration. The Hobnail pattern was the firm's No. 323.
232.-235. *Water Set (pitcher and tumblers on tray).*
236. *Cruet or Oil,* ***237.*** *4½" Square Nappy,* ***238.*** *"O" size Jug, or Creamer.*
239. *Covered Butterdish,* ***240.*** *Toy Tumblers.*

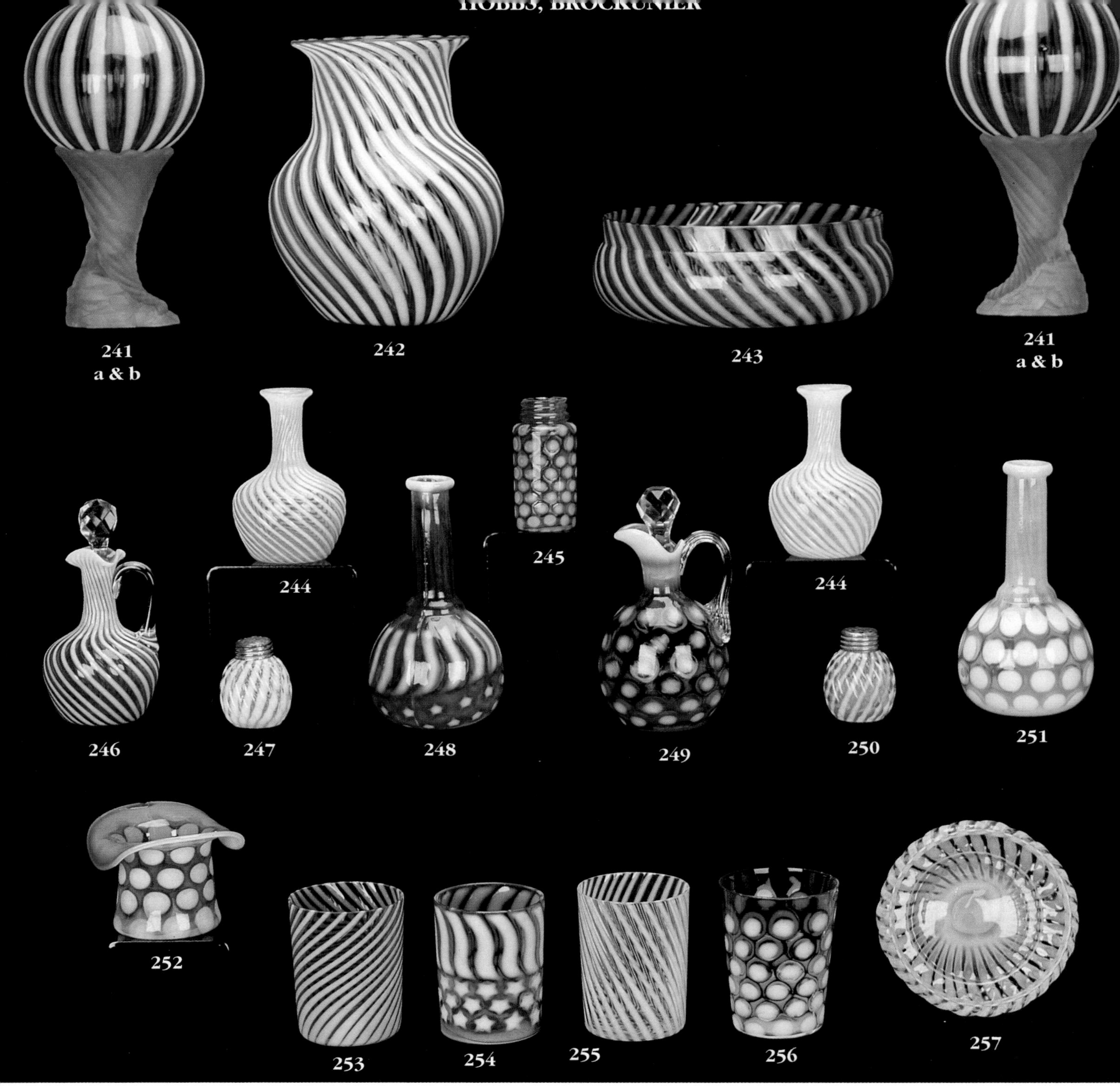

A collection of Hobbs Opalescent Blown Ware:
241. a & b. *Pair of Ruby Opalescent striped Witchballs resting on pressed cornucopia-shaped stands,* ***242.*** *Ruby Opalescent Striped Vase, 8½" tall,* ***243.*** *No. 325 Bowl in Ruby Opalescent.*
244. *Pair of Crystal Opalescent Bottles,* ***245.*** *No. 216 Polka Dot Salt or Pepper Shaker in Ruby Opalescent.*
246. *No. 325 Ruby Opalescent Cruet,* ***247.*** *Crystal Opalescent Striped Salt,* ***248.*** *No. 293 Stars and Stripes Bitter Bottle in Ruby Opalescent,* ***249.*** *No. 312 Polka Dot Oil or Cruet in Ruby Opalescent,* ***250.*** *Pale Yellow Opalescent Striped Salt,* ***251.*** *Crystal Opalescent Bitter Bottle (probably not Hobbs, Brockunier) in Coin Spot pattern.*
252. *Novelty Hat in Ruby Opalescent (probably not Hobbs, Brockunier) in Coin Spot pattern,* ***253.*** *No. 325 Ruby Opalescent Tumbler,* ***254.*** *No. 293 Stars and Stripes Ruby Opalescent Tumbler,* ***255.*** *No. 325 Crystal Opalescent Tumbler,* ***256.*** *Polka Dot-type Ruby Opalescent Tumbler,* ***257.*** *Pale Yellow Opalescent Striped Nappy or Small Bowl.*

258. *No. 325 Barber Bottle in Ruby Opalescent,* ***259.-262.*** *Four examples of Hobbs No. 323 Hobnail Bitter Bottles in Crystal Opalescent, Ruby, Canary Opalescent and Sapphire.*
263. *No. 338 Bitter Bottle in Sapphire Opalescent,* ***264.*** *No. 325 Square Barber Bottle in Ruby Opalescent,* ***265.-266.*** *No. 325 Bitter Bottles in Sapphire Opalescent,* ***267***. *No. 325 Bitter Bottle in Ruby Opalescent.*

268.-271 *. Four Glass Bells –*
*While these novelties cannot definitely be attributed to Hobbs, the three ruby pieces do resemble the company's Coin Spot pattern (**268.**), No. 207 Swirl (**269.**) and No. 323 Hobnail pattern (**271.**). All four bells have similarly-shaped handles.*

Examples from Hobbs No. 230 Neapolitan line in Ruby glass (R to L, starting at the top): ***272.*** *Pitcher,* ***273.*** *Spooner,* ***274.*** *Bowl,* ***275.*** *Creamer,* ***276.*** *Celery Vase.*

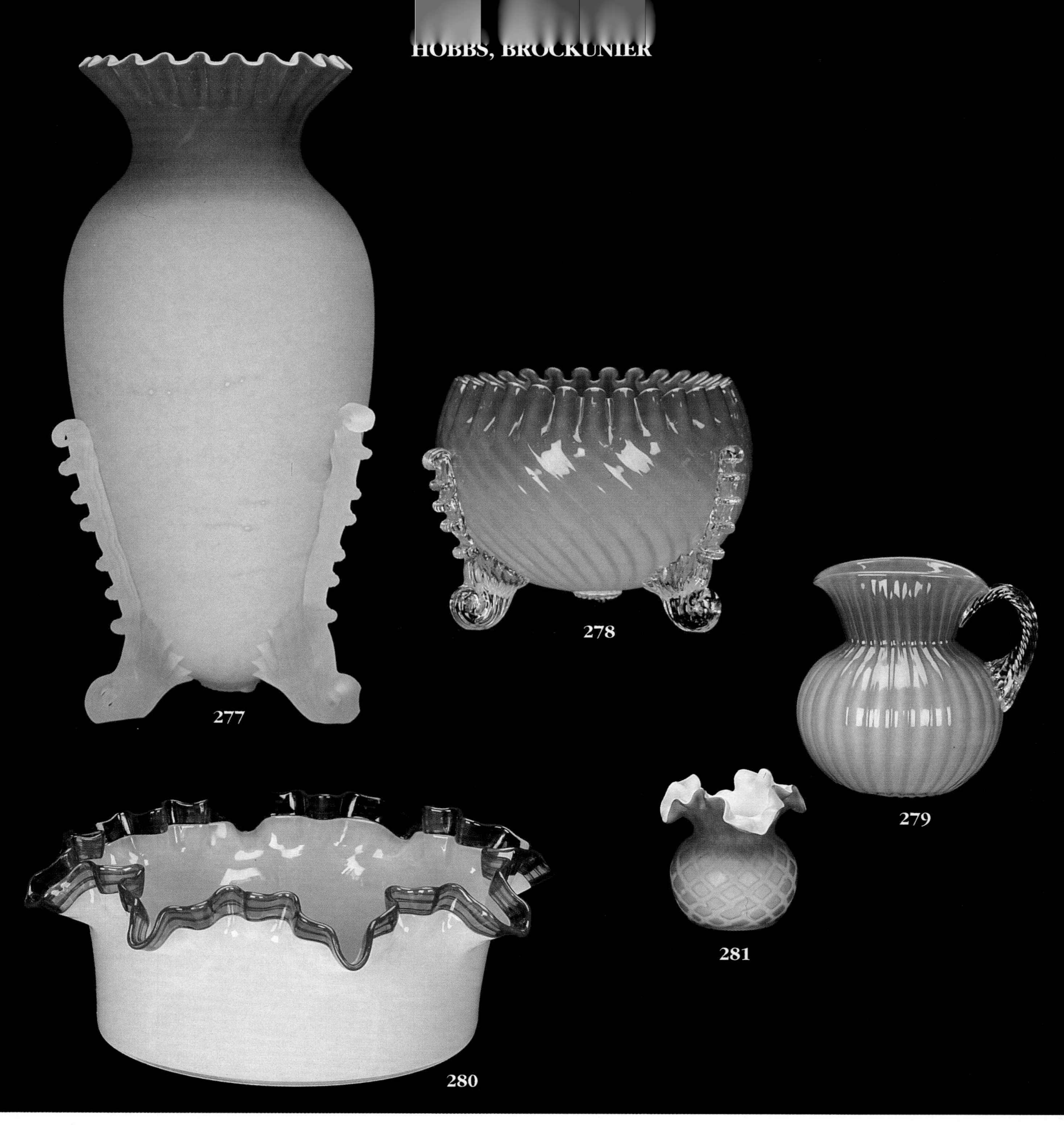

Hobbs No. 230 Neapolitan line: ***277.*** *No. 230 Vase in Frosted Ruby, height 14¼",* ***278.*** *No. 230 Nut Bowl in Ruby,* ***279.*** *No. 230 Cream Pitcher in Ruby.*
280. *No. 206 Bowl in Opaque Yellow Glass with Ruby Edge,* ***281.*** *Mother of Pearl Satin Glass Vase with Ruffled Edge.*

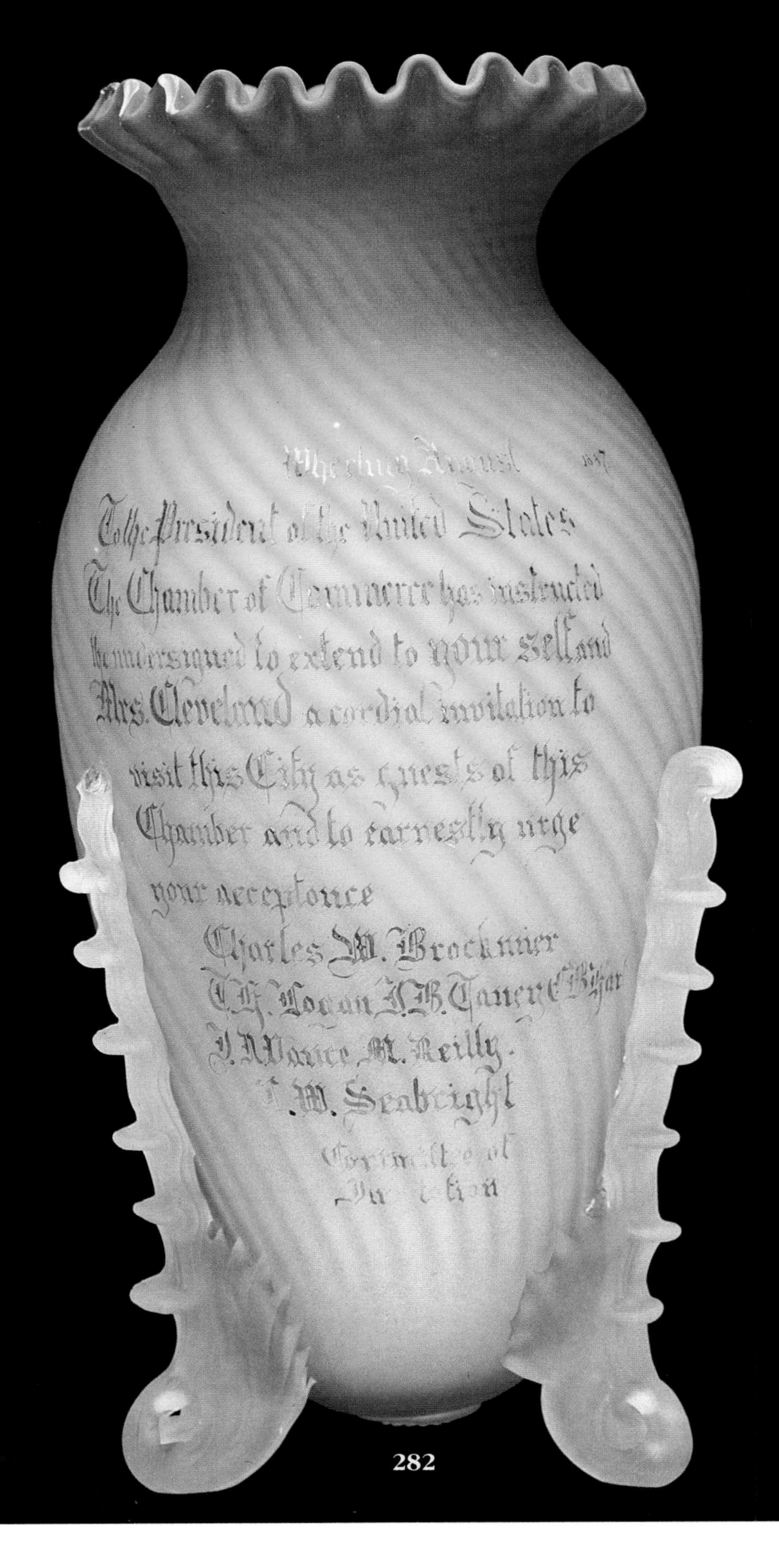

282. *The Cleveland Vase*
This piece was actually an invitation issued to President and Mrs. Grover Cleveland to visit Wheeling. It is signed by members of the Wheeling Chamber of Commerce, including Charles Brockunier and dates to August, 1887. The vase is a special creation from Hobbs No. 230 Neapolitan line. Height 14¼".

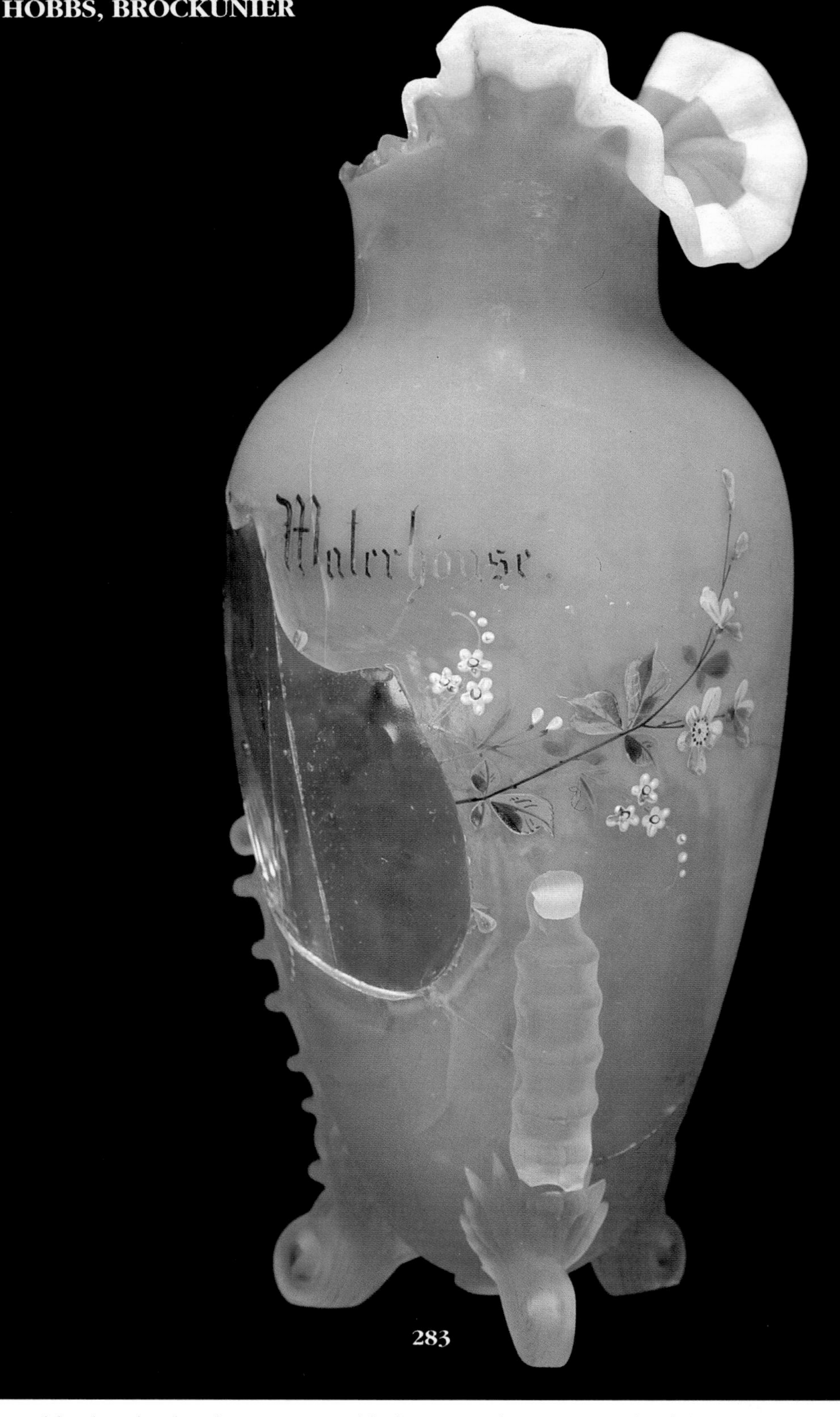

__283.__ This Vase, like the Cleveland Vase pictured before it, is also an example of the No. 230 Neapolitan line. The creamy yellow edge is reminiscent of the firm's No. 205 and No. 206 bowls. Although it was found in very poor condition (the clear portion in the center is actually a repair), one can see the hand-painting on this piece. The name "Waterhouse" represents a prominent Wheeling family, and the vase was probably specially decorated for them.

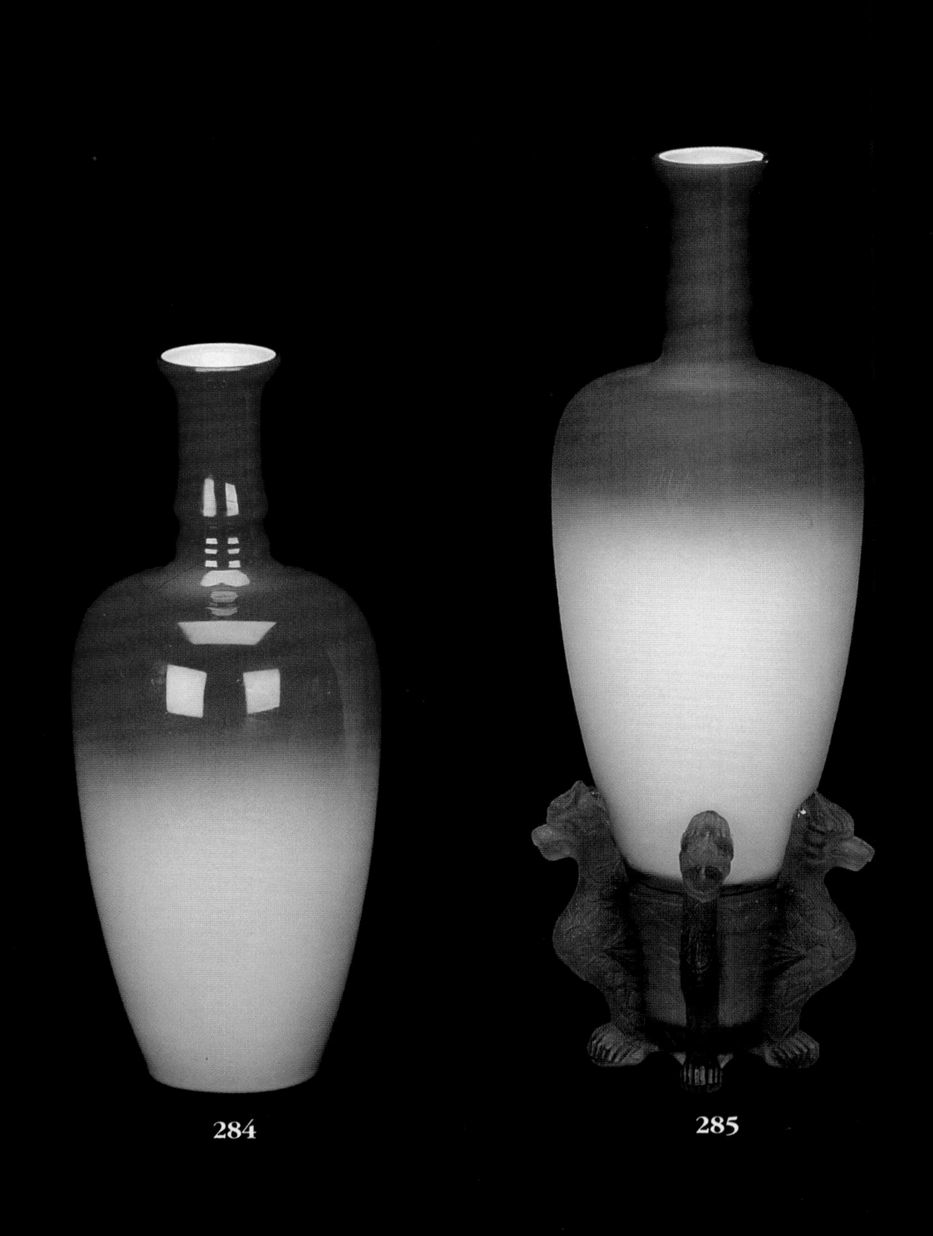

Two examples of the Morgan Vase in Wheeling Peachblow. ***284.*** *has the shiny, or Coral finish.* ***285.*** *has been treated with acid, in what was called by the company a Lusterless finish. Height of the vase is 8".*

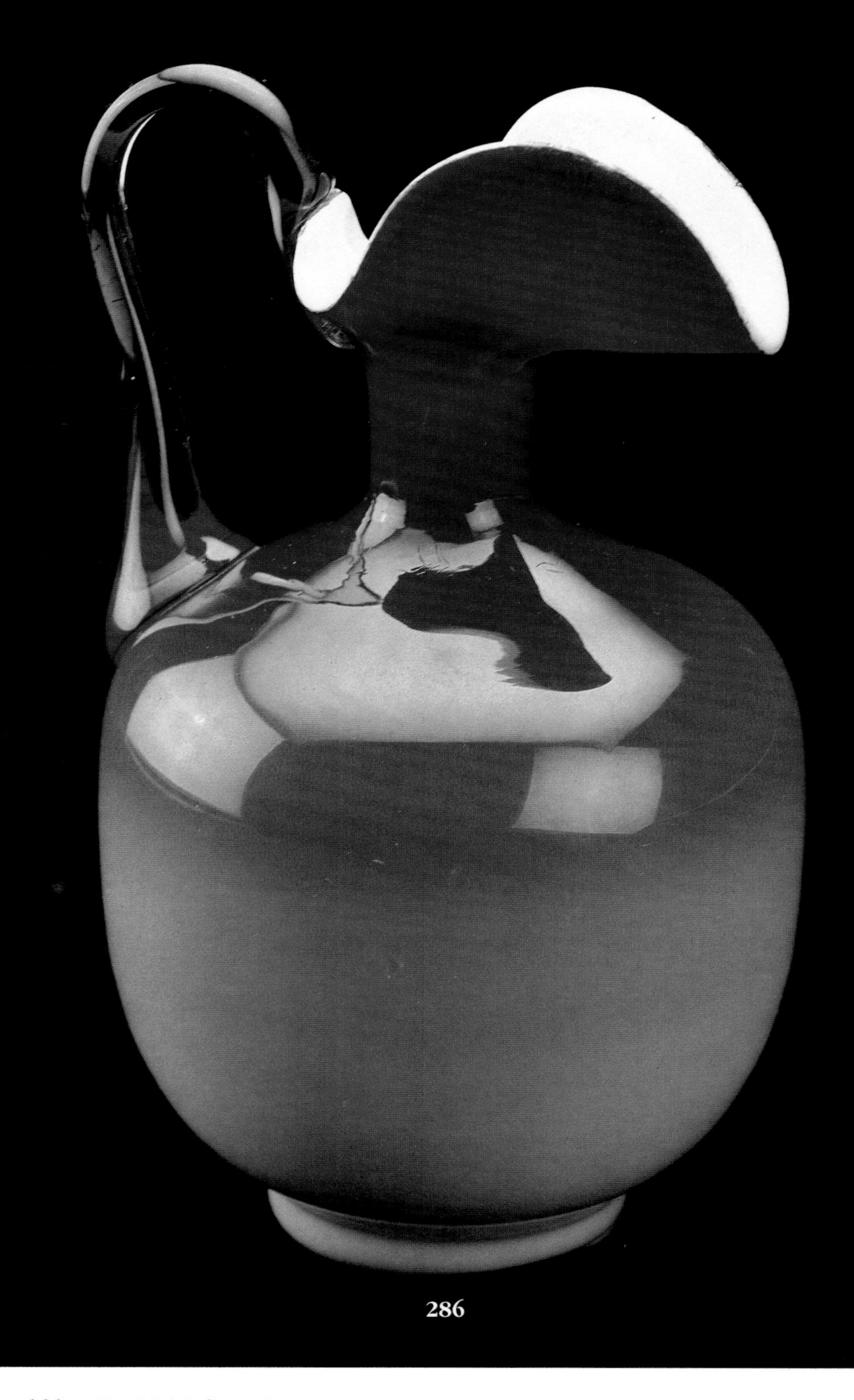

286

286. *Wheeling Peachblow No. 324 Pelican Jug.*

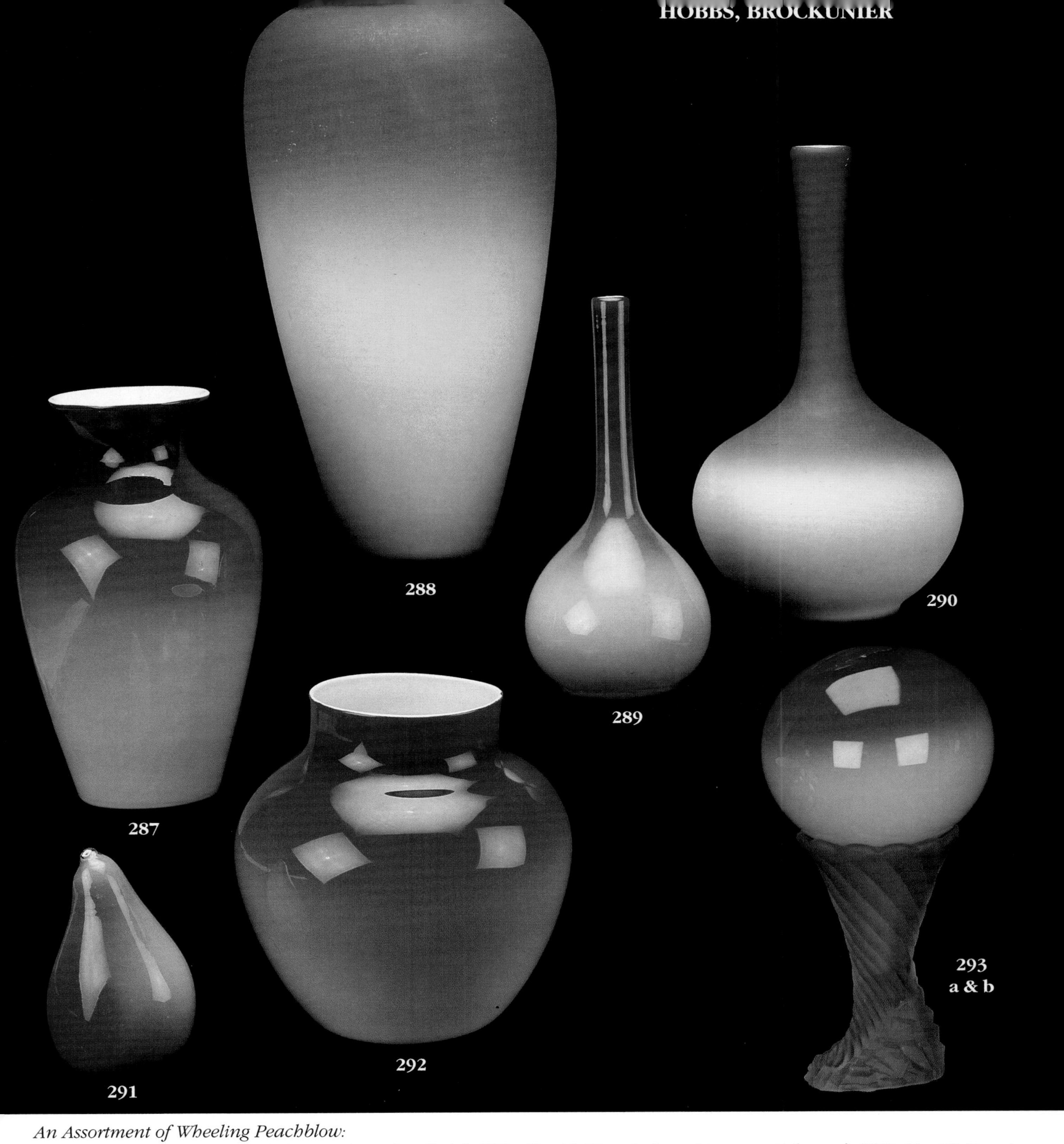

An Assortment of Wheeling Peachblow:
287. *No. 6 Vase,* ***288****. No. 18 Vase in Lusterless finish,* ***289.*** *No. 11 Vase (referred to as a stick vase),* ***290.*** *No. 13 Vase in Lusterless finish,* ***291*** *. Peachblow Pear,* ***292.*** *No. 5 Vase,* ***293. a & b.*** *Witchball resting on frosted cornucopia-shaped stand.*

Wheeling Peachblow:
294. *319 No. 5 Jug.*
295. *No. 91 9" Tankard,* ***296. and 297.*** *No. 236 Tumblers,* ***298. -299.*** *No. 321 Tumbler and Tankard.*

300. *Wheeling Peachblow Night Lamp. Collectors call this style a "Gone with the Wind" lamp. Height 21", including chimney.*

An assortment of Wheeling Peachblow Tableware:
301. *No. 4 Decanter.*
302. *No. 322 Claret Jug,* ***303.*** *and* ***304.*** *No. 236 Tumblers, with Coral and Lusterless finish, respectively.*
305. *No. 314 Celery Vase,* ***306.*** *No. 93 Finger Bowl,* ***307.*** *No. 312 Oil or Cruet (note the original amber stopper),* ***308.*** *and* ***309.*** *No. 1 Spooner and Creamer,* ***310.*** *Salt or Pepper Shaker.*

311. *and* ***312.*** *Pitcher and Tumbler. This is a variant of Wheeling Peachblow where the pieces are finished with spatters of glass and spangled with mica flecks. Like the spangled Peachblow Vase on the cover of this book, these were not standard production items of the company, but represent the artistic expression and ability of Hobbs workers.*

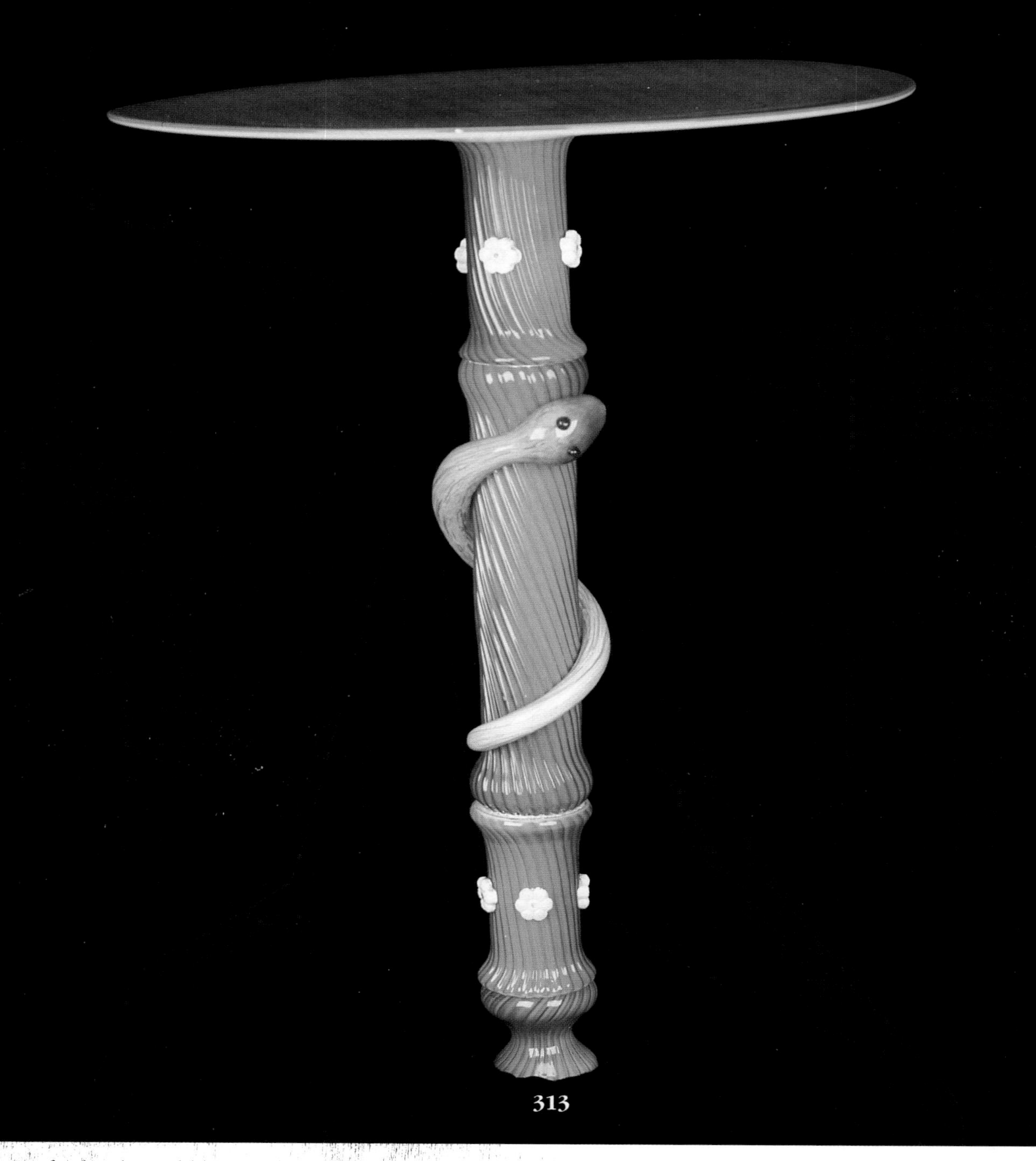

313

313. *One-of-a-kind Peachblow Table. Local legend states that this whimsey, embellished with a brown snake and white floral prunts, was made at Hobbs, Brockunier.*

A collection of Hobbs Lamps:
314. *No. 326 A. Hand Lamp in Sapphire Opalescent with Crystal Base,* ***315.*** *Stand Lamp in Ruby Opalescent Swirl pattern with Crystal Base,* ***316.*** *Stand Lamp with Blown and Engraved Ruby Font and Opal Cloverleaf Base. Features John H. Hobbs patented connector.*
317. *Stand Lamp with Opal Base. Features Hobbs patented connector. Height 11½".* ***318.*** *Stand Lamp in Crystal Opalescent Swirl pattern with Crystal Base.* ***319.*** *Miniature Lamp in Ruby Opalescent Swirl pattern with Crystal Base.*

320

320. *Hanging Lamp with a ribbed pattern shade in Gold Ruby. The piece rests in a brass frame.*

GLASS WORKS
J.H. HOBBS, BROCKUNIER & Co
U.S. MAIL
GLASS WORKS OF J. H. HOBBS, BROCKUNIER & CO.
COR. OF 36TH & McCULLOCH STS. WHEELING, WEST VA.
JOHN H. HOBBS. JOHN L. HOBBS. WM LEIGHTON JR. CHARLES W. BROCKUNIER

Two Panel with Diamond Point Bowls or Compotes made in a Cobalt and Crystal combination: ***321.*** *9" Covered Bowl, High Foot,* ***322.*** *9" Bowl (missing cover), high foot.* ***323.*** *6" Sweetmeat (missing cover).*

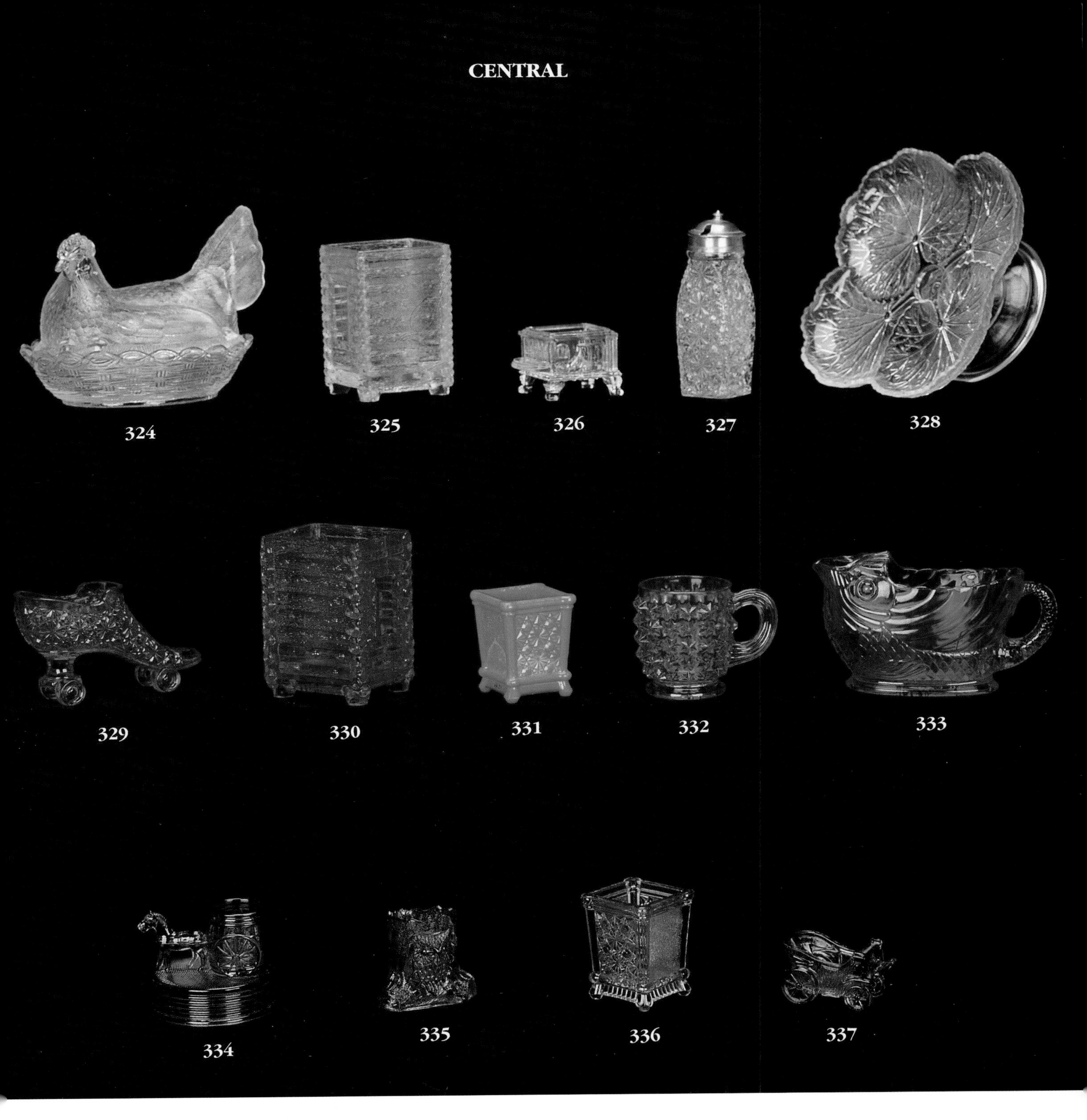

A Colorful Assortment of Central's Novelty Items:
324. *No. 707 Hen on Nest Covered Egg Dish in Canary Yellow,* ***325.*** *No. 748 Log Cabin Spooner in Canary Yellow,* ***326.*** *No. 822 Stove-shaped Salt in Canary Yellow,* ***327.*** *No. 822 Cruet in Canary Yellow (part of a Caster Set),* ***328.*** *No. 763 Lily Pad 8" Comport, Canary Yellow.*
329. *No. 831 Slipper on Skates in Electric Blue,* ***330.*** *No. 748 Log Cabin Spooner in Electric Blue,* ***331.*** *No. 782 Match Box in Opaque Blue,* ***332.*** *No. 876 Effulgent Star Toy Mug in Electric Blue,* ***333.*** *No. 824 Fish Creamer in Electric Blue.*
334. *No. 865 Horse and Barrel Match Box in Amber,* ***335.*** *No. 866 Owl in Tree Trunk Match Box in Amber,* ***336.*** *No. 782 Match Box in Amber,* ***337.*** *No. 16 Open Carriage Salt in Amber.*

An arrangement of Central's No. 775 Pressed Diamond pattern tableware:
338.-340. *Canary Yellow Water Tumbler, height 10", Covered Bowl, Salt or Pepper Shaker.*
341.-343. *Amber 9" Comport, Spooner and Creamer.*

Central's No. 796 Lattice Thumbprint pattern:
344. *and* ***346.*** *Covered Sugar Bowls in Amber and Electric Blue,* ***345.*** *Creamer in Electric Blue,* ***347.*** *Base of a Butter Dish (missing cover) in Electric Blue.*
348. *Covered Butter Dish,* ***349.*** *8" Comport, Canary Yellow,* ***350.*** *Master Salt, Canary Yellow.*

A Collection of Central's Engraved Pieces. ***351.*** *Bell, decorated with a looped engraving,* ***352.-354.*** *Three pieces of stemware featuring a Grape and Vine design,* ***355.*** *Champagne Glass with a Griffen design,* ***356.*** *Custard Cup decorated with a geometric pattern. Items* ***357.-360.*** *are engraved with thistles. The thistle engraving was featured in the January, 1909 issue of* American Pottery Gazette *under the heading "New Deep Plated Etchings" by the Central Glass Works.*

Chapter Four

East Wheeling Glass Works
(Central Glass Company)

See Figure 386.

G. Eason Eige

EAST WHEELING GLASS WORKS
(Central Glass Company)

By G. Eason Eige

In 1863 Western Virginia declared itself a separate state becoming West Virginia. The Civil War was on and Virginia was physically and emotionally at the center of turmoil. Sentiment divided, those living west of the Appalachian Mountains felt far from the government of the Confederacy in Richmond. These were people who identified more with the 19th century midwest of Western Pennsylvania, Ohio and Kentucky, dependent on the Ohio River and its tributaries for commercial uses, carrying raw materials to industry and finished products to market. Roads and railroads were quickly being improved as well, making the population of West Virginia more independent than ever.

It was spring of 1863 when the Oesterling, Henderson & Company was opened by a group of Wheeling glass blowers. They pooled their experience and a meager $5,000 to purchase an abandoned building in which they began their small operation. These were William K. Elson, Peter Cassell,

Print from the Atlas of the Upper Ohio River Valley *showing the Central Glass Company as it appeared in 1877.*

James Leasure, Roy Combs, John Henderson and two men who were to become well known for their design patents - John Oesterling and Andrew Baggs.

Mr. Oesterling, as president, stood out for his able management skills, carefully guiding the fledgling company. James Leasure was the plant manager. The firm was immediately appreciated for its quality goods. It was not long before the men purchased an East Wheeling distillery and pork packing house. In 1867 they obtained a charter as a joint stock company under the new name Central Glass Company. Their capital was by then $80,000. The company soon grew to a worth of $260,000 according to a story in the *Wheeling News Register* on January 11, 1942. The article goes on to say:

> The company had its own coal mine, with some fifty acres of good coal land, and its own coke plant. In 1872, a third furnace was added to the two already in operation, and a large structure to be used as warehouse, office, and packing room, was erected on the west side of McColloch street. This building was connected with the factory by an elevated bridge over McColloch street. The factory had also been enlarged and improved by the addition of a mould and mechanics' shop, cutting shop, pot-making rooms, blacksmith shop, engine houses, carpenter's shop, coke ovens, mixing room, and two buildings which housed six annealing ovens.

Not much is known about the earliest products, but by the beginning of the 1870s Central was making a good selection of bar goods, imaginative table wares and lamps. These were to remain their range of production into the last decade of the 19th century.

The buildings which made up the Central Glass Company could only be described as impressive and extensive. Complete with large furnaces and up to date pressing equipment there were also warehouses, barrel-making workshops, offices, and rail lines which ran directly to the shipping department. The factory and buildings were located at Fifteenth and McColloch Streets on Wheeling Creek. An illustration of the model complex appeared in the *Atlas of the Upper Ohio River*, published in 1877. It shows Central Glass Company as a busy industry, one of Wheeling's great manufacturers in a city built on manufacturing. Central was indeed one of the largest glass houses in the country in 1877. By 1879 Central was shipping lots of fifteen to twenty tons to Europe and as far as Australia via the Ohio and Mississippi Rivers.

Relatively little has been published about this enormous and prolific glass manufacturer. A carefully sifted outline of the management history of the Central Glass Company is available in Albert Christian Revi's book titled *American Pressed Glass and Figure Bottles* ©1964, page 108. In that account Mr. Revi has clearly drawn from an earlier book by Josephine Jefferson titled *Wheeling Glass*, published in 1947. Revi stated:

> William K. Elson left the firm to become the manager of the Belmont Glass Works at Bellaire, Ohio, and Andrew Baggs became manager of the La Belle Glass Company at Bridgeport, Ohio. Mr. Castle left the company to attend to his many investments, and Henderson was reported to be "doing well in Pittsburgh" in 1879.
>
> The Central Glass Company exhibited at the San Francisco Exposition in 1881, showing many of its pressed glass tableware designs.
>
> In 1887 Mr. Oesterling died, and Nathan B. Scott was appointed to the presidency of the firm. The factory burned down in 1888 but was very soon rebuilt; meantime, orders were filled from a large stock on hand. In 1891 Central joined the United States Glass Company, becoming "Factory 0." The new owners wanted an open shop, but the men refused to allow it; consequently the plant was inactive from 1893 to 1895. In 1896 a new company was formed using the old name, the Central Glass Company [Works], with Nathan B. Scott, Peter Cassell, L. F. Stifel, and Joseph Speidel.

This brief, but pioneering, history of the Central operation illustrated their No. 438 or Star and Diamonds pattern, the No. 140 or Cabbage Rose pattern and a page from an undated catalogue illustrating children's toy mugs in Rabbit and Elephant motifs along with three hen on nest covered egg dishes of individual to large sizes, a duck on nest (acid etched), owl pickle (acid etched), leaf pickle, lily pad comport and an oval 8 in. dish, No. 764, often found today in blue glass. Mr. Revi listed some of the table patterns made by Central Glass Company using one or more catalogues (source not given) which are probably different catalogues than the ones owned by the Mansion Museum, Oglebay Institute. Prominent among those patterns illustrated by Revi are Cord and Tassel, Log Cabin (No. 748), Rose (No. 140), Leaflets (No. 585), Nail City (No. 555), Prism and Diamond Band (No. 438) and Panel with Diamond Point (No. 439).

Two Central Glass Company trade catalogues are owned by the Mansion Museum. These documents are an invaluable primary source of information, useful in identifying products of the company at the time of their publication. The earlier catalogue was mentioned by Minnie Watson Kamm in her *Pitcher Book Vol. VI*, published in 1949 and again in 1954. On page 95 of that book Mrs. Kamm included the following in notes on the Central factory:

> "Central put out a splendid trade catalog in 1881, a copy of which the writer has examined, for it is preserved at the Oglebay Institute, Wheeling. It illustrated hundreds of articles made in anticipation of the San Francisco Exposition in September of that year and is thus inscribed."

This 1881 *Illustrated Catalogue of Flint Glassware* does have a handwritten inscription in pencil, written on the inside cover, which reads "Sample for San Francisco Ship Aug. 24th 1881. A relatively small catalogue (9¼" x 12⅛") it contains just forty-one pages. The first eleven pages depict barware including a chart of "patterns of engraving for stem ware" on page 11. There are forty-five numbered designs shown, but their numbers suggest that as many as 336 variations may have been available.

Pages 12 through 19 include tableware in familiar Central patterns such as Rose (No. 140), Wheat in Shield (No. 234), Prism and Diamond Band (No. 438) and Panel with Diamond Point (No. 439), all popular designs in 1881. That is interesting because Rose (or Cabbage Rose) was a patented pattern designed by John Oesterling in 1870. Another older pattern Oak Leaf Band (No. 152) also remained active, available in limited forms in the 1881 catalogue. Lighting goods appear on pages 27 through 35 and on pages 38 and 39. On page 37 are eighteen pieces of Leaflets (No. 585) pattern tableware. Toward the end of this catalogue the pages contain a mix of plain patterned, somewhat institutional looking tableware, bar goods and more kerosene lamps. This catalogue is in fragile condition, but is of great value in its suggestion that familiar designs of the early 1870s remained in production for more than a decade.

A second Central Glass Company trade catalogue in the archives at the Mansion Museum, Oglebay Institute, seems to have not been used by modern authors to illustrate the products of this important manufacturer. This catalogue contains one hundred-eighteen pages. Products represented seem to be somewhat evenly divided into three categories. Those are barware through page 37, table patterns on pages 38 through 84 (page 85 is missing) and kerosene lamps on pages 86 through 118.

Old glass trade catalogues were frequently not dated making an assigned date speculative. Popular patterns remained in production for years with others being discontinued. New designs were added to replace them. The second Central Glass Company catalogue at Oglebay dates from about 1885. On page 39, pickle jars from table sets of the 1870s appear along side a pickle jar in Pressed Diamond pattern dating from the mid 1880s. Earlier pat-

Page 39 of a Central Glass Company trade catalogue, c. 1885.

Illustration from Central catalogue showing patterns 438 and 439.

terns such as Log Cabin remain only in selected forms along side more current designs. A full three pages (pages 59-61) are dedicated to thirty-two pieces of Pressed Diamond tableware dating from the mid 1880s. Everything from an individual butter pat to nine sizes of flat bottom bowls were offered. On page 65 is a water set in Pressed Diamond pattern which shows an additional pitcher with two tumblers plus a waste bowl sitting on matching tray. Still more shapes appear in the form of a goblet (page 28), oil bottle (page 35), individual salt (page 38), and celery (page 45). Total number of shapes illustrated in this catalogue comes to forty-one, suggesting that this was a current and popular pattern at the time. See page 94 for color illustration of Pressed Diamond pattern in the Mansion Museum collection. Many other patterns illustrated in this Mansion Museum owned catalogue are hold-overs from the mid 1870s.

Many other fascinating patterns of tableware appear in this trade catalogue. There is a group of four patterns which are all Central designs of remarkably similar character. They are No. 794 (Rope, plain/engraved) No. 796 (Lattice Thumbprint), a similar pattern with vertical optic band (not illustrated in this trade catalogue) and the Barrel pattern (number is illegible in the catalogue) found on page 84. All of these were produced in crystal, canary, amber and blue glass.

At first it seems unreasonable for a glass manufacturer to offer so many nearly identical patterns concurrently. Yet when considering the quantity of glass that Central was selling it becomes clear that in order to fill such demands a single mold would probably be insufficient to make the pieces required.

Two conventional but popular patterns were Central's No. 438 and 439. Pattern No. 438 is known to collectors today as Prism and Diamond Band. The full line of wares included a cordial, wine, claret, champagne and goblet. On page 26 of the Central Glass Company 1885 trade catalogue are all these stems shown next to the goblet, claret and wine of the No. 439 (or Panel with Diamond Point) pattern. No fewer than fifty-one different shapes constitute the offering in No. 439 pattern. In this pattern, only selected shapes appear to have been made in color. Panel with Diamond Point wines are abundant in colors popular at Central - canary, blue and amber. Rare are the stemmed compotes in No. 439 which were made with cobalt glass. These are seen on page 92 from the Mansion Museum collection. One compote has a cobalt stem while the other has a cobalt bowl on clear stem. Cobalt was a color also used for rare pieces in Central's Shell pattern and very rarely for candlesticks in Picture Window pattern.

Central patterns of the 1880s include their No. 730, No. 810, No. 829, and No. 876. These patterns were not included by Mr. Revi or Ruth Webb Lee. No. 730 is a geometric boxy pattern with oval window shown with a wheel etched design on page 39 of the 1885 catalogue. On pages 72 and 73 appears No. 810 pattern which is similarly wheel etched around a clear band above a pressed cut style pattern of diamonds and jewels with a distinctive cruciform finial. Pattern No. 829 (unnamed) on page 76 of the 1885 catalogue is shown with and without wheel engraved vine. This is a somewhat ungainly pattern with vulnerable protruding handles which may account for how few are seen today. Finally pattern No. 876, Effulgent Star, is shown on page 79 of the old catalogue. This slightly better-known pattern and No. 810 (Tudor) are familiar to kerosene lamp collectors rather than to table pattern enthusiasts.

On May 27,1892 an article of extreme interest appeared in the *Wheeling Daily Register*. The story has to do with one of Central's most noteworthy glass patterns, Silver Age (or U. S. Coin) pattern issued to celebrate the centennial of the founding of the United States Mint.

> Patterns Destroyed: The Coin Designs of the Hobbs and Central Factories Demolished.
>
> On Wednesday, Mr. McSweeny, an agent of the

United States Treasury Department seized a lot of molds in the United States Glass Company's factory "H" and "O" in this city. The molds were used for a novel design of lamp, with facsimile representations of United States coins of different denominations stamped upon them, which have been manufactured by the Central and Hobbs factories since they joined the United States Glass Company. The imitations were alleged to be in violation of the law. There was no objection to the lamp, but the authorities thought there was a possibility that the molds might be used for counterfeiting. Yesterday that part of the molds containing the coin design were destroyed, and the matter will be allowed to drop. The extreme penalty for the offense is a fine of $100.

Yesterday, under the direction of Mr. McSweeny, a workman took a chisel and cut off the design of the coins from the different molds. A Register reporter saw Manager Scott of factory "0," yesterday, and he stated that the loss will be merely nominal, as any other design can be substituted for the coin. He thought a figure of Columbus or Queen Isabella would be very appropriate. The coin idea was a novel one, and there was a strong demand for the lamps. The United States Glass Company will be allowed to dispose of all the lamps it has in stock, and jobbers will be given the same privilege.

This much revered pressed glass pattern was being produced simultaneously by both Central Glass Company (Factory 0), and the Hobbs Glass Company (Factory H), both part of the United States Glass Company.

Although the Central Glass Company appears to have conceived the Silver Age pattern in 1891 prior to merging with the United States Glass Company, by 1892 the coin glass molds had been issued to two or more factories by the new management. Thus in the United States Glass Company catalogue of 1891 were illustrated tablewares in the coin designs. These included creamer, sugar, spooner, butter, salver (cake stand), water set (pitcher, two goblets, waste bowl and undertray), beer mug, tumbler, wine, claret, champagne, footed ale, finger bowl, 4½" comport (sauce), celery, 6", 7", 8" and 9" covered nappies, 4", 4½", 6", 7", 8" and 9" nappies, pickle dish, oblong dish, cake plate (bread plate) and a salt and pepper shaker tray with standing toothpick holder. Other pieces in this pattern include compotes on high stand (open and covered), vinegar cruet, gallon pitcher, toothpick holder, syrup, and stand lamps in several sizes.

Molds for the Silver Age pattern were made by the Hipkins Novelty Mold Shop, Martins Ferry, Ohio. The pattern was No. 15005. One interesting account of the history of this pattern appeared in *Coins* magazine, May 1980.

As Mr. Scott suggested in his newspaper interview of May 27,1892, the pattern later developed as Columbian Coin was sold as a commemorative souvenir.

The 1942 article in the *Wheeling News Register* continues:

Illustrations of four covered sugars in Central patterns No. 794 (plain and engraved), No. 796 and the Barrel pattern.

The history of the period from 1879 to 1917 was interestingly related to the News Register by John Yeager of McColloch Street, who began as an errand boy and became secretary-treasurer of the company. Mr. Yaeger was with the Central during its period of greatest production and prosperity. He said in part:

> I went to work for the Central Glass Company in 1879 as an errand boy. I was then 12 years old. We had no typewriters, telephones, or adding machines. John Oesterling was president of the company, and Nathan Bay Scott was secretary. H. E. Waddell was our traveling salesman and William Goehring was bookkeeper. In 1883, N. B. Scott became president.

On July 1, 1891, the Central Glass Company merged with seventeen other glass manufacturers to form the enormous United States Glass Company. Central was known as

Factory 0. Daniel C. Ripley became the first president of the United States Glass Company, with each member company retaining it own officers. It was hoped that by joining together they would all survive an economically difficult time. Glass company administrators pushed hard for a non-union shop causing a strike at Central from 1893 to 1895.

By January 4,1896 Factory O pulled away from the United States Glass Company and became Central Glass Works. Some of the former operators were again in control, including Nathan B. Scott, L. F. Stifel, Joseph Speidel and Peter Cassell. This purchase was recorded in *China, Glass and Lamps*, January 8, 1896. Incorporation took place for the new owners February 8,1896. Their capital amounted to $500,000, one hundred times Central's initial worth. The following entry appeared in the January 29,1896 issue of *China, Glass and Lamps*.

> Glassmaking was resumed at the Central Glass Works this week and everything is moving along satisfactorily. The management is much pleased with the start made. Only one furnace is in operation but the others will be started when the trade justifies it. Some handsome orders have already been received from old customers of the Central and others promise to remember the company. Several of the former customers have already written words of encouragement, saying that they will be glad to renew their relations. The outlook seems very bright.

One of Central's pressed tableware patterns from the late 1890s appeared in the *Glass and Pottery World* on page 70 of the February issue, 1897. The pattern is illustrated in the form of a four piece table set, ie., creamer, covered sugar, spooner and butter dish. Ruth Webb Lee included this pattern in her book *Victorian Pressed Glass*, plate 48, no. 1, calling it Helene pattern. In her text, Mrs. Lee incorrectly attributed Helene to A. H. Heisey, but admits that she has lost her notes on the pattern. This is one link between the previous United States Glass Company association and the restructuring of 1901 following a major fire at the plant. Not surprising, Helene emulated the geometry of cut glass so popular at the time.

With a good reputation and lots of hard work the owners were beginning to turn a profit again by 1898. In April of 1901 the following advertisement appeared in *China, Glass & Pottery Review*.

> Central Glass Works, Wheeling, W.Va., Manufacturers of BAR GLASSWARE, pressed and blown, cut, etched and engraved. Branch offices: John H. Dobbs, 66 W. B'way (also Boston and the New England States), Geo. R. Reinhart, 619 Arch St., Phila. Pa., Green & Seeman, 21 S. Charles, Baltimore, Md., H. E. Waddell, room 502, Journal Bldg., Chicago.
>
> The contract has been awarded to the Central Glass Co. of Wheeling, W.Va., to furnish the GERMAN VILLAGE at the PanAmerican Exposition in Buffalo with all the glassware and ornaments needed during the season.

Business was good at Central until October 10,1901 when the factory again burned down. That fire was terrible. Only because the company warehouse was overstocked, were goods available to fill orders while new buildings could be constructed. By March of 1902 the factory was ready to make glass; however, a decision was made to concentrate on the manufacture of bar and hotel goods.

The company's Board of Directors included N. B. Scott, Louis Schaub, Louis Stifel, Dr. R. W. Hazlett, Peter Cassell, Joseph Speidel, Sr., John Frew and William Goehring. At that time the company employed nearly seven hundred.

From *China & Glass Trade Directory* for 1936.

> Central Glass Works, Wheeling, W.Va.
> Jess W. Speidel, president; Carl Schmidt, vice-president; E. J. Schaub, secretary and treasurer; Sidney Morgan, factory manager. 3 furnaces, 36 pots. High grade tableware; gold decorated and cut stemware and tumblers; etched tableware, hotel and bar glassware.

The *House Furnisher and China, Glass & Pottery Review* for May 1901 reported the following about stemware from the Central Glass Works.

> The Central Glass Works, Wheeling, W.Va., have put out the most beautiful line of iridescent stemware the trade has yet seen. All the colors of the rainbow are reflected, yet at first glance one sees only a beautiful clear crystal. The goods are astonishing in value at the prices asked.

Their iridescent stemware seems somewhat early for glass of the sort to be appearing on the market. Iridescent wares are generally associated with the post-World War I through the 1920s. The taste of the time demanded paper thin glasses, light stemware and delicate colors or colorless tableware until at least the mid 1920s. Central satisfied these desires with a remarkably changed line befitting public taste. No longer were they making old style pressed pattern glass.

The depression of the 1930s closed the plant for a short time, but it was again reopened in 1933 and was engaged in the manufacture of all kinds of bar goods. By 1939 competition from foreign wares imported into this country reached such proportions that the Central Glass Works was finally closed for good. The Imperial Glass Company acquired their molds and machinery in 1939. Central was never again to reopen.

Central Glass Co.

Pattern Number	*Pattern Name*
135	Barrel Thumbprint
137	Central Colonial
139	Crystal
140	(Cabbage) Rose
145	Leaf (Loop)
146	?
150	?

152	Oak Leaf Band
153	Honeycomb
163	Ripple
189	?
234	Wheat in Shield
280	Flower in Diamond Band
365	Mountain Laurel
438	Prism and Diamond Band
439	Panel with Diamond Point
555	Nail City
585	Leaflets
610	Thumbprint Band
650	Gadroon and Cross (Dot and Dash)
651	Bead and Chain
705	Simplicity
720	Corner Medallion
730	Unnamed (Oval with Fan Corners) plain/engraved
740	Strawberry Diamond plain/engraved
748	Log Cabin
775	Pressed Diamond
783	?
794	Rope, plain/engraved
795	Rope, ribbed optic
796	Lattice Thumbprint (Rope and Thumbprint)
810	Tudor (Diamond Cane) plain/engraved
829	Oesterling, plain/engraved
835	Daisy & Button (variation)
838	Barrel (pg. 84,1885 catalogue)
870	Picture Window, plain/ engraved
876	Effulgent Star, (Allover Stars)
877	Flute Band
881	Blocks
884	Unnamed (Swirl & Concave Band)
895	Unnamed (Three Vertical Band Thumbprint)
960 (950?)	Whirlpool
999	Swirl and Dot
15005 (U.S. Glass Co. #)	U.S. Coin (Silver Age)
?	Columbian Coin (Spanish Coin)
?	Cord and Tassel
?	Rococo
?	Scroll with Acanthus
?	Shell

References Consulted

J. Stanley Brothers File, Rakow Library, Corning Museum of Glass, Corning, New York.

Bailey, Lois R. and Don, "Coin Glass: Where the Numismatic and Antique Hobbie Meet," *Coins,* Krause Publications, Inc. ©1980, Vol. 27, No. 5, May 1980.

Eige, Eason, *A Century of Glassmaking in West Virginia,* Huntington Galleries (Huntington Museum of Art), ©1980.

Jefferson, Josephine, *Wheeling Glass,* The Guide Publishing Company, ©1947.

Jenks, Bill and Jerry Luna, *Early American Pattern Glass 1850-1910,* Wallace Homestead Book Company, ©1990.

Kamm, Minnie Watson, *Pattern Glass Pitchers,* Vol. III, Vl, Vll, Vlll, Mrs. Oliver Kamm, ©1954.

Lee, Ruth Webb, *Early American Pressed Glass,* Lee Publications ©1960.

Lee, Ruth Webb, *Victorian Glass,* Lee Publications, ©1944.

Revi, Albert Christian, *American Pressed Glass and Figure Bottles,* Thomas Nelson Inc., ©1964.

Timmerman, Tim, *U. S. Coin Glass: A Century of Mystery.* 1992.

Weatherman, Hazel Marie, *Colored Glassware of the Depression Era 2,* Weatherman Glassbooks, ©1974.

Welker, John W. and Elizabeth F, *Pressed Glass in America Encyclopedia of the First Hundred Years. 1825-1925,* Antique Acres Press, ©1985.

An arrangement of Central's No. 140 Rose pattern, sometimes known to collectors as Cabbage Rose:
361. *9" Covered Bowl, High Foot,* ***362.*** *8" Covered Bowl, High Foot,* ***363.*** *7" Nappy,* ***364.*** *Celery Vase.*
365. *and* ***366.*** *Pickle Dishes. Although both are similar in size and pattern, item 366 is much thicker and heavier than item 365. Upon close examination, it appears that item 366's Rose pattern matches all the other pieces in the collection as well as the pattern in the catalogue pages, while item 365 does not. Therefore, item 365 is probably not Central.* ***367.*** *12" Salver.*
368. *Water Goblet,* ***369.*** *Egg Cup,* ***370.*** *8" Oval Dish.*

Five examples of the No. 152 Oak Leaf Band pattern: ***371.*** *9" Covered Bowl, High Foot,* ***372.*** *Water Goblet,* ***373.*** *Celery Vase,* ***374.*** *4½" Nappy,* ***375.*** *7½" Nappy.*
Central's Cord and Tassel pattern: ***376.*** *Stand Lamp, height 8¼",* ***377.*** *Tumbler,* ***378.*** *Water Goblet,* ***379.*** *8" Oval Dish,* ***380.*** *9" Comport.*
381.-383. *No. 234 Wheat in Shield pattern Spooner, Creamer and Cruet.*

384. *14" Hollow Stemmed Salver in the No. 150 pattern.*

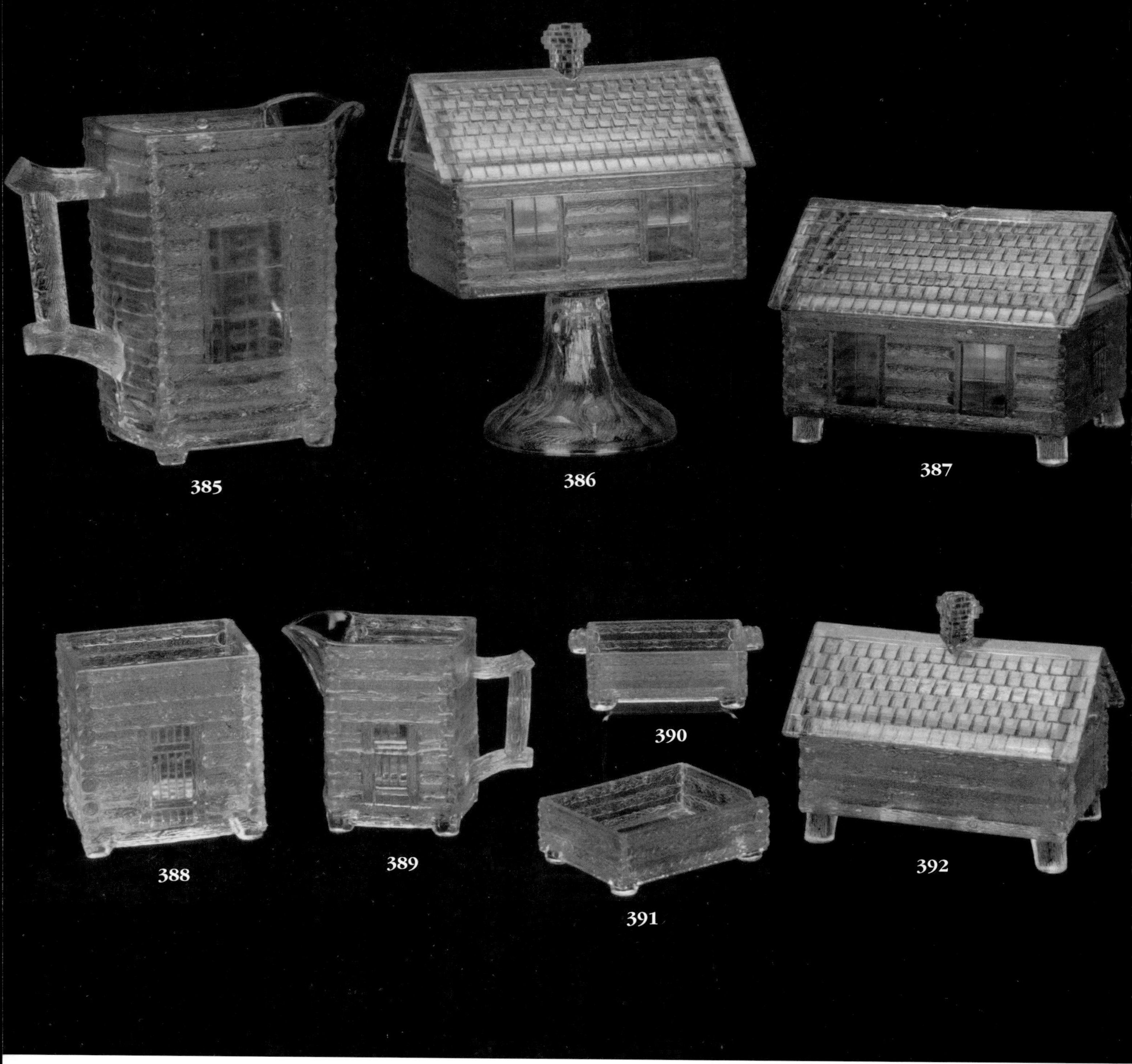

Central's famous No. 748, or Log Cabin pattern:
385. *Pitcher, 8½" high,* ***386.*** *7" Covered Bowl, High Foot,* ***387.*** *7" Covered Bowl, with the inscription "Jas. Lutted Buffalo N.Y. USA" stamped on the inside of the bowl.*
388.-389. *Sugar (missing the lid) and Creamer,* ***390.*** *4" Comport,* ***391.*** *4" Nappy,* ***392.*** *Covered Butter Dish (handles have been broken off).*

An assortment of No. 439, or Panel with Diamond Point pattern tableware:
393. *8" Comport, High Foot,* ***394.*** *9" Comport, Low Foot,* ***395.*** *11" Salver.*
396. *Spooner,* ***397.*** *Pitcher,* ***398.*** *8" Plate,* ***399.*** *Celery Vase.*
400. *Horseradish or Mustard (missing lid),* ***401.*** *Pickle Jar (missing cover),* ***402.*** *5" Nappy on Foot,* ***403.*** *and* ***404.*** *Wine and Water Goblets.*

Three examples of Central's No. 438 Prism and Diamond Band pattern: ***405.*** *7" Bowl, Low Foot (missing cover),* ***406.*** *Celery Vase,* ***407.*** *Spooner.*
408. *No. 870 Picture Window 8" Comport,* ***409.*** *No. 650 Gadroon and Cross Covered Bowl, High Foot.*
Three pieces of the No. 585 Leaflets pattern: ***410.*** *Pickle Dish,* ***411.*** *and* ***412.*** *Creamer and Covered Sugar.*

413. *No. 146 Large Goblet,* ***414.*** *and* ***415.*** *Loop pattern 8" Comport and Celery Vase.*
416. *No. 960 Whirlpool pattern Goblet,* ***417.*** *and* ***418.*** *No. 146 Wine and Cordial Goblets,* ***419.*** *No. 884 Celery Glass.*
Four Salts: ***420.*** *No. 189,* ***421.*** *No. 140 Rose pattern,* ***422.*** *No. 439 Panel with Diamond Point,* ***423.*** *No. 152 Oak Leaf Band.*

An assortment of Central's Bar Ware:
424. *No. 455 Centennial Ale or Pilsner,* ***425.*** *Beer Glass,* ***426.*** *No. 522 Weiss Beer Glass,* ***427.*** *Knights of Labor Beer Glass.*
428. *1876 Centennial Beer Mug,* ***429.*** *No. 276 Sham Claret,* ***430.*** *No. 529 Beer Mug.*
431. *No. 659 Tumbler,* ***432.*** *Beer Mug,* ***433.*** *No. 444 Centennial Pony Mug.*

A Variety of Central's Novelties:
434. *No. 747 Fish Condiment Dish, etched;* ***435.*** *No. 819 Swan Oval Dish,* ***436.*** *No. 691 Cherub Candlestick, partly etched;* ***437.*** *No. 758 Pheasant Oval Covered Dish, etched cover.*
438. *No. 579 Salt or Pepper Shakers, etched;* ***439.*** *No. 727 Duck Oval Covered Dish, etched;* ***440.*** *No. 823 Pickle Dish,* ***441.*** *No. 732 Owl Pickle Dish, etched.*

442.-445. *No. 794 Celery Vase, Covered Sugar, Spooner and Creamer, decorated with Engraving No. 215.*
446. *No. 720 Corner Medallion pattern Creamer, decorated with Engraving No. 189.*

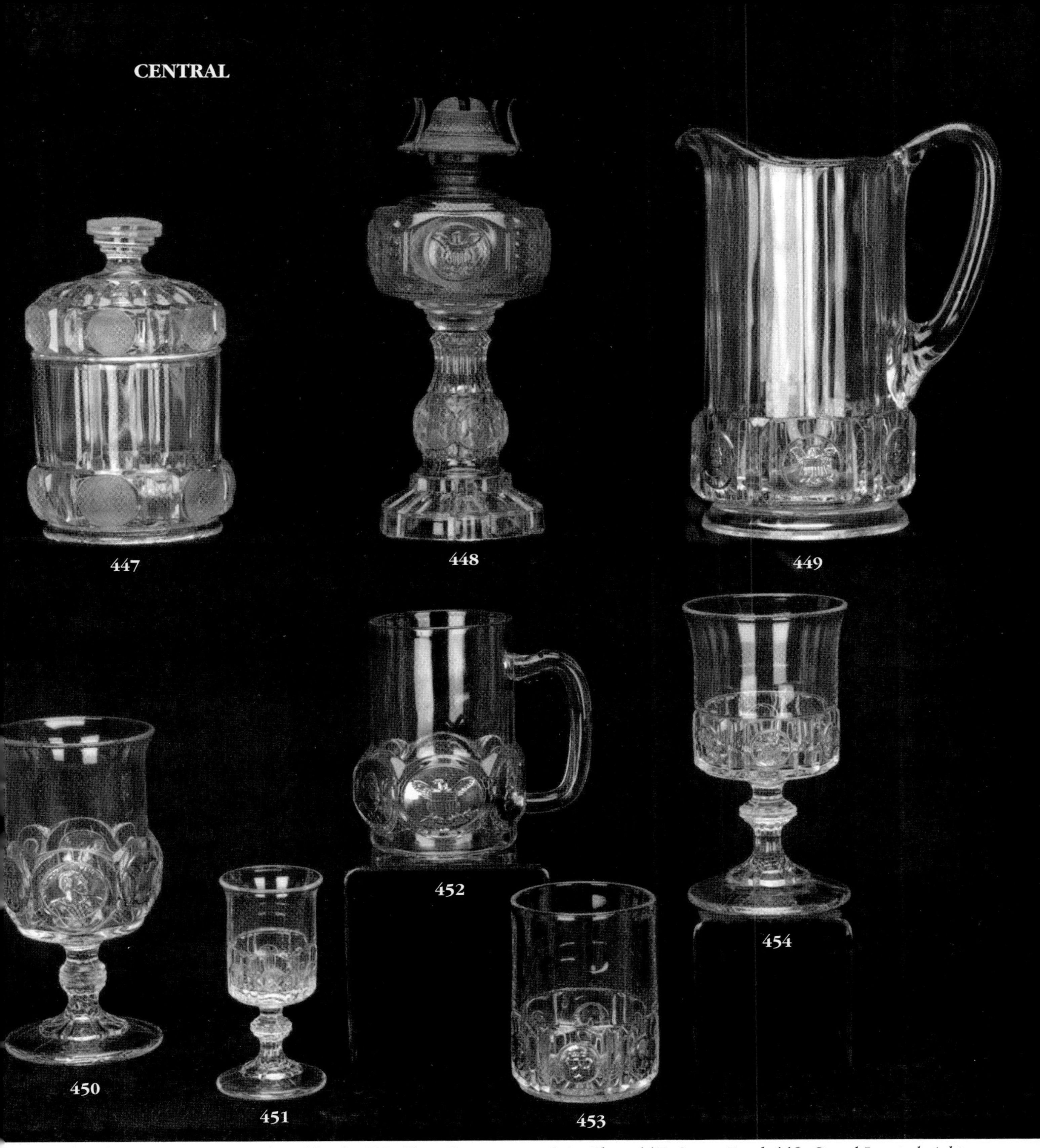

Central's Silver Age pattern, produced by the U.S. Glass Company as Coin Glass: ***447.*** *Sugar Bowl,* ***448.*** *Stand Lamp, height 7½",* ***449.*** *Pitcher.*
450. *Columbian Coin Goblet, a product of the U.S. Glass Company. Coins are painted with Gilt decoration.* ***451.*** *Wine Glass,* ***452.*** *Columbian Coin Beer Mug, with coins painted in Gilt decoration;* ***453.*** *Columbian Coin Tumbler, Coins painted with Gilt decoration;* ***454.*** *Water Goblet.*

Central's Silver Age pattern, produced by the U.S. Glass Company as Coin Glass:
455. *Covered Compote, height 10½".* ***456.*** *Stand Lamp with Amber Stained Coins,* ***457.*** *Celery Vase,* ***458.*** *U.S. Glass Columbian Coin Pitcher, Coins painted with Gilt decoration;* ***459.*** *Stand Lamp.*
460. *Cake Plate,* ***461.*** *Beer Mug,* ***462.*** *Cruet (note original stopper),* ***463.*** *Pickle Dish,* ***464.*** *Preserve Dish.*
465. *Tumbler,* ***466.*** *Toothpick,* ***467.*** *Covered Butter Dish,* ***468.*** *Salt or Pepper Shaker (missing pewter top),* ***469.*** *Footed Nappy,* ***470.*** *Creamer.*

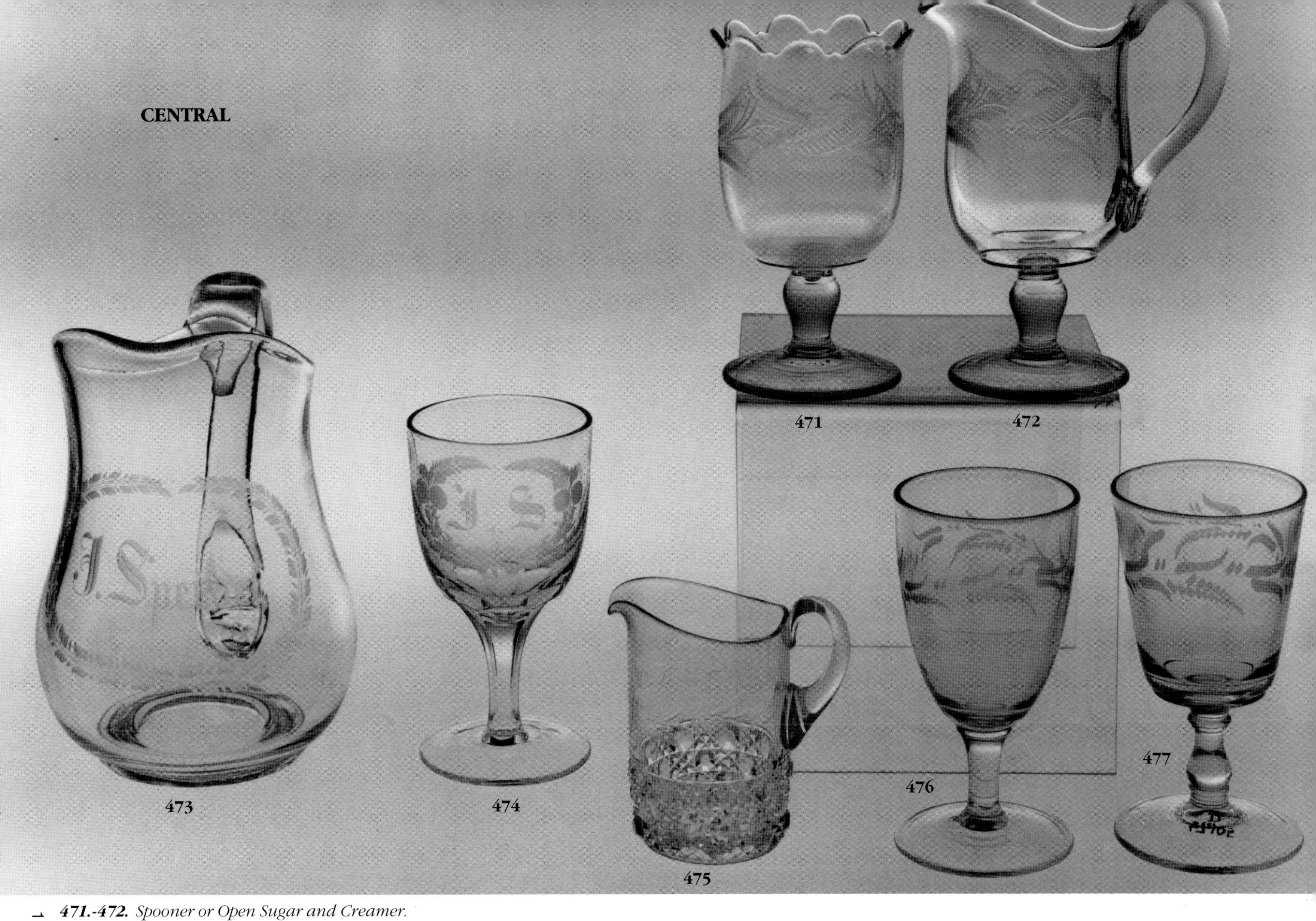

471.-472. *Spooner or Open Sugar and Creamer.*
473.-474. *No. 155 Half Gallon Jug and No. 386 Goblet. Both are engraved with the name or initials for Joseph Speidel, a chief stockholder in the Central Glass Works.*
475. *No. 810 Tudor pattern Creamer,* **476.** *No. 567 Goblet decorated with Engraving No. 185,* **477.** *No. 705 Goblet decorated with Engraving No. 185.*

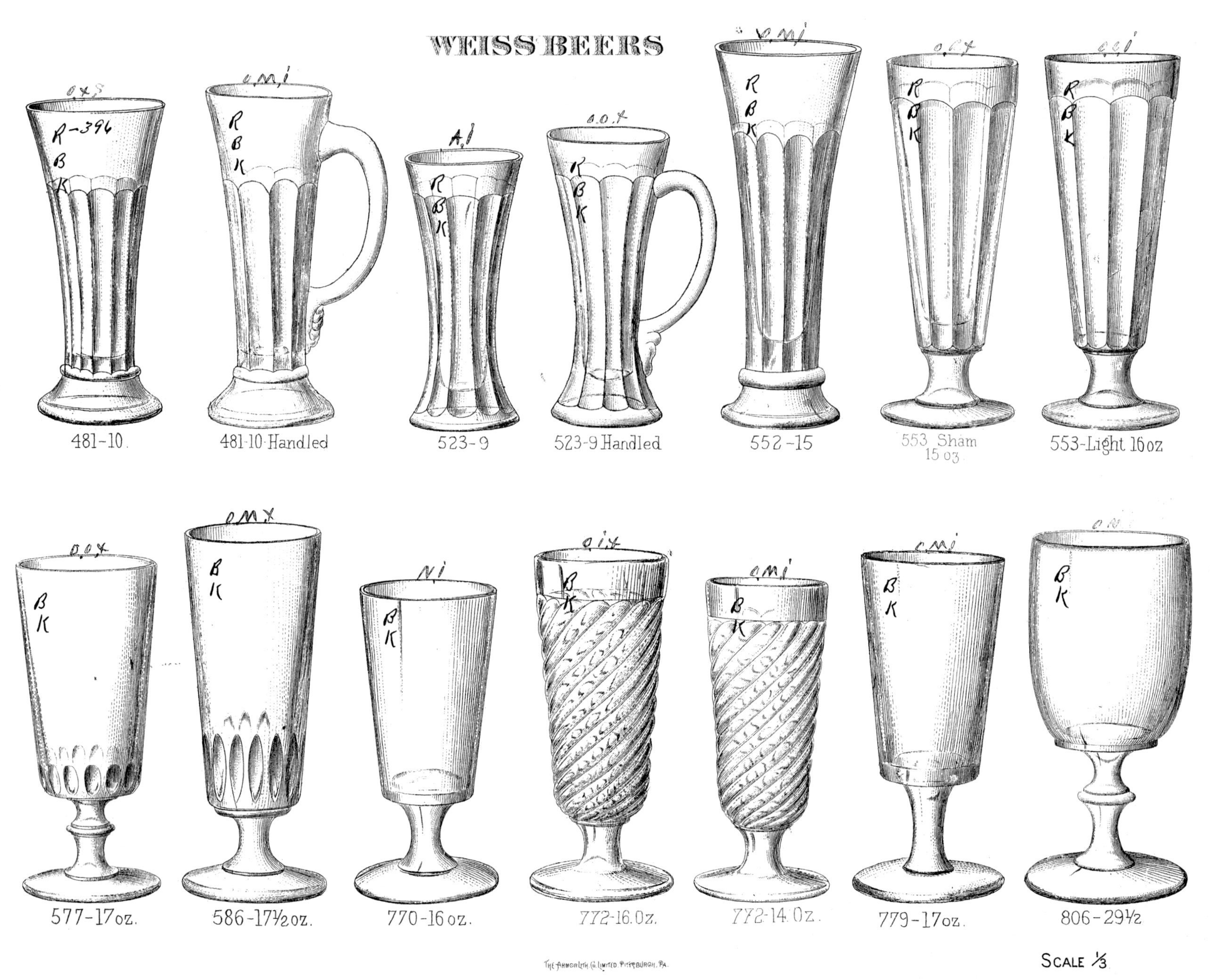

Central catalogue page depicting a series of beer glasses produced by the company.

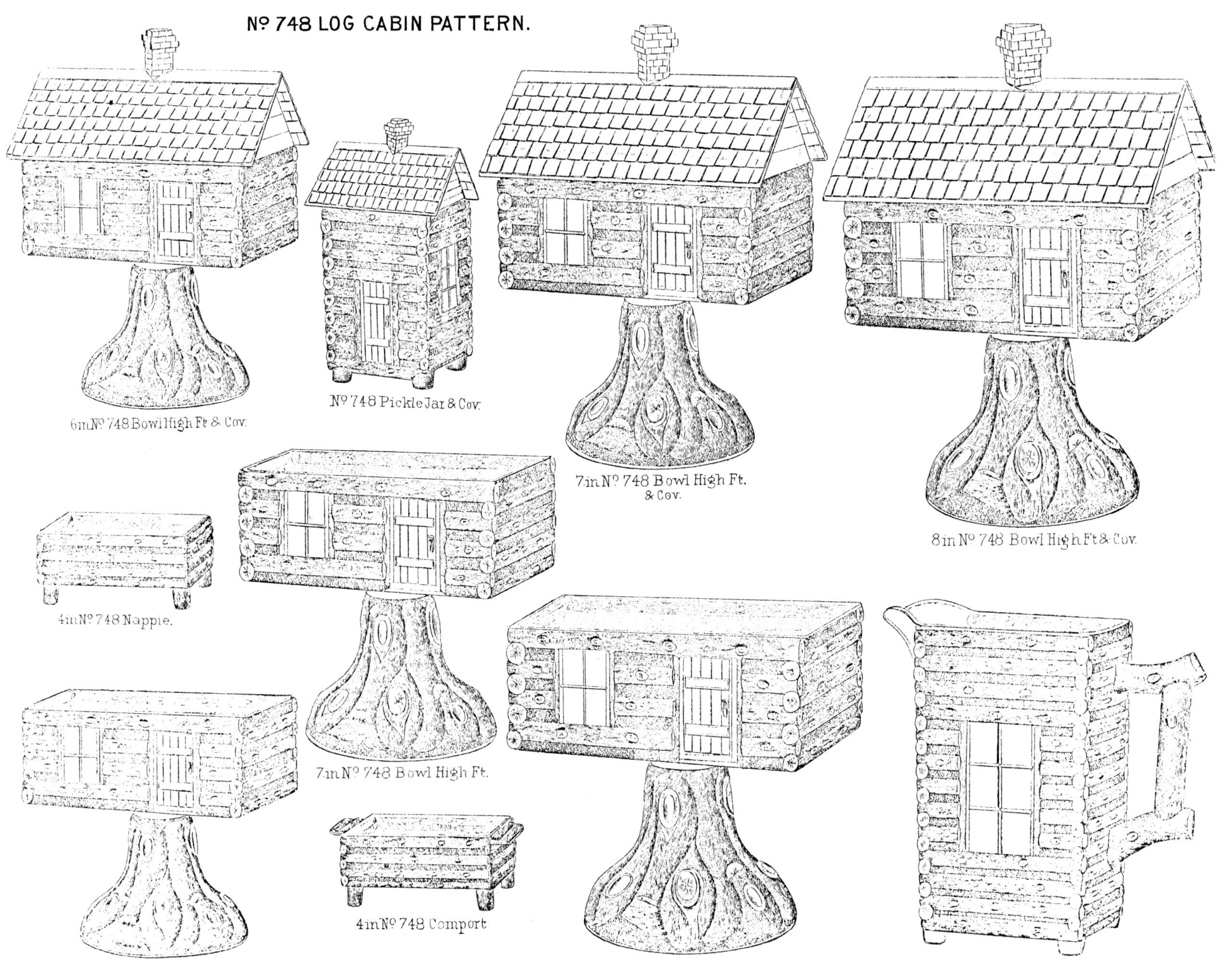

Various pieces made in Central's Log Cabin pattern are shown on this page taken from a company trade catalogue.

Several novelty items which were made by Central are shown on this trade catalogue page.

478.-479. *Matching Candlesticks and Compote, Cobalt Blue and Opal combination. Height of the candlesticks is 15".* ***480.*** *Magenta Compote, diameter 11". These pieces were produced by the Central Glass Works after 1900.*

Tableware made by the Central Glass Works after 1900. All feature a Chinese Red to Clear color combination, and are decorated with a wide gold band.
481. *Plate, 11½" diameter,* ***482.*** *Bank Bowl on Black Base,* ***483.*** *Handled Tray (the gold decoration is of Holly leaves).*
484. *Open Compote,* ***485.*** *Candlesticks, height 9",* ***486.*** *Bank Bowl.*

The articles on this page were made at the various factories with which Harry Northwood was associated in the 1890s. **487.-488.** *Netted Oak tumbler and pitcher in decorated opal glass (Indiana, Pa., c. 1898).* **489.** *No. 285 Aurora pitcher in rubina with elaborate etching (Martins Ferry, c. 1890).* **490.-491.** *Blue opalescent (originally called "Pearl Blue") Intaglio tumbler and pitcher (Indiana, Pa., c. 1899).* **492.** *Rubina/flint opalescent pitcher (Indiana, Pa., c. 1898).*
493. *Grape and Leaf creamer in opal glass (Indiana, Pa., c. 1898).* **494.-495.** *Canary opalescent Trough and Pump novelties (Indiana, Pa., c. 1899-1900).* **496.** *No. 333 (Leaf Mold) pattern, spooner in Royal Silver glass (Martins Ferry, c. 1892).* **497.** *No. 287 Royal Ivy tumbler in "spatter" glass (Martins Ferry, c. 1890)*.**498.-499**. *Ivory glass Pagoda spooner and Nautilus covered sugar bowl (Indiana, Pa., c. 1899). Panelled Sprig creamer in "granite ware" treatment (Ellwood City, Pa., c. 1894).* **501.** *Blue opalescent No. 562 novelty vase (Indiana, Pa., c. 1899).* **502. and 504.** *Ivory glass Inverted Fan and Feather salt shaker and turquoise Pagoda salt shaker (Indiana, Pa., c. 1899).* **503.** *Cactus pattern salt shaker in opaque green (Ellwood City, Pa., c.1895).* **505. and 507.** *No. 263 (Leaf Umbrella) salt shaker in rose du barry and sugar shaker in light yellow (Martins Ferry, c. 1899).* **506.** *No. 315 Royal Oak covered butter dish in rubina (Martins Ferry, c. 1891).*

508.-509. *Scroll with Acanthus berry bowl and sauce dish in flint opalescent, c. 1904.* ***510.-513.*** *Drapery pitcher in blue opalescent; spooner, creamer and covered sugar bowl in flint opalescent (note gold decoration), all c. 1907-08.*
514.-515. *Regent berry bowl in green and jelly compote in amethyst, c. 1903-1904.* ***516. and 518.*** *Scroll with Acanthus covered butterdish in crystal with gold and enamel decoration (c. 1904) and spooner in Mosaic glass, c. 1903.* ***517.*** *Golden Holly creamer in blue opalescent with gold decoration, c.1907-08.*
519.-522. *Emerald green Regent spooner, covered sugar, creamer and pitcher with gold decoration, c. 1903-1904.*

523.-526. *Four pieces in canary opalescent: Carnelian jelly compote and spooner, c. 1904; Four Pillars vase; and Grape and Cable two-handled bon bon, c. 1910 (this piece has a Basketweave pattern on the exterior).*
527.-530. *Note the elaborate handpainted decoration on this crystal Mikado table set (spooner, covered butterdish, covered sugar bowl and creamer), c. 1904.*
531. *Pearl Flowers card receiver in green opalescent, c. 1906.* ***532.*** *Bushel Basket novelty in dark amethyst, c. 1910.* ***533.*** *Shell and Wild Rose card receiver in amber, c. 1906.*

534. *Emerald green Greek Key and Scales bowl with crimped edge (note red/gold 'goofus' decoration).* ***535.*** *Crystal Poppy and Scroll plate.* ***536.*** *Crystal Strawberries bowl with crimped edge (Basketweave exterior).*

537. and 540. *Emerald green Poppy shallow bowls (540 is crimped and decorated with heavy gold paint), c. 1906.* ***538.*** *Flint opalescent basket from the Intaglio line, c. 1906.* ***539.*** *Flint opalescent Greek Key footed, crimped bowl with red and heavy gold decoration.*

541. and 544. *Poppy jelly compotes (541 is decorated with heavy gold paint).* ***542.-543.*** *Double Loop sugar basin in green (note gold decoration) and small creamer in dark blue.*

545.-547. *Crystal tumblers and pitcher with hand-painted floral decoration, c. 1905-08.* ***548.*** *Crystal No. 31 (Belladonna) pitcher with gold bands and hand-painted decoration, c. 1907-08.* ***549.-550.*** *Singing Birds decorated tumbler and pitcher, c. 1912.*

551.-553. *Inverted Thumbprint, Oriental Poppy and decorated tumblers in blue.* ***554.-557.*** *Crystal No. 31 (Belladonna) covered sugar bowl and butterdish; blue No. 31 (Belladonna) spooner and covered sugar bowl (note the various hand-painted decorative motifs on these pieces).*

558.-565. *Note the various hand-painted floral motifs on these decorated tumblers in emerald green and decorated wines in crystal, all c. 1906-08.*

Crystal glass was a Northwood favorite for decoration with gold and ruby or pale purple. All pieces here are c. 1906-1912.
566. *Gold Rose pitcher with "maiden's blush" decorative treatment.* ***567.-568.*** *Golden Cherry tumbler and pitcher.* ***569.*** *Strawberry and Cable tankard pitcher.*
570.-571. *No. 12 berry bowl and sauce dish.* ***572.-574.*** *Grape and Lattice sauce dish, tumbler and berry bowl.* ***575.-576.*** *Cherry and Cable spooner and berry bowl.*
577. *Plums and Cherries covered bowl.* ***578.-581.*** *Peach sauce dish, sugar bowl base, spooner and creamer.*

Gold decoration was applied to various shades of transparent green glass at the Northwood plant between 1906-1912.
582. *Teardrop Flower pitcher.* ***583.*** *Regal covered sugar bowl.* ***584.*** *Oriental Poppy tankard pitcher.* ***585.-586.*** *Peach tumbler and pitcher.*
587.-589. *Teardrop Flower covered butterdish, spooner and creamer.* ***590.*** *Posies and Pods berry bowl.*
591.-594. *Emerald green Peach table set-- spooner, creamer, covered butterdish and covered sugar bowl.*

Northwood's pattern No. 19 was introduced in 1907. Collectors today call it Memphis. Items are well-known in crystal (Figs. 676-680) as well as emerald green, but canary is quite scarce.
595. *Canary No. 19 (Memphis) spooner.* ***596.-598.*** *Emerald green No. 19 (Memphis) pitcher, sauce dishes and berry bowl (note gold decoration).*

Opalescent glass was a popular Northwood product, especially between 1905 and 1915, when these pieces were made. ***599. and 604.*** *Tree Trunk and Leaf Columns vases in flint opalescent.* ***600. and 603.*** *Diamond Point vase and unknown pattern vase in blue opalescent.* ***601.*** *Flint opalescent Roulette bowl.* ***602.*** *Peacocks on the Fence ruffled bowl in blue opalescent.* ***605.*** *Pearl Flowers card receiver in blue opalescent.* ***606.-607.*** *Poinsettia Lattice bowl and Leaf and Beads card receiver in flint opalescent.*

608. and 611. Flint opalescent Regal covered sugar bowl and sauce dish. ***609.*** *Flint opalescent Beads and Bark vase.* ***610.*** *Flint opalescent Ocean Shell vase.* ***612.*** *Flint opalescent Graceful vase.*

Northwood's "Golden Iris" made its debut in 1908-09. These items and those on the next page were made between that time and about 1914. Carnival glass collectors call this color "marigold" today.
613.-614. *Ruffled bowls in Peacocks on the Fence and Good Luck (note the Ribbed exteriors).* ***615.*** *Raspberry milk pitcher.*
616. *Shell and Wild Rose ruffled bowl.*
617. *Daisy and Plume footed rose bowl.* ***618.-621.*** *Grape and Gothic Arches spooner, covered butterdish, creamer and tumbler.*
622. *Bushel Basket round novelty.* ***623.-625.*** *Tumblers in Singing Birds, Dandelion and Springtime.*

626.-628. *Grape and Cable fruit bowl, pitcher and oval berry bowl.*
629. *Beads ruffled bowl.* ***630.*** *Wishbone footed bowl with ruffled edge.* ***631.-632.*** *Grape and Cable sauce dish and berry bowl.* ***633.*** *Lustre Flute tumbler with ruffled top.* ***634.-636.*** *Sherbet dishes or nut bowls in Interior Swirl and Flute patterns.* ***637.*** *Springtime tumbler.* ***638.*** *Grape and Cable two-handled bon bon with Basketweave exterior.*

Many different items in Northwood's Grape and Cable pattern were made in purple Carnival glass between 1910 and 1914. ***639, 640. and 642.*** *Grape and Cable tankard pitcher, two sizes of tumblers.* ***646.*** *Candleholder/lamp with shade.* ***643.-644.*** *Two-piece fruit bowl and inverted base.* ***645.*** *Cracker jar.*

646. *Three-toed berry bowl.* ***647. and 650.*** *Berry bowl and matching sauce dish.* ***648.*** *Plate with ruffled edge.* ***649.*** *Footed sauce dish.*

651.-655. *Four-piece table set--spooner, covered butterdish, creamer and covered sugar bowl--along with a smaller creamer.*

656.-657. *Oriental Poppy pitcher and tumblers in purple Carnival glass, c. 1911-12.*

658.-659. *Purple Carnival glass Grape and Cable master punch bowl on base with matching cups, c. 1911.*

Chapter Five

H. Northwood & Company 1902-1925

See Figure 750.

James S. Measell

H. NORTHWOOD & COMPANY, 1902-1925

By James S. Measell

In the fall of 1901, the Wheeling Board of Trade sought investors as well as a glassmaker to re-open the Hobbs, Brockunier factory, which had been idle since 1894, shortly after it was acquired by the United States Glass Company. The Board struck success when two seasoned glassmen, brothers Harry and Carl Northwood, formed H. Northwood & Co. with their wealthy uncle, Thomas Dugan of Ellwood City, Pa.

According to the *National Glass Budget* (May 17, 1902), the Board raised $10,000 to help finance the venture. The plant was renovated and new equipment installed so that glass production could begin in July. The August 24, 1902, issue of the *Wheeling Intelligencer* lauded "the exertions of the board of trade of Wheeling" and listed the plant "among the foremost industries of Wheeling."

The Northwood concern soon became one of the leading establishments in the American glass tableware industry in the early twentieth century. For more than two decades, the Northwood name was associated with many different kinds of glass — pattern glass, decorated ware, imitation cut glass, opalescent novelties, Carnival glass, lighting goods, stretch glass and a succession of unusual opaque colors.

The Northwood Men

No strangers to Wheeling by 1902, Harry and Carl Northwood were sons of the famous Stourbridge, England, cameo glass artisan John Northwood, who was known worldwide for his replication of the Portland vase. Harry Northwood, who was born in 1860, emigrated to the United States in November, 1881, and found employment at Hobbs, Brockunier as a glass etcher in the department headed by Otto Jaeger. His fiance, Clara Elizabeth Beaumont, came to Wheeling the following spring, and they were married by the Rev. J. W. Griffith on May 27, 1882, at the Jacob Street home of John Walford, another Hobbs, Brockunier worker. Blessed with artistic talent, Harry Northwood won three first premium awards at the West Virginia State Fair on Wheeling Island in September, 1882, for etched glass, a display of glassware, and "oil painting from nature" (*Crockery and Glass Journal,* September 28, 1882).

Harry Northwood left Hobbs, Brockunier in early 1884 to join the La Belle Glass Co. in Bridgeport. This enterprise made much of Northwood's Stourbridge roots, and he was listed as "Designer and Metal Maker" in the firm's advertising when the factory was destroyed by fire in late

***660.-662.** Three pieces of Grapevine and Cherry Sprig--covered sugar bowl, creamer and butterdish.*

HENRY HELLING, PRES'T. H. FLOTO, TREAS. A. W. KERR, SEC'Y.

THE NORTHWOOD GLASS CO.

Martin's Ferry, Ohio.

MANUFACTURERS OF

BLOWN TABLEWARE, WATER SETS, FANCY GOODS, DOME SHADES, GAS GLOBES, ETC.

In all the LATEST COLORS and EFFECTS, including RIB, DIAMOND, SPOT, DEW DROP, SATIN FINISH, etc.

Mr. Harry Northwood (late of La Belle Glass Works), of Stourbridge, England, Metal Maker, Designer, and General Manager.

General Traveling Salesman, S. C. Dunlevy.

Ad from Crockery and Glass Journal *(January-September, 1888)*

September, 1887. Within a few months, former investors in the La Belle concern joined with several prominent Martins Ferry businessmen to launch the Northwood Glass Co. in that Ohio River city.

The Martins Ferry plant was reasonably successful, despite its relatively small size. Northwood made several lines in rubina glass (Figs. 489 and 492), a technique he probably learned at Hobbs, Brockunier. Cased glass was featured in the No. 263 line, which is now known as Leaf Umbrella (Figs. 505 and 507). Spattered and spangled effects were also made (Figs. 496-497).

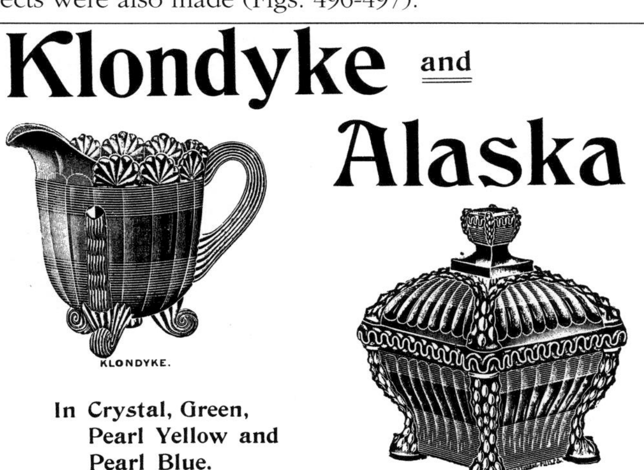

In Crystal, Green, Pearl Yellow and Pearl Blue.

Opalescent and Decorated Lemonade Sets IN LARGE VARIETY AND AT RIGHT PRICES.

THE NORTHWOOD CO.,

INDIANA, PA.

NEW YORK,	PHILADELPHIA,	BALTIMORE,
Frank M. Miller,	Fitzpatrick & Pascoe,	Andrew J. George.
76 Park Place.	930 Arch Street.	

WEST, Carl Northwood. EAST, George Mortimer.

Ad from China, Glass and Pottery Review *(February, 1898).*

Harry and his wife built a large home at Broadway and Monroe in Martins Ferry, and they journeyed overseas several times. In 1889, Harry Northwood and George Pownall, head of the glass cutting department, went to the Paris Exposition, probably with John Northwood. Carl Northwood, who had been born in 1872, visited Martins Ferry on several occasions before emigrating in June, 1891, to join his brother in the glass business.

In the fall of 1892, the Northwood Glass Co. relocated to Ellwood City, Pa., where a new plant was built by town boosters including Thomas Dugan. Harry Northwood was manager and glassmaker, and Carl Northwood covered the South as a salesman for the firm. Little advertising was done, so not much is known about the company's products. Decorated opal (milk glass) was made, as were several pale opaque colors (Fig. 503) which the firm called "neutral tints" in one of its few advertising notices in 1895.

The glassmaking venture at Ellwood City struggled for several years. After poor sales at the annual glass exhibit at Pittsburgh's Monongahela House, the Northwood men resigned abruptly to go to Indiana, Pa., in February, 1896, to re-open the glass factory built by the townspeople for the short-lived Indiana Glass Co., which closed in 1893 about a year after its inception. Local businessmen had tried for several years to attract an experienced glassmaker to Indiana.

Northwood's Intaglio (Fall, 1908, Butler Brothers).

These Northwood crystal pieces were made between 1906 and 1915.
***663.** Holiday round tray.* ***664.** Grapevine and Cherry Sprig/Frosted Fruits berry bowl.* ***665.** Poppy and Scroll round plate.* ***666.** No. 21 (Flute) spooner.* ***667.** and* ***669.** Atlas Creamer and spooner.* ***668.** Regal pitcher.* ***670.** Strawberry and Cable goblet.* ***671.** Grape and Lattice pitcher.* ***672.** No. 14 (Valentine) ruffled bowl.* ***673. and 675.** Atlas sauce dish and berry bowl.* ***674.** Grapevine and Cherry Sprig sauce dish.*

The Northwood Glass Co. at Indiana, Pa., was an unqualified success, as new lines in pressed and blown pattern glassware soon caught the public fancy and sold well. In mid-1898, Harry Northwood created an opaque Ivory (called "custard" today) glass for pressed ware, and several new lines were produced in decorated ware (Figs. 498-499). During the times of the Gold Rush, the Northwood produced pressed ware patterns dubbed Klondyke and Alaska which, from all reports, were remarkably popular. A blown line of pink opalescent (now called "cranberry opalescent") glass was well-received, too.

In late 1899, the Northwood Glass Company was absorbed by the National Glass Company, a Pittsburgh-based conglomerate which controlled some nineteen glass tableware firms in Maryland, Pennsylvania, West Virginia, Ohio and Indiana. Harry Northwood and Carl Northwood

Photo, (June, 1906) of Northwood workers. Note No. 12 pitcher near the mould.

Decorating room at H. Northwood and Co. in June, 1906. The No. 12 pattern is being ruby-stained, and many plain tumblers are ready for decoration. Foreman Carl Northwood, wearing a light shirt and a cap high on his head, is standing in the rear of the photo, between a woman in a dark dress and a support post.

went to England to manage the London sales office of the National Glass Company. By June, 1901, the National was in financial straits. The Northwood men returned to the United States, and the Board of Trade soon attracted them to Wheeling, where Factory H of the United States Glass Co. had been idle for some time. Ironically, this was the same plant in which Harry Northwood had begun his career some two decades earlier when the concern was the famous Hobbs, Brockunier firm.

Butler Brothers catalogue (February, 1912).

At first, the Northwood enterprise was financed by its namesake and his uncle, Thomas Dugan of Ellwood City, Pa. The Wheeling Board of Trade raised $10,000, and the U. S. Glass Co. held a mortgage for $20,000. Despite some difficulties in readying the plant for production, the furnaces were in operation by July, 1902. Harry Northwood served as vice-president and general manager of the firm until his death in 1919, and Carl Northwood (who died in January, 1918), was both a salesman and in charge of the decorating department. Harry Northwood's son, Harry Clarence Northwood, was also a salesman, although he was based in Cincinnati for many years; he passed away in 1923.

When the Northwood firm incorporated in June,1905, several of Wheeling's leading businessmen became associ-

676.-680. *No. 19 (Memphis) punch cup, master punch bowl on base, handled nappy, fruit bowl on base and deep berry bowl. The nappy carries an advertising message ("Pickering/Furniture/Carpets/10 & Penn/Nuf Ced") as does the deep berry bowl ("From/Keech's/Furniture/Carpets/923-931/Penn Ave/Pittsburg").*

HARRY NORTHWOOD. THOS. DUGAN, (of Ellwood City, Pa.)

H. NORTHWOOD & CO.,

MANUFACTURERS OF

CRYSTAL COLORED AND OPALESCENT GLASSWARE, PLAIN AND DECORATED.

WHEELING, W. VA.

NEW YORK, FRANK M. MILLER. 25 WEST BROADWAY.

This letterhead was used in 1905.

ated with the company. George E. House, president of House and Hermann Home Furnishings, became president of H. Northwood Co.; he had been an influential member of the Wheeling Board of Trade when the Northwoods decided to come to Wheeling. Matthew H. McNabb was manager of the Lyceum Advertising Agency in Wheeling, and John R. Mendel was a principal in the Mendel Brothers Pearl Laundry.

Northwood Products, 1903-1908

The first pressed tableware line made by Northwood at Wheeling was called "Carnelian," and attractive advertisements appeared in several trade journals in January, 1903. Articles were made in three opalescent colors— flint, blue and canary—and most are decorated with gold (Figs. 523-524 and 793), but Ivory pieces are decorated with green and gold.

Carnelian was soon followed by a short-lived assortment of Mosaic glass in purple and white. Several novelty vases were made, and a pattern now called Scroll with Acanthus was introduced (Fig. 518). Among the items known are the berry set, table set and water set as well as cruet, jelly compote, toothpick holder and salt/pepper shakers. Mosaic glass was difficult to make, and Northwood's production probably lasted only a few months.

Also among the early products at Wheeling were decorated or opalescent lemonade sets—pitchers accompanied by six matching tumblers and a metal tray. The decorated sets invariably feature handpainted floral motifs, and the tumblers are decorated on one side only (Figs. 558 - 562). Northwood's opalescent Poinsettia and Daffodils are both well-known in several opalescent colors—flint, blue, canary, green and ruby.

The next major table pattern, Regent, was introduced in mid-1903, although advertising continued well into the next year (Figs. 514-515, 519-522 and 793-796). In September, 1904, Harry Northwood patented a "process of decorating glassware with liquid gold" (U. S. Patent #770,867). Northwood's patent was used for a later line called "Verre D'or" (French for "glass of gold"). As with the Regent line, heavy gold decoration stands out on royal blue, amethyst and emerald green glass. A few pieces are known in Ivory, too (Fig. 735). *Glass and Pottery World* (August, 1906) reported that the designs for the Verre D'or line were inspired by "the decorations in the Court Theater, Wheeling."

Another 1904 pattern, Mikado, is one of the most elaborate of Northwood's decorated lines, and the influence of oriental taste is apparent. Crystal items with stippled backgrounds are decorated with ruby stain and gold, and the petals of each flower are delicately shaded with red, yellow, green and either blue or light purple (Figs. 527-530). The Encore line from 1906, like Mikado, is decorated with ruby stain and gold, but the effect is less dramatic.

Diadem debuted in 1905. Clear glass examples resemble cut ware, but Diadem (Figs. 790 and 810-811) is also known in opalescent glass (flint, blue, and canary). Another imitation cut glass motif was called simply No. 12. Introduced in 1906, this line consisted of numerous "open stock" items, ranging from the table set and pitchers to a punch bowl and handled baskets. G. Sommers and Co., a Minnesota whole-

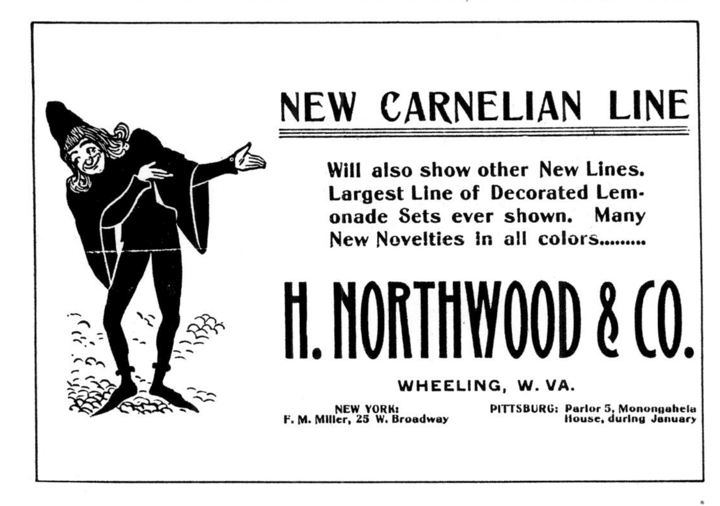

Style! What Is It?

Style is an intangible expression of exquisite taste
and refinement which is beyond the power
of mere words. It is found in

Northwood's New Glass Lines for 1907

Over 100 new patterns in water sets alone.
Ten entirely new shapes in jugs and tankards.
The famous line of

"Verre D'Or" Glass

has been lengthened, both in "Sateena" and "Intaglio." The new crystal lines are radically different from anything ever offered. See our large January exhibit at the Monongahela House, Pittsburg, or write to the factory or these representatives for catalogues : : : :

New York . . . . . . Frank Miller, 25 W. Broadway
New England . . . . Chas. J. De La Croix
Cleveland . . . . J. G. Anderson, 502 Arcade
Baltimore . . . . Green & Thomas, 33 S. Charles St.
Buffalo . . . . Chas. Lantaff, 523 Main St.
Chicago . . . W. E. Cummings & Co., 160 State St.
Milwaukee . . . . . E. Bersback, 250 West Water St.

H. Northwood Company

Wheeling, W. Va.

Ad in Glass and Pottery World *(January 20, 1907).*

Gold Rose (Butler Brothers catalogue, 1910).

Grape and Cable sets from a Butler Brothers catalogue.

sale house, offered 72 pieces for $6.04. The No. 12 line may be decorated with ruby stain and gold (Figs. 570-571). Photographs taken inside the Northwood plant in June, 1906, show this pattern.

In late 1905, the Northwood firm began to mark many of its pressed pieces with a block N, underlined and enclosed within a circle. This mark was often featured in the company's advertising, and glass collectors today are well aware of this distinctive Northwood mark. Surprisingly, the design was never officially registered as a trade mark by the firm, and its use seems to have been discontinued about 1915. Many Carnival glass items bear the Northwood mark (tumblers are marked on the inside, but the placement of the mark varies on other articles).

Northwood's Drapery is known in both flint and blue opalescent, accented with heavy gold decoration on the vertical ribs and rims (Figs. 510-513). Northwood's Teardrop Flower pattern, made ca. 1906, occurs in amethyst, blue, light green and crystal. Like many of the other Northwood patterns from this period, Teardrop Flower (Figs. 582 and 587-589) occurs in table sets, water sets, and berry sets as well as a condiment set consisting of salt/pepper shakers and a cruet.

The No. 31 line was a short one, consisting of water set, table set and berry set. Heacock named this pattern Belladonna in a column for the weekly *Antique Trader* in 1975. Both crystal and blue items were produced, and articles may be decorated with either geometric or floral motifs (Figs. 554-557 and 784-785).

Lustre Flute pieces (Butler Brothers catalogue, Fall, 1908).

Grape and Cable in a Butler Brothers catalogue, 1912.

The Regal line was introduced in late 1906. Crystal and emerald green (sometimes gold decorated) Regal pieces are known, but the opalescent hues—flint, blue, green—are of most interest to collectors today (Figs. 583, 608 and 611). Regal water sets, berry sets and table sets were featured in Butler Brothers catalogs in 1907. In addition to the celery vase, today's collectors have also found cruets and salt/pepper shakers.

Both No. 21 and Atlas are Northwood colonial-style lines, but they are difficult to find today. Crystal table sets, berry sets and water sets are known, but the most striking articles have a "maiden's blush" ruby-stained effect and are decorated with gold (Figs. 821-822). Most pieces seem to be marked with the N-in-a-circle.

A new pattern for 1907 was "Golden Cherry," which could be either Cherry and Cable or Cherry Thumbprints. These feature light ruby/purple stain as well as gold decoration (Figs. 568 and 575-576). The Northwood firm apparently had insufficient production capacity to meet demand for these lines, so the company sent teams of workmen and the moulds for Cherry and Cable to the New Martinsville Glass Manufacturing Company. The Northwood's mould room foreman, George Matheny, had formerly been associated with the New Martinsville concern.

Gold Rose items typically have the N-in-a-circle. Table sets, water sets and berry sets were illustrated in a fall, 1910, Butler Brothers catalog, which also mentioned the two colors made, "solid wine ruby and emerald green." Crystal glass articles often have the "maiden's blush" treatment (Fig. 566) as well as gold decoration on the flowers.

Grapevine and Cherry Sprig, which was named by Heacock, is so unlike other Northwood patterns from 1903-07 that one might overlook it but for the N-in-a-circle. The crystal articles—table set, water set and berry set—are rel-

Ad for Northwood wares, December 29, 1906, including the Intaglio, Verre D'or and Regal lines.

This letterhead was used in 1906.

atively heavy, and some have gold decoration on the rims. The peg-like feet are different from virtually every other known Northwood pattern. The grapes and cherries may be satin finished with acid, giving rise to another name sometimes applied to this pattern—Frosted Fruits (Figs. 660-662, 664 and 674).

The Lustre Flute line was a contemporary of pattern No. 19 (now called Memphis) as well as Cherry Thumbprints, for these three are shown together in a Butler Brothers catalog from the fall of 1908. The opalescent effect is generally heavy on Lustre Flute items, and pieces may be trimmed in bright gold. A small creamer and open sugar are known in emerald green, as is the punch cup.

The Peach pattern, which is perhaps better known as Northwood's Peach, is well-established in Carnival glass circles. One may be surprised to see the "Peach" decorated with ruby-stain, and such pieces are quite scarce (Figs. 578-581). Posies and Pods (Fig. 590) may have been produced prior to 1905, for only the large berry bowl bears the N-in-a-circle mark, despite the fact that numerous items are known—water set, berry set and table set. Crystal pieces are sometimes decorated with gold and a light ruby stain.

Northwood's featured patterns for 1908 were No. 19 which is now known as Memphis, and a line called Golden Holly, which is now called simply Holly or, more often, Panelled Holly. Memphis is well-known in crystal (Figs. 676-680) and emerald green (Figs. 596-598), usually decorated with gold, and the pattern was later used for iridescent production. Several clear articles feature advertising messages (Figs. 678 and 680). Memphis pieces in canary are quite scarce (Fig. 595). The Panelled Holly line is best known today in a vibrant opalescent blue (Fig. 517) with heavy gold decoration on the holly leaves and in flint opalescent with red (ruby-stained) and green decoration.

The best source of information about Northwood glass from 1903-1908 is a factory catalog issued in the fall of 1906. In addition to some of the patterns discussed above, this catalog illustrates items ranging from the No. 14 pattern (Fig. 672) and decorated wine sets (Figs. 563-565) to impressive epergnes (Fig. 724). An extensive line called Intaglio is also featured. Crystal Intaglio items are decorated on the undersides with red and gold paint which is not fired on. Collectors often refer to this ware as "goofus glass," although the name has no historical basis. The decorative effect is sometimes a bit garish, but the Northwood plant also made some some interesting examples in opalescent glass and in emerald green (Figs. 535-541 and 544).

Carnival Glass

From 1908 to 1915, the Northwood plant produced large quantities of pressed glass which was sprayed while hot with various solutions of metallic salts. Known as "dope ware" to the glassworkers, this is Carnival glass to the many

From Pottery, Glass and Brass Salesman.

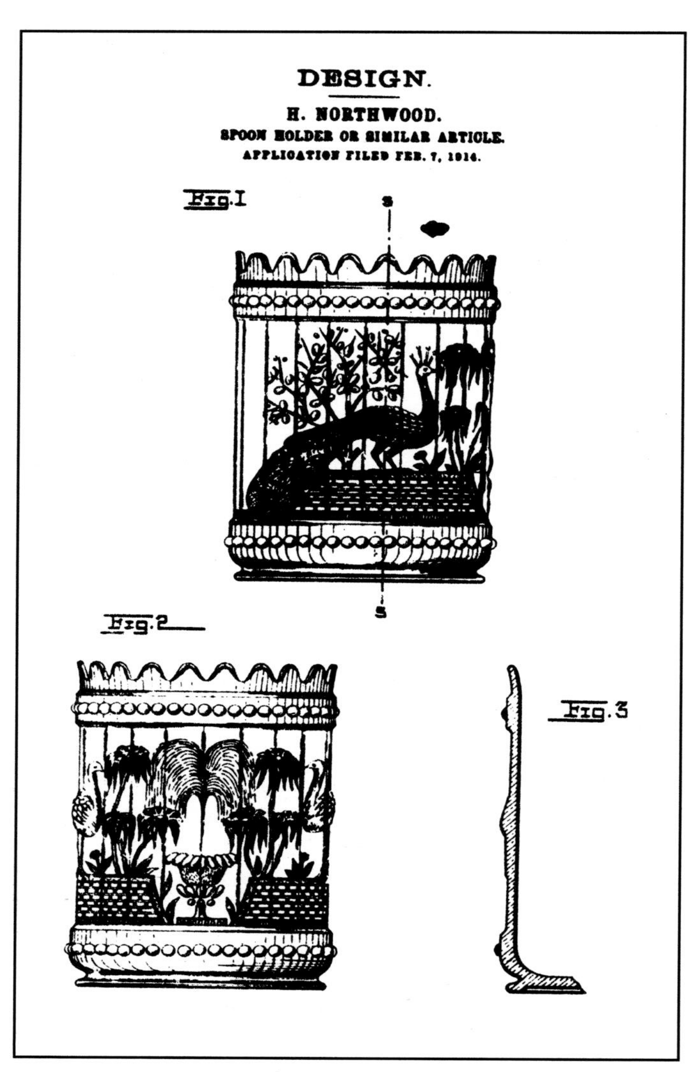

Design patent for Peacock at the Fountain.

avid collectors who seek it today. Although the Northwood plant was not the first to market this glassware, the firm was close on the heels of its originator, the Fenton Art Glass Company of Williamstown, West Virginia. Competition was keen in this area, and Northwood vied with other concerns, such as the Millersburg and Imperial plants in Ohio and the Westmoreland and Dugan firms in Pennsylvania. Despite the large quantities of such glass to be found today, the Carnival glass era actually spanned less than a decade (1908-1915), although the Dugan's successor, the Diamond Glass-Ware Company, continued to produce iridescent lines in Indiana, Pennsylvania, until its demise in 1931.

The Northwood's first iridescent hue, introduced in late 1908, was Golden Iris, and it is called marigold Carnival glass today (Figs. 613-638). Two new colors, Pomona (green) and Florentine (blue), were marketed in early 1910, and three more shades— Azure, Pearl and Emerald—were added about two years later. Described as "softer tones" by the trade press (*Pottery, Glass and Brass Salesman*, January 4, 1912), these are now known as ice blue, white and ice green, respectively.

Although the moulds for some earlier lines were also used for Carnival glass, the Northwood and other firms sought to create distinctive patterns for the new ware. Usually, the four piece table set—creamer, spooner, covered sugar bowl and covered butterdish—was made at first. When a pattern proved popular, items such as water sets and berry sets could be quickly added to the line. The motifs were almost never protected by design patents, and manufacturers were not above introducing similar patterns to capitalize upon the success of a rival firm.

Although its original name remains a mystery, the Northwood pattern which debuted in 1910, now known as

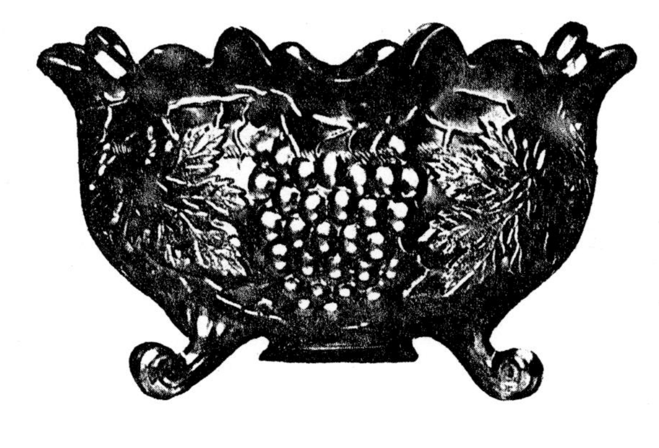

The
H. Northwood Glass Co.
WHEELING, W. VA.

For the past quarter century the last word on American Colored Fancy Glassware has always been "NORTHWOOD." The name to-day stands out more prominently than ever. His latest creations "Golden Iris," "Pomona" and "Florentine," all of changeable metallic sheen, are the most beautiful examples of iridescent glass in the market. In Novelties of every description, Punch, Orange and Fruit Bowls, etc. Don't miss seeing them when in New York.

From Pottery, Glass and Brass Salesman *(February 23, 1910).*

The Very Latest **Northwood Creations**

Wonderful Imitations of the Richest Marbles

BREĆ-CIATED MARBLE
(Patent Pending)

MOTTLED AGATE
(Process Patented)

ETRUSCAN
(Protected by the Patent on Agate)

SATIN SHEEN
A New Iridescent Glass of Rich and Delicate Coloring

ROYAL PURPLE and
VENETIAN BLUE
All That the Names Imply

Blown Decorated Lemonade and Wine Sets—Epergnes—Flower Blocks and Birds

And When You Want Light—Then it's "LUNA" Glass

Illustrations and Prices for the asking. It will be our pleasure to serve you

H. NORTHWOOD CO. WHEELING WEST VIRGINIA

NEW YORK
C. J. De la Croix, 19 Madison Ave.

BALTIMORE
Green & Thomas, 33 S. Charles St.

CHICAGO
Kelly & Reasner, 30 E. Randolph St.

From the February 8, 1917, issue of Pottery, Glass and Brass Salesman.

Grape and Cable, was surely the firm's most ambitious undertaking in Carnival glass (Figs. 639-655 and 658-659). Many different articles occur, including a puff box and hat-pin holder, various sizes of bowls and comports, whiskey decanters with shot glasses, a large punch bowl with base and matching cups, and a candlestick holder with matching shade.

Among the other well-known Northwood patterns in Carnival glass are these: Acorn Burrs (Figs. 687-688), Good Luck (Fig. 614), Greek Key, Hearts and Flowers, Peach, Peacocks on the Fence (Figs. 613 and 740), Peacock at the Fountain (Figs. 690, 783 and 814-816), Oriental Poppy (Figs. 656-657), Poppy Show, Raspberry, Rose Show, Singing Birds (Fig. 623), Springtime, and Three Fruits. Although a few items in these patterns may be known in colored and/or opalescent glass, these patterns were undoubtedly intended for production in iridescent (Carnival) glass. Only Peacock at the Fountain was protected by a design patent (#46,059 issued July 7, 1914).

Although much Carnival glass was intended as table-ware, the Northwood firm developed quite a few novelty items which functioned as card receivers, vases (Figs. 696-711) or simply decorative objects.

Lighting Goods

The natonwide transition from kerosene and gas lighting to electricity had a great effect upon glassmaking firms, and H. Northwood Co. moved from limited production of kerosene lamps and gas shades to become a large-scale manufacturer of various lighting goods around 1920.

The earliest kerosene lamps, made about 1906-07, were relatively simple in design. A grape motif (Fig. 763) may have been the forerunner of the Grape and Cable pattern used extensively for Carnival glass.

After several years of experiments in 1911-12, Harry Northwood developed Luna glass, an alabaster-like, opaque white glass which diffuses electric light. Some shades (Figs. 758 and 760) have the word LUNA in block letters in the fitter area, and this is helpful to separate Northwood's shades from similar products made by other firms such as Beaumont, Haskins, Jefferson and Macbeth-Evans. Northwood patented several designs as well as tools and techniques for drilling holes in these shades for hanging (U. S. Patent # 1,276,683).

Some Luna shades were treated with the iridescent spray mixtures (Fig. 759), and the Luna glass formula was also used to make bookends and paperweights featuring the likeness of a bear (Fig. 751). The bear was mentioned in the May 25, 1916, issue of *Pottery, Glass and Brass Salesman.*

In 1914-15, the Luna Ivory color was added, and these attractive shades may be decorated with a brown stain (Figs. 755 and 761-762). Some are quite large, having a diameter of 24" and weighing about 35 pounds. At the same

RAINBOW

The very name is suggestive. The radiance and colorings of this Ware are among the most beautiful ever achieved by skilled artists in the decorative glassworker's craft.

Rainbow Ware is subject to imitation from many sources, yet its beauty of shape and design, and its originality of colors remain unequaled. Its appeal is instant and universal to those who appreciate beautiful glassware, and wish to use it in decorating and beautifying the home.

The Rainbow Line

is offered in a variety of unusually beautiful colors. Three of these, Blue, Topaz and Russet, are transparent and iridescent, reflecting from their specially treated surfaces all the values of light in the vari-colored hues of the rainbow. The other two colors are opaque and include the popular Jade Green, and a new shade known as Chinese Coral. This new color is a distinctly novel introduction in colored glass but its vividness of coloring has led to wide acceptance where a bizarre decorative note is desirable.

The entire Rainbow line is obtainable either in plain colors or decorated with a band of coin gold. This produces a striking effect, adding appreciably to the beauty of any of the colors with which it may be used.

The universal recognition accorded the Northwood name wherever quality glassware is known has come only with the knowledge gained through many years close association with the glass working industry. Established as one of the pioneer glass factories on the American continent, Northwood leadership in design and manufacture has been consistently maintained.

Northwood designs are created by artists of traditional talent and long experience and are carried out by workers who spring from generations of skilled artisans in the glassworking craft.

Thus it is that a piece of glassware, known to be of Northwood origin, carries with it the fullest assurance of originality, novelty and inherent quality.

PRICE LIST

MARCH 1, 1924

	List, Colors	List, Gold Band
Nos. 616-617-660-661-718 (Roll Edge) Bowl and Base	$16.80	$23.00
Nos. 647-648-649-673-697-717 Bowl and Base	20.00	26.00
No. 662 Bowl and Base (same shape and size as No. 617)	16.00	22.00
No. 663 Bowl and Base (same shape and size as No. 660)	16.00	22.00
No. 669—8" Bowl and Base (same shape as No. 620)	14.00	18.00
Nos. 692-693-694 Bowl and Base	11.50	15.00
No. 620 Bowl and Base	21.00	27.00
No. 638 Bowl and Base	12.00	16.00
Nos. 640-641-642 Bowl and Base	11.25	15.00
No. 658—7" Candle-stick	9.00	12.00
No. 657—8" Candle-stick	10.50	13.75
No. 651—10½" Candle-stick	30.00	35.00
No. 659 Candy Jar and Cover	13.50	18.50
No. 636 Candy Jar and Cover	17.50	22.75
No. 643 Candy Jar and Cover	13.50	18.50
Nos. 644-645-646 Ftd. Bon Bon	8.00	10.50
Nos. 652-653-654-655-656 Ftd. Comport	8.00	11.50
No. 666 Ftd. Comport	16.00	19.50
No. 637 Ftd. Comport	8.00	10.50
No. 650 Baked Apple Dish	6.00	9.00
No. 301—4½" Nappy	3.00	4.50
Nos. 613-618 Vase	12.00	17.00
No. 569 Sweet Pea Vase (Rolled or Flat Top)	8.00	11.50

	List, Colors	List, Gold Band
No. 668 Wall Vase	16.00	22.00
No. 559 Jug and Tumbler	15.00	20.00
No. 621 Mayonnaise Bowl	8.00	10.50
No. 670 Finger Bowl	6.00	8.50
Nos. 671-672 Bulb Bowl	6.00	8.50
Nos. 301-701—6" Butter Plate	4.00	6.50
No. 622 Salad Plate	8.00	11.50
No. 630—8½" Luncheon Plate	12.00	15.50
No. 639 Service Plate	8.00	13.50
No. 631 Cake Plate	12.00	17.50
No. 703—11" Plate	8.00	13.50
No. 595 Turtles	7.50	....
No. 594—2½" Flower Block	3.60	....
No. 594—3½" Flower Block	5.00	....
No. 5 Crystal Coaster	1.30	....
No. 5 Colored Coaster	1.60	3.25
No. 640 (Small) Black Base	4.00	....
No. 638 (Medium) Black Base	5.00	....
No. 616 (Large) Black Base	6.00	....
No. 669 (Special) Black Base	5.00	....
No. 620 (Special) Black Base	6.00	....
No. 674 Plate	6.00	8.50
No. 685 Sherbet	4.50	6.50
No. 675 Handled Candle-sticks	8.00	12.00
No. 676 Candle-stick	7.00	10.50
No. 989—11" Swung Vase	6.00	8.00
No. 816—11" Swung Vase	6.00	8.00
No. 930—15" Swung Vase	12.00	15.00

	List, Colors	List, Gold Band
No. 576 Flower Pot and Saucer	18.00	28.00
Nos. 677 to 684 Footed Bowls	24.00	30.00
With Black Foot	28.00	35.00
Nos. 713-714-715 Ftd. Bowls	18.00	22.50
With Black Foot	21.60	24.00
No. 688—8 Pc. Ice Tea Set—Hld. Tum.	36.00	60.00
No. 691 Covered Almond or Bon Bon	18.00	23.00
No. 695—8½" Candle-stick	10.50	13.75
No. 696—10" Candle-stick	12.00	16.00
No. 698 Handled Tray	14.00	20.75
No. 699 Cheese and Cracker Set	22.50	30.00
No. 700—7 Pc. Water Set	30.00	45.00
No. 704 Deep or Roll Edge Mayonnaise	8.00	11.50
No. 705 Tall Comport	12.00	17.00
No. 706—Ash Tray	4.00	8.00
No. 707—3 Ft. Bowl Reg.—Cupd.—Fld.	7.00	10.50
No. 708—8½" Candle-stick	10.50	13.75
No. 709 Black Stand for No. 647	10.00	....
No. 710 Black Stand for No. 640	8.00	....
No. 711 Black Stand for No. 692	8.00	....
No. 712 Black Stand for No. 616	10.00	....
Nos. 716/695 Console Set (11½" Roll Edge Bowl)	36.50	Special
Nos. 692/695 Console Set	30.00	Special

This photo appeared in the 1911 Yearbook *of the Wheeling Board of Trade.*

time, Grape and Cable tableware in this same color was being marketed as Antique Ivory, although its success seems to have been limited (Figs. 727, 729-731 and 733-734).

The Luna formula was also the basis for glass which was decorated to simulate marble (Figs. 753-754). These were called Brecciated Marble, Mottled Agate and Etruscan, and they were protected by several patents (#1,217,490 issued February 27, 1917; and #1,229,315 issued June 12, 1917). This ware is difficult to find today, and it may have been intended for use as store fixtures rather than for public consumption.

The Northwood firm also produced some reverse painted shades. These are about 4" in diameter at the bottom and are designed to rest upon a flat disk which has an opening for the electrical fixture. The shades are known in three colors—pale pink, pale yellow-orange and light blue (Figs. 756-757). The painted decorations range from simple geometric motifs to elaborate outdoor scenes. The shades diffuse the light nicely, and the overall effect is pleasant.

Stretch Glass

About 1917 or 1918, Northwood revived production of his iridescent glass, but the distinctive "stretch" effect is quite different from Carnival glass. Unlike Carnival glass, stretch pieces are usually plain articles which lack a distinctive pattern. While Carnival glass was shaped, usually by the pressing process, before being iridized, stretch glass was sprayed before a skilled finisher brought the object to final form by flaring, cupping, paddling or a similar technique. The finishing operation creates the onion-skin appearance that characterizes most stretch glass.

Pattern names were largely obsolete by this time, and most articles were simply assigned a three digit number to differentiate them from one another. Some 30 different articles were listed and illustrated in a small folder issued by the factory about 1919-20. Five years later, over 80 items were listed (see p. 150).

Many articles in Northwood's stretch glass, which was called Cobweb or Rainbow, are quite similar to wares made

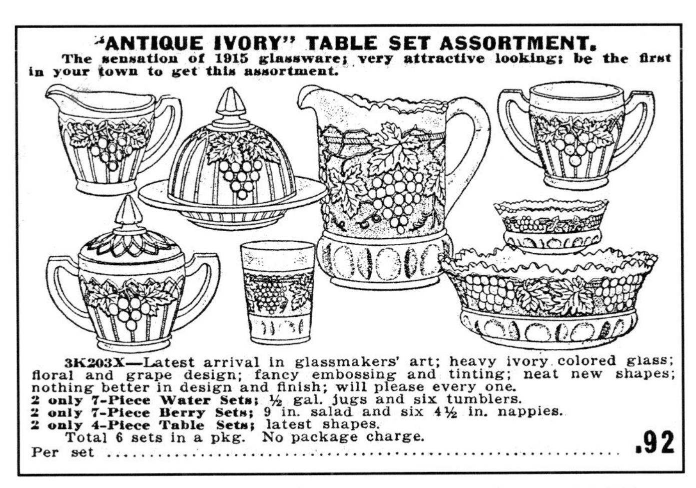

"ANTIQUE IVORY" TABLE SET ASSORTMENT.

The sensation of 1915 glassware; very attractive looking; be the first in your town to get this assortment.

3K203X—Latest arrival in glassmakers' art; heavy ivory colored glass; floral and grape design; fancy embossing and tinting; neat new shapes; nothing better in design and finish; will please every one.
2 only 7-Piece Water Sets; ½ gal. jugs and six tumblers.
2 only 7-Piece Berry Sets; 9 in. salad and six 4½ in. nappies.
2 only 4-Piece Table Sets; latest shapes.
Total 6 sets in a pkg. No package charge.
Per set .... .92

Antique Ivory ware (G. Sommers catalogue, 1915).

"ANTIQUE IVORY" DINING SET ASSORTMENT.

C1771—Extra heavy ivory glass, finest finish, asstd. grape and trellis embossed designs.
2 only 7-pc water sets—½ gal. jug, ht. 8 in. SIX 4¼x3¼ tumblers to match.
2 " 7 " berry sets—8½ in. large berry bowl, SIX 4½ in. deep nappies to match.
2 " 4 " table sets.
6 sets in bbl., 60 lbs. Set, 95c

Butler Brothers catalogue (Spring, 1915).

by the Fenton Art Glass Company and the Diamond Glass-Ware Co. Northwood's stretch glass is best known in Topaz (canary) and Blue (Figs. 770-771, 835-836 and 838), although a few pieces in Pearl (white) and in Royal Purple are known today. Production of stretch glass continued into the 1920s.

The Roaring 20s

While this era of economic expansion brought prosperity to some American glass companies, such was not the case for the Northwood concern. After the untimely deaths of Carl and Harry Northwood (in 1918 and 1919, respectively), the Wheeling-based plant began to lose ground in the highly competitive glass tableware industry.

Production of stretch glass continued into the 1920s, and Topaz Iris and Blue Iris were the Northwood's key colors. An olive-green hue called Russet (Figs.780, 809 and 830-831), which was introduced in 1922, enjoyed a measure of popularity for several years. Some new opaque colors—such as Jade Blue (Figs. 764, 772, 777-778 and 781), Jade Green (Figs. 773, 783, 823 and 824) and Chinese Coral (Figs. 774-775, 782, 806-807 and 828-829)—were developed, and a transparent hue called Rosita Amber was added in late 1924.

The Northwood firm never regained the stature it had had when Harry and Carl Northwood were at the helm. After a succession of financial problems and reversals, ranging from tax liens to legal defeats, H. Northwood and Co. closed its doors in December, 1925. An era in Wheeling had come to an end.

References

Edwards, Bill. *Northwood: King of Carnival Glass.* Paducah, KY: Collector Books, 1978.

Edwards, Bill. *The Standard Encyclopedia of Carnival Glass,* revised 3rd edition. Paducah, KY: Collector Books, 1991 .

Hartung, Marion T. *Carnival Glass Series.* Emporia, KS: by author, 1960-1973.

Hartung, Marion T. *Northwood Pattern Glass: Clear, Colored, Custard and Carnival.* Emporia, KS: by author, 1969.

Heacock, William; Measell, James and Wiggins, Berry. *Harry Northwood: The Early Years, 1881-1900.* Marietta: Antique Publications, 1990.

Heacock, William; Measell, James and Wiggins, Berry. *Harry Northwood: The Wheeling Years, 1901-1925.* Marietta: Antique Publications, 1991.

"John & Harry Northwood: A Family Tradition," exhibition catalog for the Mansion Museum prepared by Holly L. Hoover. Wheeling: Oglebay Institute, 1982.

Moore, Don. *Carnival Glass: A Collection of Writings.* Alameda, CA: by author, 1987.

Moore, Don. *The Complete Guide to Carnival Glass Rarities* Alameda, CA: by author, n. d.

Notley, Raymond. *Carnival Glass.* Shire Publications, Ltd., 1983.

Presznick, Rose M. *Carnival and Iridescent Glass.* Lodi, OH: by author, 1964-67.

Spillman, Jane Shadel. *Pressed Glass, 1825-1925.* Corning:

681.-682. *Amethyst Carnival glass Stippled Rays bowls with crimped edges.* ***683.*** *Green Carnival glass Raspberry milk pitcher.* ***684.*** *Amethyst Carnival glass Rosette bowl.*

685. *Not Northwood; this Blackberry compote was made by Fenton.* ***686.*** *Green Carnival glass Peacock and Urn ice cream dish, c. 1914-15.* ***687.-688.*** *Acorn Burrs berry bowl and covered sugar bowl in purple Carnival glass, c. 1911-12.* ***689.*** *Amethyst Carnival glass Finecut and Roses rose bowl.*

690. *and* ***695.*** *Blue Carnival glass Peacock at the Fountain tumbler and Grape and Gothic Arches tumbler, both c. 1914-15.* ***691.*** *and* ***694.*** *Amethyst Carnival glass Raspberry gravy boat and No. 19 (Memphis) punch cup.* ***692.*** *Green Carnival glass Daisy and Plume 3-footed rose bowl.* ***693.*** *Tumbler with hand painted decoration in purple Carnival glass.*

696.-697.,699. *and* ***701.*** *Tree Trunk vases, Fine Rib vase and Diamond Point vase in purple Carnival glass, all c. 1910-12.* ***698.*** *Four Pillars vase in aqua opalescent Carnival glass.* ***700.*** *Tree Trunk vase in green Carnival glass.*
702. *Graceful vase in green Carnival glass.* ***703.*** *Golden Iris Carnival glass Fine Rib vase.* ***704.-705.*** *Leaf and Beads candy dish and Beaded Cable rose bowl in purple Carnival glass.* ***706.*** *Shell and Wild Rose candy dish in green Carnival glass.*
707. *Green Carnival glass Fine Rib vase (note the jack-in-the-pulpit style).* ***708.-709.*** *Corn vases in green and ice green Carnival glass (note the husk motif on the undersides of the bases).* ***710.*** *Leaf Columns vase in green Carnival glass.* ***711.*** *Shell and Wild Rose candy dish in Golden Iris Carnival glass.*

712. *and* ***715.*** *Rainbow plate and Grape and Cable ruffled bowl in green Carnival glass (note Basketweave back).* ***713.*** *Stippled Rays ruffled bowl in purple Carnival glass.* ***714.*** *Nippon ruffled bowl in amethyst Carnival glass.*
716.-719. *Green Carnival glass Wishbone footed bowl, Fine Cut and Roses candy dish, Rainbow compote (Fine Rib exterior) and Shell and Wild Rose ruffled bowl.*
720.-723. *Green Carnival glass Rays two-handled bon bon, Lustre Flute creamer, Golden Holly two-handled bon bon (made from the spooner mould), and Rays ruffled bowl.*

724

724. *This striking epergne features a blue opalescent base and central horn with three smaller horns in crystal glass. Similar epergnes were shown as the No. 305 Flower Stand in the 1906 company catalog, and Harry Northwood registered his design for a bouquet holder with the U.S. Patent Office in 1916.*

The Northwood firm revived its Antique Ivory glass in 1914-15. Unless indicated otherwise, the items shown and on the next page were made at that time. The painted decoration shown here is called "nutmeg" by collectors.
725.-726. *and* ***728.*** *Grape and Gothic Arches tumbler, goblet and tumbler with crimped top.* ***727.*** *Grape and Cable cracker jar.*
729.-731. *Grape and Cable open sugar bowl, round plate and two-handled bon bon (both the plate and the bon bon have a Basketweave exterior.*

732. *Four Pillars vase with nutmeg-colored decoration.* ***733.-734.*** *Grape and Cable punch cup and fruit bowl with blue stain decoration.* ***735.*** *Southern Gardens 10"d. fruit dish (this was part of Northwood's Verre D'or line in 1907).*
736. *Hearts and Flowers crimped plate.* ***737.-738.*** *Poppy oval bowl and Three Fruits plate with nutmeg-colored decoration.*
739.-740. *Peacock and Urn round plate (9½" d.) and Peacocks on the Fence ruffled plate or bowl (note the faint iridescence and the gold edge).*

741.-744. *Grape and Cable large and smaller dresser trays, powder box and hatpin holder in dark transparent blue, probably c. 1913-14, when they were being advertised in Butler Brothers catalogues.*

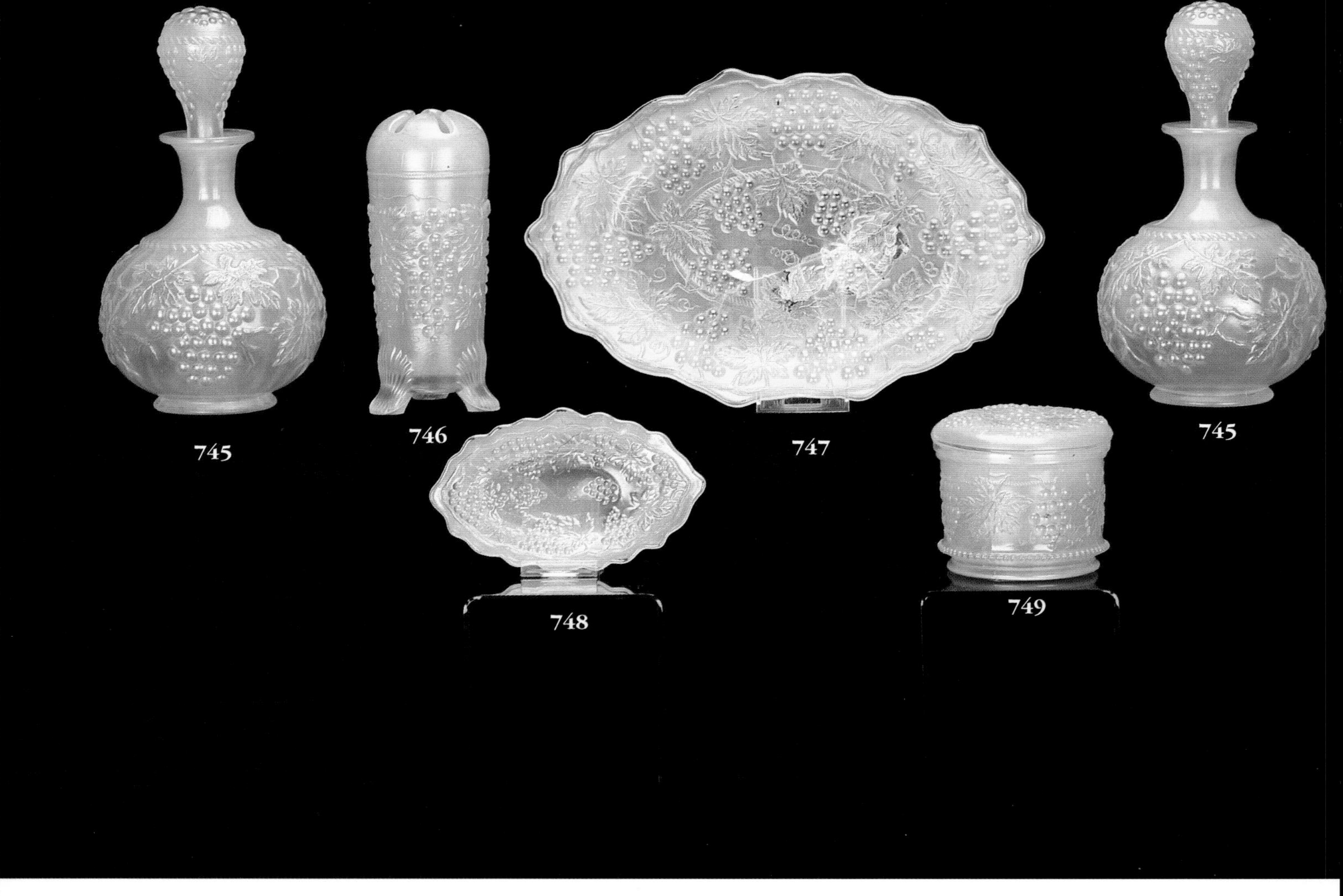

745.-749. *This decorating treatment--yellow paint on frosted crystal glass--is extraorinarily scarce, and few pieces are known to today's collectors. Shown here are Grape and Cable cologne bottles with stoppers, hatpin holder, large and small dresser trays, and a powder box.*

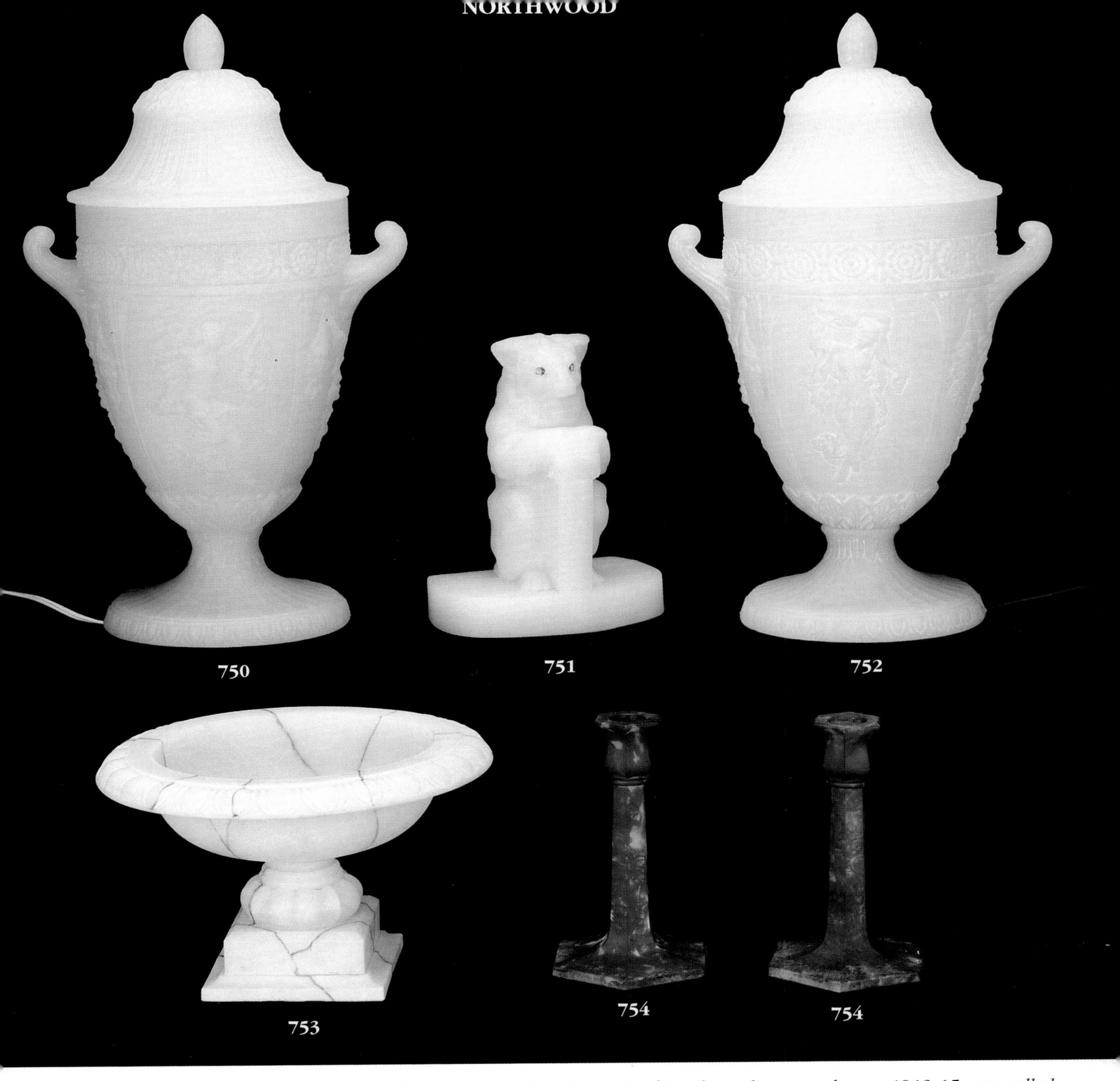

750 751 752

753 754 754

750. *and* ***752.*** *These two covered urns(746 is wired as a lamp), made of Northwood's Luna glass c. 1913-15, are called "Dancing Ladies" by collectors today; this motif inspired a line of smaller urns and vases at the Fenton Art Glass Company in the early 1930s.* ***751.*** *This Bear bookend or doorstop was made in 1916.*

753. *This two-piece compote in Northwood's "Brecciated Marble" glass was patented in 1917.* ***754.*** *Northwood patented the "Etruscan" decorating treatment used on these candlesticks in 1917.*

755. *Luna Ivory large shade.* ***756.-757.*** *Reverse-painted shades.* ***758.*** *and* ***760.*** *Luna glass shades.* ***759.*** *Luna glass shade with iridescent finish; this pattern was called Venetian in a c. 1913 catalog.* ***761.-762.*** *Ivory shades with rust-colored decoration.* ***763.*** *Early hand lamp, c. 1906, with a grape and leaf pattern on the underside of the base.*

These colonial-style sherbets and nut cups were a staple of the Northwood firm's production for many years.
764. *Jade Blue sherbet, c. 1921.* ***765.-766.*** *Blue master nut bowl and individual nut cups with silver filigree decoration, probably c. 1908-12.*
767. *Iridescent blue sherbet (note gold decorated rim), c. 1918.* ***768.-769.*** *Golden Iris Carnival glass sherbet dishes, c. 1908-1909.*

NORTHWOOD

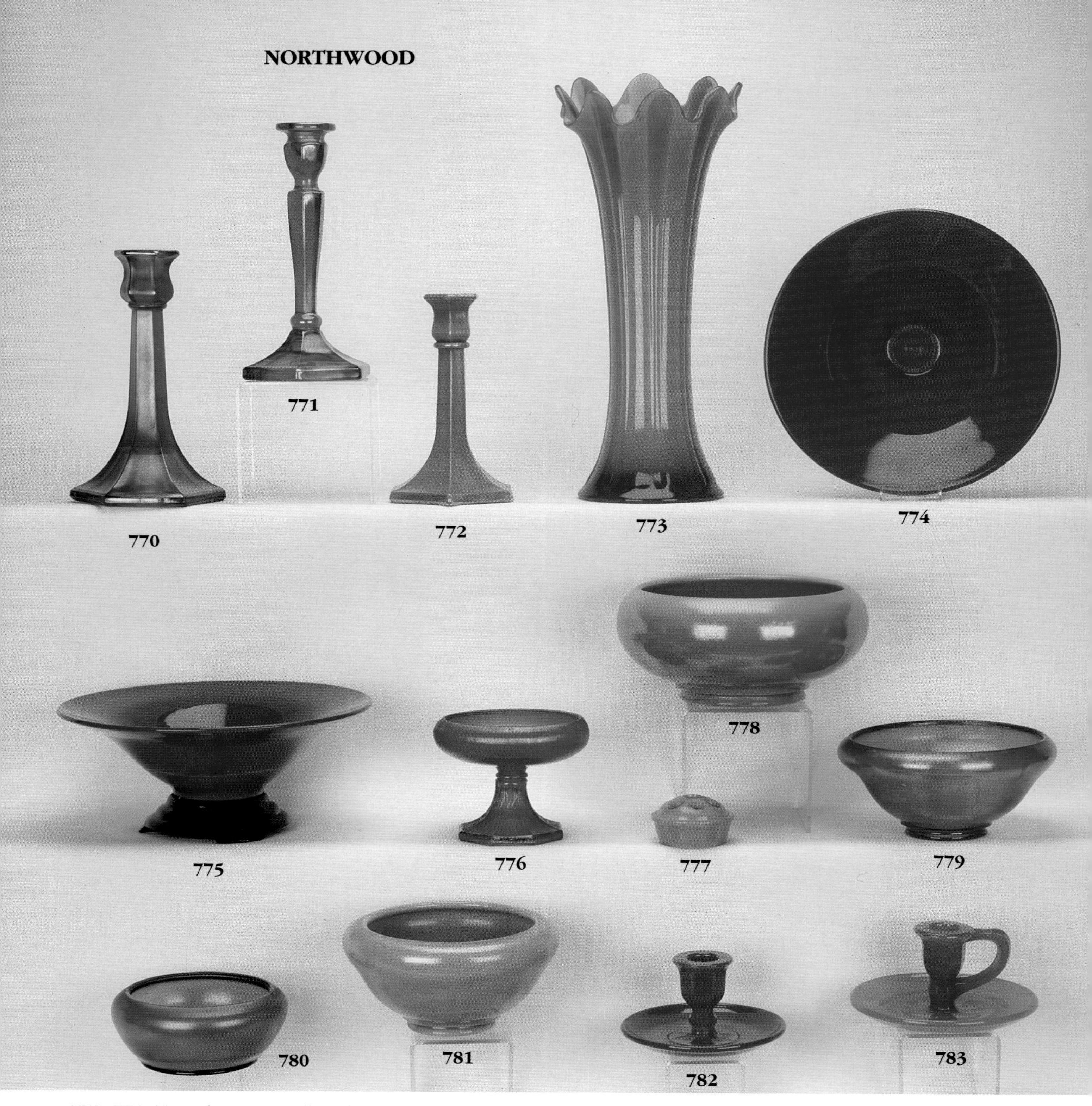

770.-771. *Two Blue Iris candlesticks, Northwood's No. 657 and No. 695.* ***772.*** *Jade Blue candlestick, No. 658, with gold decoration.* ***773.*** *Jade Green No. 930 15" swung vase.* ***774.*** *This Chinese Coral No. 692 bowl has these words in its center: "CITIZEN'S MUTUAL TRUST CO. WHEELING WVA 1924."*

775. *Chinese Coral No. 692 bowl on black base.* ***776.*** *and* ***779.*** *Iridescent blue comport and No. 693 bowl.* ***777.-778.*** *Jade Blue flower frog and No. 617 bowl.*

780. *Russet No. 670 bulb bowl, c. 1922-23.* ***781.*** *No. 640 bowl in Jade Blue.* ***782.*** *Chinese Coral No. 676 candlestick, c. 1924-25.* ***783.*** *Jade Green No. 675 handled candlestick, c. 1924-25.*

784.-785. *Emerald green No. 31 (Belladonna) berry bowl and sauce dishes with gold decoration, c. 1906-07.* ***786.*** *Crystal No. 12 covered butterdish with gold decoration, c. 1906.* ***787.*** *Golden Iris Carnival glass Peacock at the Fountain berry bowl, c. 1914.*

788.-789. *Crystal Double Loop open sugar bowl and creamer with gold decoration, c. 1909.* ***790.*** *Flint opalescent Diadem (Sunburst on Shield) open sugar bowl, c. 1908.* ***791.-792.*** *Emerald green Grape and Gothic Arches spooner and Creamer with gold decoration, 1914-15.*

793.-796. *Note the fine gold decoration on this c. 1903-04 Regent table set in amethyst--spooner, creamer, covered sugar bowl and covered butterdish.*

797. *Flint opalescent Carnelian (Everglades) covered sugar bowl, c. 1903.* ***798.*** *Canary opalescent Frosted Leaf and Basketweave creamer, c. 1904.* ***799.*** *Emerald green No. 12 creamer, c. 1906.* ***800.*** *Green tankard lemonade pitcher with hand-painted decoration, c. 1906.*

801. *Amethyst Carnival glass Rainbow bowl with crimped edge, c. 1910. Blue Scroll with Acanthus toothpick holder (note gold decoration), c. 1903-05.* ***803.-804.*** *Crystal No. 12 open sugar bowl and creamer (note gold decoration), c. 1906.*

805. *Green Carnival glass Three Fruits Medallion bowl with ruffled edge, c. 1911-12.* ***806.-807.*** *Chinese Coral No. 708 candlesticks and No. 660 console bowl, c. 1924-25.* ***808.*** *Rosita Amber No. 727 twisted vase, c. 1924-25.* ***809.*** *Russet No. 643 covered jelly or bon bon, c. 1922-23.*

810.-811. *Blue opalescent Diadem (Sunburst on Shield) creamer and open sugar bowl.* ***812.-813.*** *Golden Iris Carnival glass eight-sided Bushel Basket and Grape and Cable tray.* ***814.-816.*** *Peacock at the Fountain spooner, covered sugar bowl and creamer in Golden Iris Carnival glass, c. 1914.*

817.-820. *Decorated crystal Strawberry and Cable table set--spooner, butterdish, covered sugar bowl and creamer.* ***821.-822.*** *Atlas sauce dish and berry bowl in crystal glass with "maiden's blush" treatment and gold decoration.*

823. and 824. *No. 725 candlesticks in Jade Green (c. 1924-25) and Topaz (not iridized: c. 1919-1925).* ***824.*** *No. 719 6" candlestick in Jade Green, c. 1924-25.* ***826.-827.*** *Rosita Amber No. 643 covered jelly or bon bon and No. 717 twisted vase, c. 1924-25.* ***828.-829.*** *Chinese Coral No. 678 bowl (note black foot) and No. 717 twisted vase, c. 1924-25.*

830.-834. *Russet No. 649 bowl, No. 718 bowl (note gold edge), No. 647 bowl, No. 659 1/2 lb. candy jar, and No. 636 1 lb. candy jar--all c. 1922-23.*

835.-836 and 838. *Blue Iris No. 647 bowl, No. 617 bowl (gold decoration by the Lotus Glass Co. of Barnesville, Ohio) and No. 669 bowl with black base (the base is marked "669")--all c. 1919-23.* ***837.*** *Topaz Iris No. 301 bowl (gold decoration by the Wheeling Decorating Co.).*

JOHN A. ARTZBERGER

Director of The Oglebay Institute Mansion Museum. Mr. Artzberger served as the Museum's Curator of Collections between 1962 and 1975. Mr. Artzberger has worked with the Museum's glass collection since 1962 and has developed a number of exhibitions and lectures on glass.

GARY E. BAKER

Curator of Glass, The Chrysler Museum, Norfolk, Virginia. In 1988 and 1989, Mr. Baker planned and supervised the reinstallation of the Chrysler's glass collection, which is particularly strong in 19th and 20th Century American and European glass.

From 1976 to 1980, he served as Curator of the Oglebay Institute Mansion Museum in Wheeling, West Virginia. He has published articles and lectures widely on American glass.

G. EASON EIGE

Chief Curator, Huntington Museum of Art. Mr. Eige has written numerous articles and exhibition catalogues on West Virginia and Ohio Valley glass. He is also the current Editor of The Glass Club Bulletin of the National Early American Glass Club. He has lectured widely on the history of glass.

Mr. Eige is author of *A Century of Glassmaking In West Virginia* and co-author of *Blenko Glass, 1930-1953*. He has organized several national circulating museum exhibitions including, *Selections from the Collection of Olga Hirshhorn*, 1979, Smithsonian Institution Traveling Exhibition Service and *New American Glass: Focus 2 West Virginia National*, 1986.

JAMES MEASELL

Professor at Wayne State University in Detroit. Dr. Measell is also Director of Glass History Research for Antique Publications of Marietta, Ohio. Along with Berry Wiggins and the late William Heacock, he is coauthor of *Harry Northwood: The Early Years, 1881-1900* and *Harry Northwood: The Wheeling Years, 1901-1925*. Dr. Measell has written several other books and articles dealing with the American glass industry.

HOLLY H. McCLUSKEY

Curator of Glass, The Oglebay Institute Mansion Museum. Mrs. McCluskey has worked for Oglebay since 1984, and she has conducted a number of classes, seminars and lectures on Wheeling glass throughout the tri-state area. She also wrote the interpretive script for the audio tour system used at the Oglebay Institute Glass Museum.

GERALD I. REILLY

Curator of Collections, The Oglebay Institute Mansion Museum. Mr. Reilly has been with the Institute since 1986 and has edited several Museum publications.

JANE SHADEL SPILLMAN

Curator of American Glass, The Corning Museum of Glass. Mrs. Spillman, who lectures widely on glass made and used in America, has written numerous articles and books on glass and lighting devices.

Mrs. Spillman co-authored (with Susanne K. Frantz) *Masterpieces of American Glass* (New York: Crown Publishers, Inc., 1990). Her book *White House Glassware: Two Centuries of Presidential Entertaining* (1989) was co-published by the White House Historical Association, the Museum, and the National Geographic Society. She is writing a book on T. G. Hawks and Company at Corning, to be published by the Corning Museum of Glass.

KENNETH M. WILSON

Mr. Wilson retired in 1987 as Senior Curator of American Decorative Arts after serving as Director of Collections and Preservation at The Edison Institute/Henry Ford Museum & Greenfield Village since 1973. He was formerly Assistant Director and Curator of The Corning Museum of Glass (1963-1973) and Chief Curator at Old Sturbridge Village. Author of *New England Glass and Glassmaking*, he co-authored *American Bottles and Flasks and Their Ancestry* with Helen McKearin in 1978. He has also written numerous articles about American glass.

Mr. Wilson is also Past President of both The National Early American Glass Club and the New York State Craftsmen, and is an Honorary Fellow of the Corning Museum of Glass.

INDEX OF INDIVIDUALS AND COMPANIES

INDEX OF PATTERNS AND ITEMS